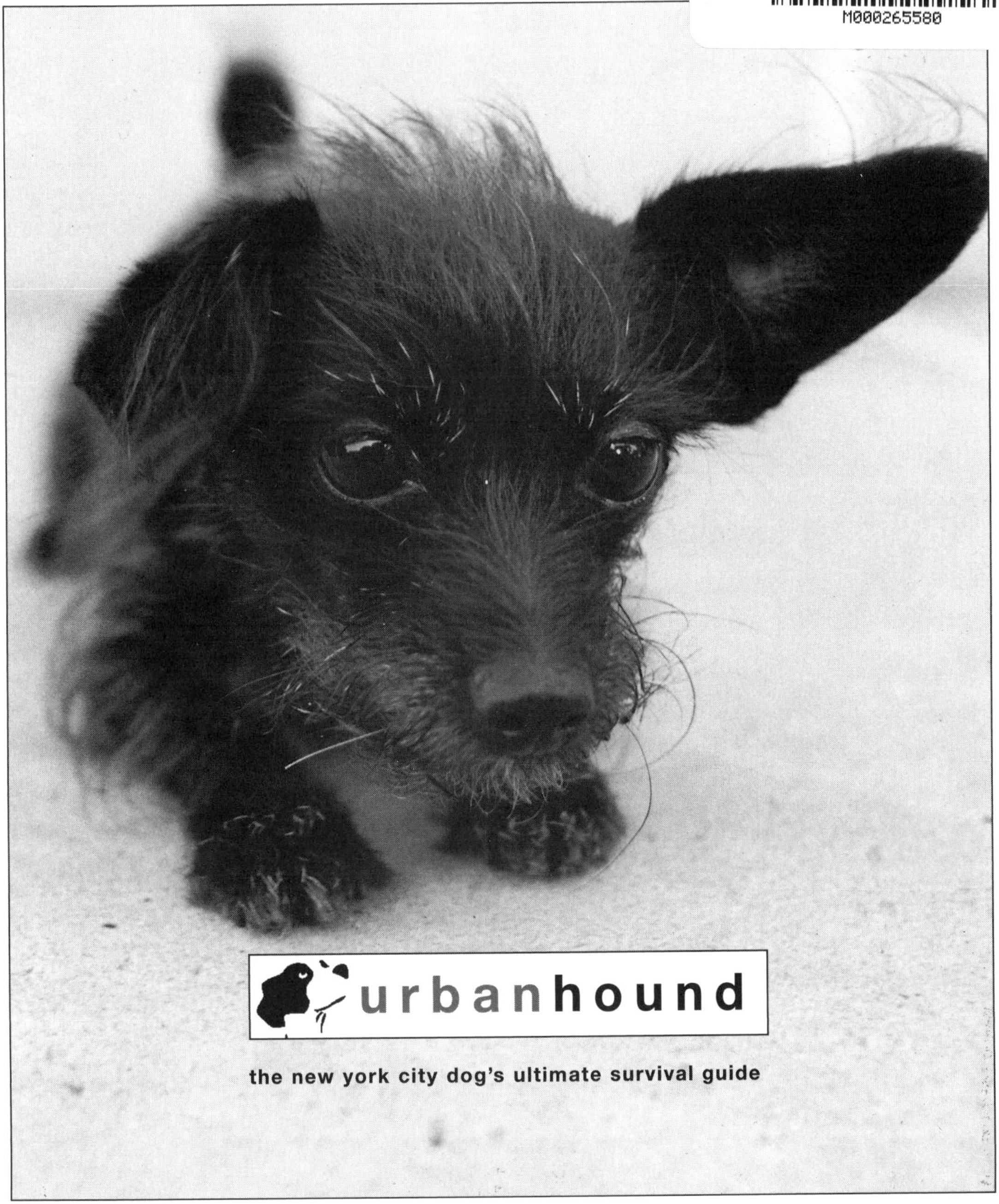

urbanhound

the new york city dog's ultimate survival guide

Photographs by Michael Nastasi

Illustrations by Stevan Jennis

urbanhound

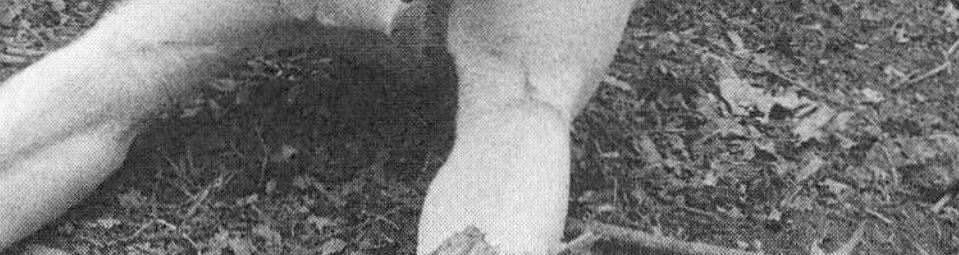

the new york city dog's ultimate survival guide

nina munk & nadia zonis

City & Company

Copyright © 2001 by Urbanhound, LLC

All rights reserved. No portion of this book may be reproduced
without written permission from the Publisher.

Cover and Interior design: Leah Lococo and Jennifer Moore,
based on the Urbanhound.com Web site designed by Crescent Logic, Inc.
Urbanhound logo: Leah Esposito
Cover and interior photographs copyright © 2001 Michael Nastasi
Illustrations copyright © 2001 Stevan Jennis

Library of Congress Cataloging-in-Publication Data
Munk, Nina.
Urbanhound : the New York City dog's ultimate survival guide /
by Nina Munk and Nadia Zonis.
p. cm.
Includes index.
ISBN 1-929439-18-0 (pb.)
1. Dogs—New York (State)—New York—Handbooks, manuals, etc.
I. Zonis, Nadia. II. Title.
SF426 .M86 2001
636.7'0887'097471--dc21 2001042432

First Edition
Printed in the United States of America
10 9 8 7 6 5 4 3 2

Publisher's Note

Neither City & Company nor the authors has any interest, financial or personal, in the locations listed in this book. No fees were paid or services rendered in exchange for inclusion in these pages. Please also note that while every effort was made to ensure accuracy at the time of publication, it is always best to call ahead to confirm that the information is still up-to-date. All area codes are 212 unless otherwise noted.

City & Company books are available at special discounts for premiums and sales promotions.
Special editions can also be created to specification. For details, contact the Sales Director.
City & Company
22 West 23rd Street
New York, NY 10010

For Mack and Masha, who inspired us to write this book

Acknowledgments

For their contributions to Urbanhound.com, and by extension to the Urbanhound book, we'd like to thank:

Geordie Allen, Andrea Arden, Jamie Attwood, Betsy Brevitz, DVM, Susan Buckley, Parke M. Chapman, Hugh Chamberlain, Andrea DiNoto (our terrific editor!), Kimberly Elman, Michele Finley, Bridget Hodge, Jennifer Keeney, Stephanie LaFarge, PhD., Sue Nastasi, Betsy Saul, Anneliese Turck, Darryl Vernon, Susan Yarnell, and Jeffrey Zahn, MD.

Many thanks as well to the members and users of Urbanhound.com, whose hounds grace the Web site and this book, and who shared their wisdom on our message boards. Also, we're grateful to the members of the Brooklyn and Manhattan Dogchat lists. They drew on their experiences as dedicated New York dog people to provide invaluable advice and guidance to us. Special thanks to Jane Cameron and Terry Fonville, MD, who created and maintain the lists. To subscribe to the DogChats, and we think you should, visit www.nycdog.org/forums.html

Please send your thoughts, ideas, corrections, and suggestions for the next edition of this book to editor@urbanhound.com.

contents

urbanhound

introduction

Not too long ago, Nina left her dog at a fancy Manhattan daycare center. That evening, on picking him up, she was handed a report card (yes, a report card) that read:

Name: Mack

Today I was very: happy & fun

My "business" was: normal

My best pals were: Wink & Sam

Fav hangout spot: playroom

Comments: Mack was absolutely marvelous today, getting along with the gang with no problems!

No doubt about it: New York dog people are a peculiar breed. Some might even say we're a bit mad. Nadia confesses that her dates are judged on how well they get along with Masha, her Shepherd-mix; she also admits (quietly) that she selected her sofa in part because it matched Masha's coat. Meanwhile, Nina's mother complains that Nina treats her dog as if he were human (he isn't?).

We've stopped explaining ourselves (why waste our breath?). In New York, it's true, there are few open spaces for a hound to chase balls or birds. Concrete is more common, by far, than grass. A veterinary checkup can cost as much as a month's rent—in any normal city. Most buildings and shops shut us out ("No Pets Allowed!"). But where else can a dog race, off leash, through the world's most famous park (Central Park, that is); compete in Halloween costume contests; hang out with friends at Coffee Barks in Prospect Park; parade at Dachshund Fiestas; or spend the afternoon at a 12,000-

square-foot indoor play center provided exclusively for hounds?

New York dog people may be nuts, but we're a force: there are between one- and one-and-a-half million hounds in this city, depending on who's doing the counting. This book is for them. It includes everything we wish we'd known when we became dog people. It answers every dog question we've ever asked ourselves. It lists all the resources a dog person in New York City could ever need. Above all, it recognizes that our dogs aren't accessories; they're our family.

Urbanhound.com, the Web site that led to this book, began when Nina got her dog Mack and started to ask questions like: Where are dog licenses sold? Are dogs allowed on Jones Beach? Can they be taken on the subway? Who's the best trainer in town? Does anyone sell a good-looking dog bed? Can dogs get West Nile Virus? No guides existed that went into that kind of detail. Surely, Nina presumed, other urban dwellers must have similar questions about their hounds—or could provide answers. Nina got a copy of *Creating Web Pages for Dummies*, learned to code HTML, and started Urbanhound.com in her living room. Almost instantly, the Web site was a hit, and it quickly became clear that Urbanhound needed to branch out and become a book.

Nadia joined Urbanhound soon after its launch. Devoted to our dogs, and determined to uncover all there is to know about canine life in the city, we've made a great team. Nina lives downtown; Nadia is uptown. Nina has a purebred dog; Nadia has a mixed-breed. Nina's dog, Mack, is crazy for agility classes; Nadia's Masha adores swimming. Because Mack tears the house to shreds when left alone, Nina is now an expert in stuffed Kongs and other remedies for separation anxiety. Because Masha can be territorial and overly protective, Nadia knows more about obedience training in this city than just about anyone.

What we have in common is this: a commitment to improving the lives of urbanhounds and their humans. We think this book does just that. We hope you agree.

1 

houndfinder

EVERYTHING YOU NEED TO KNOW ABOUT HOW & WHERE TO GET A DOG

Do I spend enough time at home? Am I prepared to take my dog out three to five times a day, in rain, sleet or snow? Am I willing to be dragged out of bed first thing Sunday morning? Do I have the patience and perseverance to train a dog? Can I afford the high cost of vet care? Does my building allow dogs? Is my life stable? If you answered yes to all those questions, then go ahead: get a dog. But first, read this chapter carefully and consult at least some of the many resources we list.

The Right Dog for You

Visitors to the Web site urbanhound.com often ask which breed of dog is best suited to city life. Honestly, there's no "right" answer. Just as there's no "typical" New Yorker, there's not one particular breed that's best for the Big Apple. The question to ask yourself is: Which breed of dog best suits my personality, habits, schedule and taste? And more importantly: Am I ready to make the serious commitment that getting a dog represents? Remember: you'll be walking, feeding, entertaining—and picking up his poop—every day for the next 10 to 15 years. If that appeals to you, you're ready to do the research that will help find the dog that's right for you.

DO I REALLY WANT A PUPPY?

Everyone loves puppies—but, like babies, they're a handful. They can't be left alone for more than a few hours at a stretch. They nip your hand and chew your furniture; they need to be housebroken and socialized. And puppies can be expensive. What's more, urban puppies—especially those raised in New York City—should not leave the house until they're around four months old. By then they've had their third set of vaccinations and are finally immune to common bacterial infections. This means that if you get your puppy when he's seven weeks old, he'll spend the next nine weeks confined to your apartment, forced to exercise, and pee and poop inside.

An older dog, on the other hand, is likely to be calmer and better behaved. She should already be housebroken and may even be obedience trained. Also adopting an older dog can mean fewer surprises: age reveals health or temperament problems that are hidden in a puppy.

But be advised: while some older dogs come up for adoption because their owners have died or moved to a place that doesn't allow dogs, others are given up because they have serious health or temperament problems.

Why You Shouldn't Get a Dog from a Pet Shop

Once you're ready to get a dog, please don't buy him from a pet shop. Buy all the supplies you need from a pet shop, but get your dog from a shelter or a topnotch breeder. Here's why:

A dog should not be an impulse buy. The decision to get a dog should not be prompted by a window display of six-week-old Pugs. If you haven't given serious thought to how a dog will fit into your life, hold off.

Dogs in pet shops are not best of show. Most pet stores sell dogs to make a profit. Good breeders, on the other hand, are in the business for the love of the breed: they work hard to produce healthy puppies free of genetic disorders; they also breed for temperament.

Buying a dog from a pet store supports puppy mills. Because pet stores need a consistent supply of dogs, they often get their dogs from large commercial breeders known as puppy mills, where dogs are churned out without regard to health or temperament. Dogs bred in puppy mills are more likely to suffer from malnutrition, disease, and genetic defects than dogs bred by dedicated, conscientious breeders.

Service counts. Few pet stores have the time or inclination to help you after you take your dog home. A good breeder, by contrast, is an invaluable source of information: she can help you pick the right breed and she'll be available for as long as your dog is alive, offering information and help each step of the way. She'll also take back your dog at any time. Animal shelters are also great resources: they make sure a dog is well-suited to a prospective owner and they provide free or low-cost spaying or neutering, microchipping (more on this in Chapter 9), and even obedience classes.

MIXED-BREED OR PUREBRED

Once you've settled the age question, it's time to decide if you'd prefer a mixed-breed or purebred dog. Here again, in both cases, there are pros and cons to consider. As an aside, if you care about such things, mixed-breed dogs are currently all the rage among celebrities and socialites.

Mixed-Breed Dogs

Pros:

- You're providing shelter to a homeless dog;
- You may be saving a dog from euthanasia;
- You're not contributing to the nation's overpopulation of pets;
- You're getting a dog for a low price and, if the dog's from a shelter, you're probably eligible for free or low-cost spaying or neutering and obedience classes;
- Your dog will be one-of-a-kind.

Cons:

- You may not be able to predict your dog's eventual size and temperament;
- You won't know the background of your dog: he may not have been cared for properly and could have health or behavioral problems.

Purebred Dogs

Pros:

- You can pick a breed that exhibits traits or skills you like;
- If you go through a top breeder, you'll get a dog that's received excellent care from birth;
- If you go through a top breeder, your dog will have been bred for good looks, excellent health and a nice disposition;
- If you go through a top breeder, you'll always have someone to turn to for help with your dog.

Cons:

- Purebred dogs may be prone to genetic disorders;
- The dog you want may not be immediately available: good breeders only breed a few litters a year;
- Your dog may cost thousands of dollars.

Choosing a Breed

Whether you settle on a purebred or mixed-breed, knowing your breeds can help you find the right dog for you. (With most mixed-breed dogs, it's possible to determine at least one or two of the breeds in its ancestry.) The American Kennel Club recognizes 148 breeds. These breeds are divided into seven broad groups, or classifications, that generally define a dog's traits: sporting, hound, working, terrier, toy, herding, and the catch-all category "non-sporting," for dogs that don't fit

The 25 Most Popular Breeds

What makes a breed of dog popular? Partly disposition; partly fashion. The Labrador Retriever has been ranked No. 1 on the list of purebred dogs registered with American Kennel Club's list since 1991. Labs now account for an astonishing 14 percent of all AKC registrations. But back in the early thirties, Boston Terriers topped the list (they've since dropped to No. 18). Then came Cocker Spaniels, Beagles and, from 1960 to 1982, Poodles. Just as quickly as a breed becomes popular, it can drop right out of favor: in 1990, 105,642 Cocker Spaniels were registered with the AKC; in 2000, the number fell to 29,393. Beware: the more popular a dog, the more likely it is to be overbred and poorly bred.

within the other groups. Apart from general appearance, breeds vary tremendously as to energy level, tendency to aggression, and responsiveness to training. For details on each of these groups, see the table on page 21. But first consider each of these issues:

Size Do you want a "pocket" dog that slips into a tote? Or an imposing dog that'll scare off potential muggers? Or something in between?

Energy Level How much time do you have to exercise your dog? Are you looking for a dog to jog with? Or do you work so hard that by the time you get home you can barely make it around the block? (Note: When it comes to dogs, energy level is often unrelated to size. Some small dogs become neurotic if they don't get plenty of exercise, while certain big breeds have a low metabolism and are happiest lounging about.)

Coat Type Are you prepared to spend $75 a month to have your dog groomed? Or do you want a wash-and-wear pet? Do you hate the thought of dog hair on your furniture, your carpet and your clothes? Is anyone in your house allergic to dog dander? (If so, your only choice is a dog that doesn't shed: Poodle, Bichon Frise, Maltese).

Behavior Are you the sort that likes the trains to run on time? Do you want a dog that obeys your every command? Generally, herding and sporting breeds are the easiest to train because they like following commands.

Temperament Every breed has good and bad traits. The question is: Which traits can you live with? (See box on page 21.)

KID-FRIENDLY BREEDS?

Parents often wonder which breeds of dog are best with children. Unfortunately, there's no right answer. Many families choose Labradors and Golden Retrievers because these breeds are generally gentle with youngsters. But the fact is no one breed can be guaranteed to be better with kids than any other. What counts is a dog's temperament, which has more to do with breeding than with the type of breed. A poorly-bred Golden Retriever may be more likely to bite a child then a laid-back Pit Bull who's been raised with love from the get go. If you're looking to get a dog for your son or daughter, do your research: if it's a purebred you want, find a top breeder who focuses on breeding for good temperament; if you plan to adopt a dog from a shelter, hire a skilled trainer to help you assess the dogs for aggression and possessiveness (see Chapter 6 for names of some of the city's top trainers).

Resources to Help You Select a Breed

WEB SITES

Urbanhound's Breed Finder

www.urbanhound.com/houndFinder/breedFinder.html

Tell Urbanhound what you are looking for in a dog, and the site will help select the best breeds for you. This breed finder is limited to the 50 most popular AKC breeds in America.

Breed FAQ Homepage

www.k9web.com/dog-faqs/breeds/

This stripped-down site, maintained by Cindy Tittle Moore, contains some of the most detailed information on around 100 dog breeds, all of it written by enthusiastic volunteers and compiled from dozens of sources. Not all breeds are included, and the quality of the information is uneven, but this site is still a wonderful resource.

The American Rare Breed Association
www.arba.org
The place to go for info on breeds that are not recognized by the AKC, from the South Russian Ovtcharka to the Nova Scotia Duck Tolling Retriever.

The Dog Owner's Guide: Choosing the Right Dog
www.canismajor.com/dog/tchoose.html
This superb site is a compilation of helpful articles that have appeared in a bi-monthly tabloid newspaper called Dog Owner's Guide that's distributed free in Ohio, Kentucky, and Indiana.

BOOKS

The New Encyclopedia of the Dog, by Bruce Fogle, DVM (DK Publishing, 2000)
Choosing a Dog: Your Guide to Picking the Perfect Breed, by Nancy Baer and Steve Duno (Berkley Books, 1995)
ASPCA Complete Guide to Dogs, by Sheldon L. Gerstenfeld, V.M.D., with Jacque Lynn Schultz (Chanticleer Press, 1999), available online at www.petsmart.com/aspca/dog.main.shtml
The Right Dog for You: Choosing a breed that matches your personality, family and lifestyle, by Daniel F. Tortora (Simon & Schuster,1983)
Paws to Consider: Choosing the Right Dog for You and Your Family, by Brian Kilcommons and Sarah Wilson (Warner Books, 1999)

DOG SHOWS

Visiting a dog show gives you a chance to meet a range of breeds as well as their breeders and handlers. Westminster, the largest dog show in the country, takes place every February at Manhattan's Madison Square Garden. For information, visit www.westminsterkennelclub.org. A listing of smaller dog shows throughout the year can be found at the InfoDog.com at www.infodog.com/showinfo/showMain.htm

PUPPY CONSULTANTS

Some dog trainers offer advice on the best breed for you, and will research and locate a well-bred pup:

Understanding Breed Groups

AKC Group	Bred to	Traits	Includes	Possible drawbacks
SPORTING	Find and retrieve game	Active, friendly, and alert	Retrievers, Spaniels, Setters	Without plenty of exercise, sporting dogs can become destructive and neurotic.
HOUND	Track game	Tough, courageous, and hearty	Beagles, Dachshunds, Greyhounds	Stubborn nature makes them hard to train. Driven by tracking instinct, hounds are not suited to be off leash. Some make a "baying" noise that can be annoying.
WORKING	Guard, pull sleds, rescue	Highly intelligent and strong-willed	Rottweilers, Siberian Huskies, Great Danes	Large and strong, can be aggressive and territorial.
TERRIER	Hunt and kill rats and other vermin	Scrappy, self-confident and relentless	Jack Russells, Westies, American Staffordshires (aka, Pit Bulls)	Stubborn and demanding, can be hard to obedience train. Originally bred to fight to the death, they rarely back down—even in the face of danger.
TOY	Be pets	Small stature	Chihuahuas, Mini Poodles, Pugs	May be fragile and prone to yapping.
HERDING	Herd livestock	Intelligent, alert, highly responsive	German Shepherds, Border Collies, Welsh Corgies	Without plenty of stimulation, may become destructive. Can be territorial, sometimes "herding" young children.
NON-SPORTING	Nothing specific. These dogs don't fit in other groups	Various	American Eskimos, Lhasa Apsos, Bulldogs	Various

- The Educated Puppy & Dogs Too, 718-788-3602. www.educatedpuppy.com
  Their Canine Research Service costs $50 an hour or $30 for a half-hour.
- Empire of the Dog, 917-723-5233. www.empireofthedog.com. Aside from helping with purebred puppies, they'll also help you assess and select a dog from a shelter. Prices begin at $40.
- Follow My Lead, 212-873-5511. Their Pre-Puppy Consultation costs $100.

Adopting a Dog

When visiting a shelter, it's hard not to be moved by the vast number of dogs who need homes. If compassion for these homeless dogs motivates you to donate needed money, time, or supplies to a shelter or rescue group, that's great. But don't let your emotions drive your decision to adopt an animal. If a dog interests you, take time to evaluate his or her health and temperament (a great guide to evaluating shelter dogs is Sue Sternberg's *A Guide to Choosing Your Next Dog from the Shelter,* a booklet available for $10 from www.suesternberg. com). Don't be impulsive: leave empty handed if you don't find a good match. Chances are you will find what you are looking for at another shelter, or on another day. If you are looking for a specific breed of dog, let the shelter know so they can contact you if the dog you want shows up.

Be warned: adopting an animal from a good shelter isn't easy. At the North Shore Animal League, for example, one in three applicants is turned down. A volunteer for the rescue group Might Mutts proudly told us, "It's easier to receive a pistol permit than to get a dog from us." Most shelters won't let you adopt a puppy unless you work at home or have very flexible hours. And they forbid getting a dog as a gift for someone else. See the box on page 24 for a sampling of the questions you'll be asked before being permitted to take home a dog.

LOCAL SHELTERS AND RESCUE GROUPS

There are hundreds of shelters and rescue groups in the New York area. By far the biggest is the city pound, known in New York as the Center for Animal Care and Control (CACC). With a branch in each borough, the CACC finds homes for more than 10,000 animals a year.

We include detailed information in this chapter on the eight big shelters in and around New York City—plus one of the City's better-known small rescue groups, Mighty Mutts. But there are many other smaller, specialized animal rescue groups in the New York region. The best known among them:

- New Yorkers for Companion Animals on Manhattan's Upper East Side (www.geocities.com/Heartland/Plains/5418/nycaadoptions.html), 212-427-8873;

- Save Our Small Dogs, in southern New Jersey (http://sosdogs.petfinder.org);
- The Staten Island Council for Animal Welfare (www.petfinder.org/shelters/NY34.html), 718-761-6678;
- S.A.V.E. in Queens (www.saveanimalrescue.org), 718-358-0774;
- Rondout Valley Kennels, two-and-a-half hours north of the city in Accord, NY (http://web2.petfinder.org/shelters/NY58.html), 845-687-7619.

If you want to adopt a specific breed, contact that breed's rescue group. Virtually every breed has a national rescue club, and most have regional ones as well. To find a breed rescue group, go to this page on the American Kennel Club Web site: http://www.akc.org/breeds/rescue.cfm. Using a good Internet search engine like www.google.com, you should be able to find rescue groups for breeds that are not recognized by the AKC. If you're interested in adopting a retired racing Greyhound, see the box on page 33.

Before you visit in person, check out a shelter's Web site: most of them are updated at least once a week and include photos of available dogs. As well, the ASPCA, Bide-a-Wee, CACC, and many other shelters and rescue groups list their dogs on Petfinder, an online adoption database with about 40,000 listings from shelters natonwide (www.petfinder.com).

Center for Animal Care and Control (CACC)

www.nycacc.org

Since 1995, the not-for-profit Center for Animal Care and Control has been under contract to be New York City's official dog pound. With a shelter in each of the five boroughs, the CACC maintains 13 vans to pick up lost, abandoned or injured animals around the City. As well, the CACC cares for impounded dogs. Around fourteen-thousand dogs and cats are adopted each year from the CACC.

Because it's the only shelter in the City required to take in all stray or abandoned animals (and because there's a limited amount of space and money to care for these animals), the CACC euthanizes dogs that are not adopted. In 1999 (the latest year we have statistics for), 60,000 dogs and cats came through the CACC. Of those, 38,000 were put down.Together, the CACC's five shelters have room for around a thousand dogs and cats; for one good reason or another, only a fifth of that number is available for adoption. About half the animals at the CACC have been given up by their owners; the other half are strays brought in by the CACC's rescue vans, police or the public. Most dogs are mixed breeds; around 30 percent are purebred.

So, You Want to Adopt a Dog

Any good shelter or rescue group will ask a series of questions before letting you take home a dog. Here's what you can expect to be asked:

- Have you ever had another pet?
- If so, what happened to it? (They don't want to hear that it ran away from home.)
- Does your building permit dogs?
- Do you have children?
- How many hours a day will the dog be alone? (Don't request a puppy if you're not prepared to stay at home most of the day.)
- Did you have your last dog or cat neutered or spayed? (To a shelter, the right answer is yes.)
- What do you do for a living? (By which they hope for some idea of what you earn: people often abandon dogs because they can't afford them.)

The CACC charges $60 for mixed-breed dogs and $100 for purebreds. The price includes pre-adoption medical care and vaccines, de-worming, spaying or neutering, and microchip ID (see page 147). To adopt a dog, you must fill out a pre-adoption form, and be interviewed by an adoption counselor. You need two forms of ID, one character reference who can be reached by phone, and a copy of your lease or a letter from your landlord saying you're allowed a pet. Normally the process takes about an hour.

Manhattan: 326 E. 110th St, New York, NY 10029. 212-722-3620. Nearest subway: 6 train at 110th Street. Open seven days a week, 11 A.M. to 6 P.M.

Brooklyn: 2336 Linden Blvd, Brooklyn, NY 11208. 718-272-7200. Nearest subway: 3 train at New Lots Avenue. Open Monday through Saturday, 12 P.M. to 7 P.M.; and Sunday 12 P.M. to 5 P.M.

Queens: 92-29 Queens Boulevard, Rego Park, NY 11374. 718-997-6330. Nearest subway: G or R train at Woodhaven Blvd. Open Tuesday through Saturday, 8 A.M. to 4 P.M.

Bronx: 464 E. Fordham Rd., Bronx, NY 10458. 718-733-0743. Nearest subway: 4 train or D line to Fordham Rd. (then the Bx12 bus to Fordham Plaza). Open Tuesday through Saturday, 11 A.M. through 3 P.M.

Staten Island: 3139 Veterans Road West, Staten Island, NY 10309. 718-984-6643.

Nearest subway: Sorry, you need a car to get to this one. Open Monday through Saturday, 10 A.M. to 7 P.M.; Saturday and Sunday, 10 A.M. to 6 P.M.

North Shore Animal League

www.nsal.org

The North Shore Animal League was founded in 1944 as a modest no-kill shelter in Great Neck, Long Island. It soon attracted the attention and the money of Mr. and Mrs. Alex Lewyt, animal lovers and heirs to the Lewyt vacuum cleaner fortune. So determined was Mrs. Lewyt to rescue pets from pounds, she started a volunteer rescue organization that still today collects otherwise-doomed pets from pounds as far away as North Carolina. North Shore Animal League is now the largest no-kill shelter in the world (Best Friends in Utah is bigger, but it's considered to be an animal sanctuary, not a shelter). As for Mrs. Lewyt, she is still chairman of NSAL's board (her husband died in 1988).

About 80 percent of the 200-odd dogs at NSAL are rescued from shelters that put down dogs. The remaining 20 percent are given up by their owners. North Shore turns away aggressive dogs (it only takes in dogs that can be adopted). More than half of the dogs at NSAL are puppies. Around two percent of the puppies and ten percent of the adult dogs are purebred. New dogs arrive every day, but for the largest selection, come early on Saturday. The NSAL says some 16,000 dogs were adopted last year.

There's officially no charge for adopting a dog at NSAL, but donations are suggested. Dogs leave with their first set of shots, at a minimum. As well, they come with a collar, a leash, and a sample of Iams food. The shelter offers low-cost obedience classes ($10 for five classes) and subsidized spaying or neutering. If you can't get to Long Island, look out for NSAL's mobile adoption centers (35-foot Winnebagos). They're often parked at Manhattan's South Street Seaport and at the Staten Island Flea Market. Check the Web site or call for schedules.

To adopt a dog, start by filling out the pre-adoption form (save time by filling out the pre-adoption form on NSAL's Web site before you go). You'll need two forms of ID and two people the NSAL can call as character references. While NSAL calls your references and anyone you live with (to make sure they agree with your decision to get a dog), you're sent to the "family waiting room" where a video about responsible pet ownership is on a continuous loop. Once your file's reviewed, you'll be paged. A few weeks after the adoption, the NSAL may check up on you with a phone call and, if there's a problem, will make a home visit.

Long Island: 25 Davis Avenue, Port Washington, NY 11050. 516-883-7575. Nearest train station: the Long Island Railroad at Port Washington (about a ten minute walk from the shelter). For driving directions, see the NSAL Web site. Open seven days a week; 10 A.M. to 9 P.M.

American Society for the Prevention of Cruelty to Animals (ASPCA)

www.aspca.org

Although it maintains an office in Washington to lobby for animal rights, the ASPCA is not a national organization: there is only one ASPCA, and it's in New York City. Henry Bergh founded the organization in 1866 after returning to New York from a diplomatic posting in Russia where he was appalled by the abuse of carriage horses. Well-connected and rich, Bergh successfully lobbied for the nation's first law forbidding animal cruelty. To enforce the new law, the State of New York granted the ASPCA "Humane Law Enforcement Jurisdiction," which allows ASPCA officers to be armed and to arrest people for crimes against animals. Today there are 15 ASPCA officers in New York City who break up organized cock fights, dog fights and also rescue animals that are abused by their owners. Until 1995, the ASPCA was under contract by the City to collect and, if they weren't adopted, put down stray animals. Now the ASPCA is a no-kill shelter.

More than half the dogs at the ASPCA are given up by their owners. The rest are rescued, either from abusive owners or from the city pound. Generally, fewer than 25 percent are puppies; fewer than 10 percent are purebred. Around 400 dogs are adopted from the ASPCA each year.

The ASPCA charges between $75 and $125 for adoptions, depending on the dog (puppies and purebreds are more expensive). The fee includes shots, de-worming, spaying or neutering, one free post-adoption veterinary visit and a starter kit (toys, food, a leash). All dogs come with a microchip ID. The ASPCA also offers obedience classes, animal grief counseling, and a poison control hotline ($45 a case, at 888-426-4435).

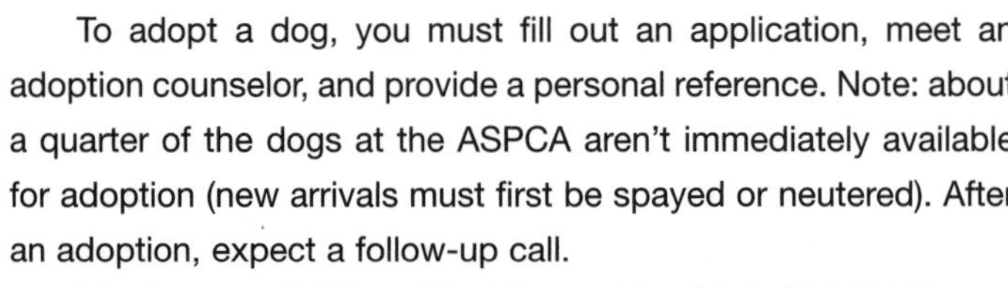

To adopt a dog, you must fill out an application, meet an adoption counselor, and provide a personal reference. Note: about a quarter of the dogs at the ASPCA aren't immediately available for adoption (new arrivals must first be spayed or neutered). After an adoption, expect a follow-up call.

Manhattan: 424 East 92nd Street, New York, NY 10128. 212-876-7700. Nearest subway: 4 or 5 train at 86th Street, or 6 train at 96th Street. Open Monday to Saturday, 11 A.M. to 7 p.m; Sunday, 11 A.M. to 5 P.M.

Humane Society of New York

www.humanesocietyny.org

The Humane Society of New York was established in 1904 to provide drinking water for New York City carriage horses and to protect animals from abuse. As horses were replaced by cars, the Humane Society shifted its focus to pets. It's now a no-kill shelter. Most of the dogs at the Humane Society have been given up by their owners. Some are rescued from the city pound. A few are strays. All dogs are "temperament checked" by the Humane Society's Bill Berloni, an accomplished dog trainer, so they can be properly matched to owners. There are many puppies here, but they're usually adopted as fast as they come in. Around 400 dogs a year are adopted from the Humane Society.

The charge for adopting a dog is $75 and up, depending on the dog. The fee includes spaying or neutering, vaccinations, and three weeks of post-adoption medical care. You also get a leash, collar, and a sample of food.

To adopt a dog, fill out the adoption form, which is available on the Humane Society's Web site, by fax, or at the shelter. You'll need two forms of ID and two personal references. If you own (or owned) a dog, you must provide the name and number of your vet. An interview with an adoption counselor takes about 15 minutes. The counselors want to meet everyone in your household (including other animals), but they ask that you don't bring young children on your first visit. Once you've been pre-approved, the counselor will show you dogs she thinks are best for you, but you can ask to see any dog and even take one for a walk. The Humane Society discourages people from taking a dog home on their first visit.

Manhattan: 306 East 59th Street, New York, NY 10022. 212-752-4840. Nearest subway: N, R, 4, 5 or 6 trains at 59th Street. Open seven days a week, 10:30 A.M. to 4 P.M.

Central Westchester Humane Society: Elmsford Animal Shelter

www.elmsfordanimalshelter.com

The Elmsford Shelter started in 1931 by sheltering animals in private homes. Now it's one of the biggest no-kill animal shelters in New York State with a 46,000-square-foot facility and five acres of land.

Because it's not easily accessible by public transportation, Elmsford is often overlooked by city folk. That's a shame: this shelter has a big selection of dogs, including purebreds and puppies. About two-thousand dogs and cats are adopted from Elmsford each year.

Prospective adopters complete a pre-adoption application, provide references and meet

How I Started Petfinder.com

My husband, Jared, and I came up with the idea for Petfinder.com over steaming plates of pasta on New Year's Eve 1995. Frustrated that our apartment complex wouldn't let us adopt a dog, we started thinking: why not help others adopt pets? What if we set up an Internet database listing adoptable pets in shelters and foster homes?

We had no expertise in computers. We knew little about the animal welfare world: at the time, we didn't even know where our local shelter was. We quickly got to work. Jared, a resident in radiology at the time, set out to program a database of pets that could be searched and organized by zip code and other criteria. Because I had done some work in graphic design, I was charged with designing the Web site. In the evenings, when I got home from my job as an urban forester for the state of New Jersey, I hit the phones to convince shelters to participate.

It was a labor of love: we spent a sizable chunk of our savings to get Petfinder up and running. But just as soon as we launched the site, we knew we'd hit a nerve. By the end of our first year—even though the site only had listings for New Jersey and New York—around a thousand people a day were checking out Petfinder. Six years later, some 50,000 people a day are visiting our site.

We quickly realized we had to expand. But we also knew it would be very costly to go nationwide. I bit the bullet, quit my day job, and devoted myself to finding sponsors for Petfinder. Thankfully, Ralston Purina came through with enough support to keep Petfinder.com free to users and to shelters and rescue groups.

Petfinder now lists more than forty-thousand pets from about two-thousand shelters and rescue groups across the nation. If you have a particular breed, size, or age of dog in mind, you can enter your criteria—and there's a good chance you'll find your dog close to where you live.

We've moved from New Jersey to Tucson, Arizona, where Jared is a Fellow in neuroradiology at the University of Arizona Medical Center by day, and a programmer for Petfinder by night. I work on Petfinder.com fulltime. We both take care of our two rescued dogs, Kobie and Max. Max found us on the streets of New Brunswick, NJ. Kobie came to us from New York's CACC, via Petfinder, of course.

Betsy Saul

an adoption counselor. The adoption fee is $75 for puppies and $65 for older dogs: it includes vaccinations, and heart-worm testing (and treatment). All animals are spayed and neutered prior to adoption.

Westchester: 100 Warehouse Lane South, Elmsford, NY. 914-592-7362 or 914-592-7334. Nearest Metro North train station is White Plains (it's a 15-minute cab ride from there). For directions by car, see the shelter's Web site. Open seven days a week, 11 A.M. to 5 P.M.

Bide-a-Wee

www.bideawee.org

One of the country's first no-kill shelters, Bide-a-Wee was founded in 1903 by Mrs. Flora D'Auby Jenkins Kibbe. Mrs. Kibbe conceived the idea during a trip to Paris where she saw an ambulance collecting stray cats and dogs for an animal adoption shelter.

Around 270 dogs were adopted from the Manhattan Bide-a-Wee last year (there are two other branches in Long Island). Most were given up by their owners; some were rescued from the city pound and other shelters that euthanize dogs. Before Bide-a-Wee takes in a dog, the shelter conducts a physical and behavioral exam. Dogs with severe or contagious illnesses, and those with serious behavioral problems are not accepted (Bide-a-Wee has a "retirement home" on Long Island for un-adoptable animals). There are usually far more adult dogs than puppies here, and many more mixed-breed dogs than purebreds.

Officially, there's no adoption fee, but Bide-a-Wee asks for a $30 donation ($55 for a puppy), which includes vaccinations, de-worming, two weeks of free vet care for pre-existing illnesses, and spaying or neutering.

If you want to adopt a dog, Bide-a-Wee will ask that you bring your entire household. You must fill out an adoption form (available on the Web site), provide references and ID, and speak to a staff member. You can play with a dog that interests you in the lobby or take him out for a walk.

Manhattan: 410 East 38th Street, New York, NY 10016. 212-532-4455. (Call or visit the Web site for information on locations in Wantagh and Westhampton, Long Island.) Nearest subway: 4, 5, 6 or 7 trains at Grand Central. Open Monday through Saturday, 10 A.M. to 6 P.M.; Sunday, 10 A.M. to 5 P.M.

Animal Haven

www.animalhavenshelter.org

Founded by a group of animal lovers in 1967 as a no-kill alternative to the city pound, Animal

Haven moved to its current headquarters in 1978. About 70 dogs a year are adopted from Animal Haven. Animal Haven is not a rescue group, so it will take in strays only when it has space. Around 90 percent of the dogs here have been given up by their owners. Fewer than 10 percent are purebreds. Fewer than 10 percent are puppies.

The $50 adoption fee at Animal Haven includes shots, spaying or neutering, tests for worms and behavior training. Plus you get an ID tag, a rabies tag, a collar, a choke chain, and a leash.

To adopt a dog, you must complete the pre-adoption form, be interviewed and provide references. If you already have a pet, or once had one, Animal Haven will ask to talk to your vet. If all goes well, Animal Haven delivers the dog to your house a few days later (assuming you live within a 150-mile radius).

Queens: 35-22 Prince Street, Flushing, NY 11354. 718-886-3683. Nearest subway: IRT #7 at Main Street. Open seven days a week, 9 A.M. to 5 P.M.

Brooklyn Animal Resource Coalition

www.barcshelter.org

BARC is a small no-kill shelter founded in 1988 by Anthony Spoto and Vincent Spinola, co-owners of BQE Pet Food and Grooming in Williamsburg. When they opened their store in 1987, they started feeding and caring for packs of stray animals living in the neighborhood. Before long they decided to help find homes for these strays. BQE Pet Food and Grooming still serves as shelter headquarters. A second building on North Ninth Street houses most of the animals.

Last year, 90 dogs were adopted from BARC. Around 60 percent were given up by their owners; 25 percent were strays (often left tied up in front of the shelter); and 15 percent were rescued from bad situations (abusive owners, for example). BARC's dogs are mainly medium-to-large-sized mixed breeds. About 20 percent are purebred and two percent are puppies.

BARC asks for a $75 "donation" as its adoption fee. The dogs here have been tested (and treated) for heart worm and have been spayed or neutered and vaccinated. Also, dogs are "socialized" and given basic leash training.

To adopt a dog, you'll need two personal references, two pieces of ID and, ideally, a lease or a letter from your landlord saying that dogs are allowed in your apartment. Before you can visit the dogs you'll be interviewed. BARC's staff will recommend dogs they think are best for you. Once you adopt, you'll get two staggered follow-up calls from BARC staff.

Brooklyn: 253 Wythe Avenue, Brooklyn, NY 11211. 718-486-7489. Nearest subway: L line at Bedford Ave. Open Monday through Saturday, 10:30 A.M. to 7 P.M.; Sunday, 12 P.M. to 4 P.M.

Adopting a Retired Greyhound

Bred for speed, endurance, and temperament, Greyhounds rarely suffer from hereditary diseases (though their deep chests make them prone to bloat, a fatal medical condition). They usually get along well with humans, including children. And, while needing plenty of exercise, they don't mind living in small spaces: they happily curl up in a ball.

On the downside, Greyhounds are unaccustomed to socializing with other breeds of dogs and can take some time to adjust to the normal life of a residential pet. As sight hounds trained to chase anything that moves, Greyhounds must always be on a leash, or kept in a secure fenced area. As well, it may take time to get them accustomed to living with small lure-like animals, such as a cat or a ferret.

Greyhounds up for adoption are usually between two and five years old. Around thirty inches high, Greyhounds weigh between 60 and 70 pounds. There are 16 recognized colors of Greyhounds, ranging from white and red to black, with almost every shade between (for a full view of all the color options, go to: www.abap.org/colors.htm).

For more information on Greyhounds, see http://aspca.org/adopt/greyhound.html and visit the sites of these national Greyhound organization sites, all of which offer links to local adoption agencies:

- The Greyhound Project, Inc at www.adopt-a-greyhound.org
- Greyhound Pets of America at www.greyhoundpets.org
- National Greyhound Adoption Program, Inc. at www.ngap.org

year; that they breed for temperament and health (not looks alone); that they are eager to make sure you're a responsible dog owner; that their homes or kennels are clean; and so on. Don't be in a rush: a good breeder is likely to have people on a waiting list. Warning: If you do get a dog from a breeder, be sure the contract states that you own the dog outright. Some breeders request that

Bringing Baby Home: How to Introduce Your Dog to a New Family Member

Question: How do I get my dogs accustomed to the presence of a new infant? Any suggestions? Or any reference material to recommend?"

Answer: If you have the slightest cause to believe that your dog is not comfortable around infants and children, you should call a good trainer as soon as possible. But if your dog seems okay around little ones, and you simply want to be extra cautious, then focus on these points:

1. **Give your dog lots of rewards in the presence of the baby.** This "classical conditioning" teaches your dog to adore the baby's presence. If you give your dog a delicious liver treat, or anything he likes, every time the baby comes in the room he will learn to associate the baby with the reward.

2. **Provide your dog his own special place to escape to when he tires of the baby.** This is especially important when your baby starts moving around.

3. **No matter how sweet your dog is, never ever leave him alone with your baby.** Many, many people come to me and ask: How do I teach my dog to babysit my child? My answer is always the same: No dog should be trusted alone with a baby.

4. **Finally, there's a good video called "Dogs, Cats & Kids" by Dr. Wayne Hunthausen, a well-known animal behavior expert.** While the video doesn't deal directly with training dogs, it does teach children how to behave safely around pets. For more information about the video, or to order a copy, visit www.dogscatskids.com.

Andrea Arden, Manhattan Dog Training

buyers sign a co-ownership contract, which under certain conditions, may allow the breeder to take back your dog and require that your dog compete in shows (partly at your own expense).

Depending on the breed of dog, you should ask if the puppy's parents have been certified by the Orthopedic Foundation for America (www.offa.org), an organization that rates a dog's risk of developing various genetic disorders, including hip dysplasia, a problem common in Labrador Retrievers and other popular large breeds. If the breed you want is prone to eye problems, find out if your breeder's dogs are registered with the Canine Eye Registration Foundation (www.vet.purdue.edu/~yshen/history.html).

New York State has a Puppy Lemon Law, but to qualify you have to get a certificate from a vet stating that your dog is "unfit" within two weeks of purchase. For more information on the law, call 1-800-771-7755 or visit the Web page of the State Attorney General at www.oag.state.ny.us/consumer/tips/pet_lemon_law.html.

Resources for Finding a Breeder

American Kennel Club Breeder Referral Search
www.akc.org/breeds/breederinfo/breeder_search.cfm

InfoDog's National Breeders Directory
www.infodog.com/brag/breedbystate/

Breeders.net
http://breeders.net/find.html

2 houndlaw

THE RULES AND REGULATIONS OF OWNING A DOG IN NEW YORK CITY

Be a responsible dog owner: obey the laws. Try to remember that many people don't like dogs or are afraid of them. Don't aggravate these people. Pick up after your dog. Keep her on a leash. Teach her not to bark when she's left alone. Be an ambassador for dogs.

The very best way to avoid trouble is to know your legal rights and responsibilities. This chapter includes a layman's guide to the basic hound laws of New York City. It also has answers to some of the most common legal queries we get at Urbanhound.com, names of some of the best pet lawyers in town, and a list of superb resources to consult for help.

The City's Dog Laws

GET A LICENSE

Any dog that's going to be in New York for more than 30 days must be licensed. And your dog's license tag must be attached to his collar whenever he leaves your house (Health Code, Section161.04). To apply for a license, call the Department of Health's Dog Licensing division at 212-676-2100 or print out the form at www.ci.nyc.ny.us/html/doh/html/vet/vetdog.html, fill it in, and mail it with a check to Veterinary Public Health Services, P.O. Box 4768, Church Street Station, New York, NY 10261-4768. Licenses costs $8.50 a year for spayed or neutered dogs and $11.50 for dogs that are not fixed.

GET A RABIES VACCINE

All dogs over three months old must be immunized against rabies (New York City Health Code, Section 11.66).

SCOOP THE POOP

Dogs owners are required to pick up after their dogs (Health Code, Section 161.03). To report dog owners who don't scoop their dogs' poop, call the City's Sanitation Action Center at 212-219-8090.

Pooper-Scooper Tips

Picking up after your dog sounds easy enough, but for reasons unknown, some dog owners just can't get it right. Herewith, a few suggestions:

What To Use: The best way to scoop poop is to use old plastic grocery bags, sandwich baggies, or special (scented!) poop bags sold by pet-supply stores (brands include: Doggie Walk Bags, Dispoz-A-Scoop, and Bags On Board). Using the bag as a glove, pick up your dog's poop, turn the bag inside out and secure it with a knot.

What Not To Use: Using newspaper to scoop poop is popular, but unwise because newspaper can't be sealed. Loose poop in a public trash can is unsanitary and smelly, especially in the summer.

What "Curb Your Dog" Means: Don't let your dog pee and poop in the middle of a sidewalk. It's rude, particularly in the summer when pedestrians wear thin-soled flip-flops. Teach your dog to do what he needs to do in the street, or at the very edge of the curb. Dogs are creatures of habit, so if you rush your dog between two parked cars as soon as you get out of your building, he'll soon catch on.

USE A LEASH

When in public, your dog must be restrained by a leash or chain no longer than six-feet long (Health Code, Section 161.05). To complain about off-leash dogs, call the Department of Health's Central Information Line at 212-442-9666.

DON'T BE A NUISANCE

You must prevent your dog from "committing a nuisance" in any public place (Health Code, Section 161.03). To report a dog that is being a nuisance, call the Department of Health's Central Information Line at 212-442-9666.

KEEP YOUR DOG QUIET

You must prevent your dog from causing "unreasonable noise" (Administrative Code, Section 24-222). To report a dog that barks unreasonably, call the City's Department of Environmental Protection at 718-699-9811.

PREVENT ATTACKS

Your dog is not allowed to attack or assault people or pets, nor is he allowed to fight other dogs (Administrative Code, Section 17-343).

Aggressive behavior may be excused if:

- Your dog attacks someone who breaks into your house;
- Your dog attacks someone who is tormenting, abusing, or assaulting him;
- Your dog attacks someone who's trying to commit a crime;
- Your dog attacks in response to pain or injury;
- Your dog attacks to protect himself, his kennels, or his offspring (Administrative Code, Section 17-347).

If your dog attacks or assaults a person or another pet, and if none of the above exceptions apply, the city may hold a hearing to decide if your dog is a "dangerous dog" (as defined by Administrative Code, Section 17-342). Based on evidence presented at the hearing, the Department of Health Commissioner can force you to:

- Register your "dangerous dog" with the City;
- Muzzle or lock up your dog;
- Take out a liability insurance policy of $100,000;
- Register your dog for an obedience class;
- Get your dog anti-bite training;
- Get the dog out of the City permanently; or,
- Have the dog put down (Administrative Code, Sections 17-344 and 17-345).

To report a dog bite, call the Department of Health's Veterinarian Public Health division at 212-676-2483. As well, all threatening dogs should be reported to the Department of Health's Central Complaints division at 212-442-1838.

Common Canine Legal Queries

The higher real estate prices go, the more we hear about landlords and co-op boards cracking down hard on hounds. But eviction notices are just one of many legal challenges confronting the city's hounds and their owners. If your dog is hit by a cab, can you sue the cabbie? What can you do if your dog is attacked by an angry Chihuahua? Is the animal hospital allowed to hold your dog until you settle the bill? (The answer to that one, by the way, is yes.)

You can get informed answers to these questions and many more by visiting Urbanhound.com, where Darryl Vernon, an attorney and defender of dogs, responds to all sorts of queries. In these pages, with help from Darryl, a partner with New York's Vernon & Ginsburg (www.lawyers.com/vernon&ginsburg), we include answers to a few of the more common canine legal questions.

But remember: this chapter is not a substitute for legal advice; it is an educational resource. If you have legal problems, hire a lawyer. If you need help finding one, consult our list on pages 43-45. We include other excellent animal law resources at the end of this chapter, on page 46.

"Because I have a dog, my landlord wants to evict me. Do I have any rights?"

First: read your lease carefully. If it includes a "no-pets clause," then, yes, your landlord can evict you. But the law allows for wiggle room. You can maneuver. Here are ways you may be able to fight an eviction notice:

The Pet Law (a.k.a., the Three-Month Rule): One way to avoid being evicted is to prove that you've had your dog in the apartment for at least three months. According to the Pet Law (officially, Section 27-2009 of the Administrative Code of the City of New York), a no-pets clause is waived if a renter keeps his dog "openly and notoriously" for at least three months before receiving an eviction notice.

Keeping a dog "openly and notoriously" means that the dog can't be hidden in a bag each time you come in and out of the building. It also means you can't lie. Telling your doorman that you're dog sitting does not count toward keeping a dog "openly and notoriously." That said, it's not hard to prove you were open and notorious. If your super, your doorman or your managing agent sees you with your dog just once, that may be all the evidence you need to build a case in your favor.

Note: just because your landlord was deemed to have "waived" the no-pets clause for your first dog, that doesn't mean you're free to get a second dog. Some recent legal decisions have said that once the no-pets clause is waived, it's waived for good. But other decisions have disagreed with that. So there's no telling which way a judge would rule on this one.

One more thing: while the Pet Law applies to all co-ops and rentals in New York City, it does not at this time apply to condos in Manhattan and the Bronx (though it does apply to condos in Queens, Brooklyn and Staten Island).

Federal Fair Housing Act: Most people know it's illegal for a landlord to use a no-pets clause to turn away a tenant who needs a guide dog. But under the Federal Fair Housing Act, which outlaws discrimination in housing, it may be illegal for a landlord to refuse a dog to anyone with a serious mental or physical disability—including HIV or AIDS, severe diabetes, high blood pressure, and depression. The key is to demonstrate that your dog is a “medical necessity,” which may simply mean he cheers you up. In one recent case, a clinically depressed tenant was “prescribed” a dog by her psychiatrist. Despite a no-pet clause in the tenant’s lease, she could not be evicted.

“My dog barks all day when I’m at work. Can I be evicted?”

Yes. But getting you out will not be easy. The law says your dog has to behave himself; specifically, Section 24-222 of the New York City Administrative Code says a dog should not “cause unreasonable noise.”

But what’s “unreasonable noise”? Hard to say. (So hard, in fact, that a court in New Rochelle recently voided an “unreasonable noise” law for being too vague.) Occasional barking, or even barking that lasts for an hour or more, probably wouldn’t be deemed “unreasonable.” The landlord would have to prove that your dog barks non-stop. To do so, other tenants have to testify that your dog barks and howls and cries all day long, and that he is therefore a “nuisance” interfering with the use of their own apartments. Even if your dog is making “unreasonable noise,” you must be given a chance to “cure” the situation.

This raises a crucial issue: if your dog barks when you’re away, do something about it! Don’t wait for an eviction notice. Don’t antagonize your neighbors. Some people are extremely sensitive to noise. Talk to your vet, hire an animal behaviorist, read about separation anxiety and obsessive-compulsive disorders in dogs. Consider getting a second dog to keep your dog company when you’re away from home. Get help.

“My dog was attacked by an angry Cocker Spaniel at the dog run. Can I sue the Spaniel’s owners?”

There’s an unwritten rule at dog runs: owners pay the medical bills of any dog attacked by their dog. In this case, that means the Spaniel’s owner should cover your dog’s veterinary costs. If he refuses, you can sue. But don’t count on getting anything more than recovery of your medical bills.

Because dogs are considered “property” in New York, you can not sue for pain and suffering, nor can you win punitive damages. (One exception: if you were close enough to the attack that you felt your life was in danger—if you were in the “zone of danger”—you could sue for pain and suffering.) Even if your dog dies from the attack, the most you can win in court, beyond your medical bills, is a sum equal to the “value” of your dog.

When it comes to the value of dogs, sentimental value doesn’t count. Courts interpret “value” literally, as in: What did you pay for your dog? Did you get her at the pound for $55? Then her value is $55. Period. (This also holds true, by the way, in veterinary malpractice suits—though you may be able to negotiate a higher out-of-court settlement. For an outstanding article about wrongful-death or -injury cases, visit www.aldf.org/damages.htm on the Animal Legal Defense Fund's Web site.)

Because the amounts likely to be recovered in such cases are so small, it's probably not worth the cost of hiring a lawyer: stick to small-claims court. If you're determined, you might try to argue that your dog—a top show dog, or a trained guard or guide dog—has greatly appreciated in value since you bought her. Let us know if you have any luck.

On a side note, if you or your dog is bitten, get as much information about the aggressor and his owner as possible (including the dog's license number, if he has one). Then call the Department of Health's Veterinarian Public Health division at 212-676-2483. They will double check that the dog's rabies vaccination is current. Under New York's "dangerous dog" law (Local Law 2 of 1991), if the dog's attack was unprovoked, the City may require the owners to muzzle or confine the dog, attend obedience class, carry liability insurance, or, in extreme cases, have the dog put down.

"My co-op board has deemed my dog a nuisance. Now they want me out. What can I do?"

A dog that urinates on the lobby furniture, races down the stairwell, growls at people, bites the doorman, attacks the mailman, jumps on children in the elevator and barks all day, is, obviously, a nuisance. Nevertheless, to prove to a court that your dog is a nuisance, your board (or, in a rental, your landlord) has to show that your neighbors are "substantially and adversely" affected by your dog's antics. The bottom line: if enough of your fellow owners (or fellow tenants) complain about your dog, you're out of luck.

That said, they can't simply toss you or your dog out of the building. More likely, your dog will be given a chance to redeem herself and learn some manners. The court may simply require that your dog see an animal behaviorist.

"When my live-in boyfriend and I broke up, he kept the dog while I looked for a new place. Now he refuses to give me custody. While living together, we both took care of the dog, but the dog is registered in my name and I took on all the associated financial responsibilities. Can I get my dog back?"

There are two crucial issues here: first, who has rights to custody; second, if you do have the rights to custody, how do you get your dog back.

Since you bought the dog and were financially responsible for the dog's welfare, it appears that you have more rights to the dog than your ex-boyfriend does. The name on the dog's license can be used as evidence of your ownership, but you should gather as many documents as possible substantiating your ownership. Finally, any agreement that was made between you and your ex regarding custody of the dog is important (ideally an agreement should be in writing, but oral agreements count too—they're just harder to prove).

Even if you can prove ownership, however, gaining custody is hard work. In this case, since you can demonstrate that the dog belongs to you, you should consider reporting a theft, asking the police to return the dog. The police, who are generally reluctant to get involved in a custody battle, will likely tell you to go to court. But you may get lucky: if your documentation is good, and you're able to enlist supervisors at the police department, you might get results from the cops.

Going to court is the last solution. Lawsuits can be effective, but they're also expensive, slow, and time-consuming. The court will try to determine what you and your ex-boyfriend intended to happen upon a breakup, and who actually owns the dog. The bottom line: the next time you walk out on a lover or a spouse, take your dog with you.

Top Pet Lawyers

Many legal disputes involving dogs can be resolved without the costly intervention of a lawyer. But in some cases, you'd best get an attorney—quickly. Eviction battles are one example. Having your dog declared "dangerous" by the city is another: if you don't act fast, the city may put down your hound.

Companion animal law is a fairly new field. Still, in New York City there are a growing number of lawyers who regularly deal with such cases. We list some of the best ones here, in alphabetical order. For names of others, call the Legal Reference Service of The Association of the Bar of the City of New York at 212-626-7373 or request a referral online at www.abcny.org/sec-bin/referral.pl. The referral service is free, and it entitles you to an initial half-hour consultation with a referring lawyer for just $25 (that fee helps defray the Legal Reference Service's costs).

Another good place for referrals is the Legal Action for Animals, an organization that defends low-income pet owners in cases against landlords at 718-544-0605. For cases outside New York, contact the Animal Legal Defense Fund, which has a network of attorneys around the country (707 769-7771, x10, or www.ALDF.org).

Frances B. Carlisle, Morrison Cohen Singer & Weinstein, 750 Lexington Avenue, Manhattan. 212-735-8600. www.mscw.com
Admitted to the New York bar in 1984, Frances earned her degree at the University of California School of Law at Davis. Because she practices in the area of trusts and estates, Frances specializes in setting up will provisions for pets, making bequests to non-profits devoted to animal issues, and establishing animal charities. She's a member of the Association of the Bar of the City of New York's Committee on Legal Issues Pertaining to Animals.

Karen Copeland, 521 Fifth Ave., Suite 1700, Manhattan. 212-560-7154.
Admitted to the bar in 1985, Copeland earned her law degree from Brooklyn Law School. Since 1995, she's largely devoted her practice to representing pet owners facing eviction and is best known for aggressively using the Fair Housing Act to defend the rights of the elderly and disabled to keep pets. Formerly on staff with the city's Housing Litigation Bureau, Karen now volunteers with Legal Action for Animals (see below).

Jeffrey D. Delott, 375 North Broadway, Suite 102, Jericho, Long Island.
516-822-6699. http://members.aol.com/delott
Admitted to the New York bar in 1990, Jeffrey earned his law degree at the University of Pennsylvania. Through his litigation and commercial law practice, he's been representing dogs and their owners since 1996.

Eric Feinberg
329 East 63rd Street, Suite 1B, Manhattan. 212-832-6667. www.doglawyer.com
Admitted to the bar in 1987, Eric got his degree at the City University of New York's School of Law. He practices real estate law, and has worked on cases involving dog owners and landlords since 1997.

Marilyne Mason, Legal Action for Animals, Kew Gardens, Queens. 718-544-0605.
After many years as a litigator for the City of New York, Marilyne founded Legal Action for Animals to help tenants in need defend themselves against landlords. An animal rights activist, Marilyne is also involved with a group called Feminists for Animal Rights.

Elinor D. Molbegott, East Williston, Long Island 516-746-6505.
Admitted to the bar in 1978, Elinor graduated from Albany Law School. Having spent more than 20 years representing various animal rights groups, she's been involved in some of the city's most important legal victories for animals, including New York's Pet Law, which expanded the rights of pet owners to fight evictions. Now a legal advisor to the Humane Society of New York, Elinor devotes most of her time to drafting animal-rights legislation, but she will occasionally take on individual cases involving egregious negligence (a dog killed by an airline or a shelter, for example).

Darryl Vernon, Vernon & Ginsburg, 261 Madison Avenue, Suite 26, Manhattan.
212-949-7300, x201. www.lawyers.com/vernon&ginsburg/
Admitted to the bar in 1982, Darryl earned his degree at Yeshiva University's Benjamin N. Cardozo School of Law. An attorney who practices real estate and commercial law, Darryl has defended dogs (and their owners) since 1983 and has been Urbanhound.com's legal columnist since the site's launch in June 2000. Many of his articles, pamphlets and case law on the subject of animal rights have been published. He is a member of the Association of the Bar of the City of New York's Committee on Legal Issues Pertaining to Animals.

Maddy Tarnowsky, 360 Central Park West, # 5E, Manhattan. 212-972-1355.
Admitted to the bar in 1988, Maddy graduated from the City University of New York's School of Law. Through her work representing tenants, especially the elderly and disabled, in housing court, she often works on eviction cases involving pets.

Joel R. Zand, 888 7th Ave., Manhattan. 212-582-3200. www.doglaw.com
Admitted to the bar in 1994, Joel earned his degree from Yeshiva University's Benjamin N. Cardozo School of Law. A real estate lawyer who specializes in co-op apartment buildings, Zand represents both tenants and landlords. He has become known for handling cases on behalf of pet owners.

Animal Law Resources

WEB SITES

ACO Fun Stop

www.acofunstop.com/newyork.htm

A resource for animal control police nationwide, this site includes the full text (in full legal jargon) of every law pertaining to animals in New York.

Animal Legal Defense Fund

www.aldf.org

This site is not easy to navigate, but buried within it are a handful of top-notch articles about recovering damages in wrongful-injury suits (www.aldf.org/damages.htm), estate planning for animals (www.aldf.org/estate.htm), and vet malpractice.

Application for a New York City Dog License: NYC Department of Health

www.ci.nyc.ny.us/html/doh/html/vet/vetdog.html

Print out this page, fill it in, and mail it, along with a check, to: Veterinary Public Health Services, P.O. Box 4768, Church Street Station, New York, NY 10261-4768

Association of the Bar of the City of New York: City Bar Online

www.abcny.org

Through its Committee on Legal Issues Pertaining to Animals, the New York Bar Association is an excellent resource for pet owners. This site offers a legal referral service and includes four terrific (and free) brochures about dog law written by attorneys:

- Providing For Your Pet in the Event of Your Death or Hospitalization
- Bringing Rex Home: A Veterinarian/Boarding Kennel's Right to Hold Your Pet Because of an Unpaid Bill in New York State
- Keeping Spot and Fluffy Home: Pets in NYC Housing
- Access Rights of People with Disabilities and Their Service Animals

ASPCA Legal Department

www.aspca.org

The ASPCA does not offer legal advice to individuals; it enforces animal cruelty statutes in New York. Nonetheless, the organization's Web site has information on animal laws, veterinary malpractice, animal abuse, and pet lemon laws. The ASPCA also publishes *Laws Protecting Animals in New York State and New York City*, a $40 book that's updated annually.

Commonly Asked Questions About Service Dogs in Places of Business: US Department of Justice

www.usdoj.gov/crt/ada/qasrvc.htm

In plain English, this Web page explains the rights of people with service animals under the American with Disabilities Act. It answers such questions as, "I operate a private taxicab and I don't want animals in my taxi . . . Am I violating the ADA if I refuse to pick up someone with a service animal?" and "How can I tell if an animal is really a service animal and not just a pet?"

DogBiteLaw.com

www.dogbitelaw.com

Maintained by Kenneth Phillips, a California-based lawyer whose practice is devoted to representing dog-bite victims, this site claims to be: "The most extensive research site for dog bite victims, dog owners, parents, journalists and others needing to learn about the legal rights of victims, how to protect children, and other aspects of the dog bite epidemic." It is exhaustive. A section for dog owners has information on liability insurance, criminal penalties for dog bites, and statutes of limitations. It also tells you what to do if your dog bites someone. A page is devoted to New York State's dog bite law (www.dogbitelaw.com/PAGES/New%20York.html).

DogLaw.com

www.doglaw.com

Maintained by New York pet attorney Joel R. Zand (see page 45), this site has useful links and facts about dog law in New York. As well, it includes the full text of some important court decisions regarding companion animals.

New York City Department of Veterinary Health

http://www.ci.nyc.ny.us/html/doh/html/vet/vet.html

This site includes the city's dog license application, which can be downloaded. But aside from that, the information here (details about the animal bite monitoring program, rabies, and animal control) is somewhat disappointing.

Nolo Press

www.nolo.com

Nolo Press publishes legal self-help guides. At this Web site you can order the company's *Dog Law* book (see p.48), find answers to some dog-law questions, download legal forms, and access a legal dictionary and encyclopedia.

NYC Top Dogs

www.nyctopdogs.com

TOPDOGS, founded by Terry Fonville, keeps tabs on the treatment of dog owners by New York's Parks Enforcement Police. This site includes an online form for dog owners to report incidents of harassment or abuse by Parks personnel.

Pet Lemon Law: Office of the New York State Attorney General

www.oag.state.ny.us/consumer/tips/pet_lemon_law.html

This Web page explains how the state's pet "lemon law" works.

Rutgers University School of Law Animal Rights Law Project

www.animal-law.org

Rutgers claims to be the first law school in the country to make animal rights part of the regular academic curriculum. The material on this thorough site covers everything from the right of students to object to vivisection or dissection in the classroom to hunting and wildlife issues to animal sacrifices and housing cases involving companion animals. One page is devoted to New York State laws regarding pets and housing (www.animal-law.org/housing/housny.html).

TenantNet

www.tenant.net.

Devoted to New York City residential tenants, and maintained by an informal network of New Yorkers involved in tenant associations and community groups, this site includes many outstanding articles about the rights of pet owners in public and private housing.

BOOKS

Dog Law, by Mary Randolph (Nolo Press, 1999).

Though it does not offer much detail about local laws, this book, written by a San Francisco-based attorney, is an excellent resource for both national and state canine legal issues. It can be ordered from the publisher at www.nolo.com, a useful Web site (see page 47). Paperback, 336 pages, $12.

3 houndplay

HANGING OUT AT DOG RUNS AND CITY PARKS

You've heard it hundreds of times: people without yards shouldn't have dogs, ever. By which is meant: people living in the city shouldn't have dogs. Rubbish! New York City offers dogs plenty of room for play. For evidence, read on.

Dog Runs

It's hard to believe that until 1990 there were no dog runs in New York City. Today, by Urbanhound.com's count, there are 38 dog runs in the city, with more on the way, including one about to open in Morningside Heights as this book was going to press. Dog runs (known as "dog parks" in the rest of the country) come in every size and condition. Some are beautifully landscaped, with benches and water fountains; others are nothing more than a small, dusty strip of pavement.

All the runs listed here are open to the public, but a few require a membership fee and one or two may have a waiting list to get in. Most are operated in conjunction with the city's Parks Department; a handful are on private land; a few are covert. But almost all the dog runs in New York are maintained by their users, who contribute time and money for upkeep. If you'd like to chip in, send a tax-deductible donation ($20 to $50 a year is suggested) to your dog run's manager. Read on to find dog runs near you, and check out Urbanhound.com for the most up-to-date listings. We've organized the list by borough and by neighborhood. Can't find one near you? Then read our guide to starting a dog run on page 65.

MANHATTAN

Inwood/Fort George/Washington Heights

Inwood Hill Park This sparse run opened in late 1999. It's still a work in progress, which is why, for both dog and human, the run is not as interesting as Inwood Hill Park itself. The park is huge, with many trails into the hill where, according to one member of Urbanhound.com, "dogs can unofficially, and unobtrusively, frolic off-leash."

Location: West 207th Street, near the baseball diamond.

Under foot: Pea gravel

Features: A water sprinkler and a separate area for small dogs is planned.

Manager: Inwood Hill Dog Run, c/o 25 Indian Road, New York, NY 10034-1017.

Rules of the Run

Rules vary slightly from dog run to dog run. This list is reprinted with the permission of Manhattan's Bull Moose Dog Run at 81st Street between Columbus and Central Park West (see page 53). We can't imagine a better set of basic rules for any dog run anywhere:

Clean Up: Immediately clean up after your dogs.

Barking: In order to keep our dog run, we must enforce the following agreement with Community Board 7. NO SUSTAINED BARKING! If barking cannot be stopped, YOU MUST LEAVE. Day or Night!

Vaccinations and Licenses: All dogs must be properly vaccinated and have a visible, current New York City dog license.

Dog Walkers: No more than 4 dogs are allowed per walker.

No Unattended Dogs Allowed: You can't clean up or break up a fight from outside.

For Those With Children: This is a dog run, not a playground. All children aged 10 and under must be accompanied by an adult and be closely supervised. NO BABY CARRIAGES, BICYCLES, ROLLER BLADES, SKATEBOARDS OR SCOOTERS. DOGS PLAY ROUGH: We strongly discourage bringing toddlers and small children inside the run. However, if you insist on taking that risk, you must closely supervise them and accept all responsibility in case of injury.

Fight Prevention: No bitches in any stage of heat may enter the run. If your un-neutered male is involved in any altercation regardless of "who started it", don't argue or blame—JUST LEAVE. If this rule is not followed, the run will have no choice but to ban ALL un-neutered males.

Correcting Behavior: If your dog is attacking, intimidating, mounting or annoying another dog, correct that behavior immediately. In addition, if anyone asks you to remove your dog from their dog for any reason, comply with no argument. If your dog continues, remove it from the run.

Breaking Up a Fight: If a fight occurs, all involved dog owners must immediately break it up.

Protecting Your Stuff: Dogs will compete for your food and your dog's toys. If this bothers you, then DON'T BRING THEM INTO THE RUN.

Don't Litter: Place all newspapers, trash and extinguished cigarettes in the garbage cans.

J. Hood Wright Park The Parks Department maintains this modest dog run because there's no active group of dog owners here.
Location: West 173rd Street, between Fort Washington Ave. and Haven Ave.
In charge: Jane Schacht, NYC Parks Dept Supervisor, 212-795-1388

Harlem

Tom's Dog Run This small run opened in March 2000. During rush hour it can be a little noisy (it's right next to the FDR Drive), but as it's the only dog run in Harlem, there's a lot here to be thankful for. The dog owners who use this run are active and enthusiastic: visit their Web site at http://tomsrun.homestead.com.
Location: Thomas Jefferson Park, East 112th Street, at First Ave.
Under foot: Wood chips
Features: Benches
In charge: Birgit Bogler, bogler427@yahoo.com and Russell Granger, russellgranger@earthlink.net

Upper West Side

Dog Run 105 It took nearly two years and $75,000, but it was worth it: the reconstruction of this dog run, completed in May 2000, has made it a model for the rest of the city. Dog Run 105 shows what can be done when the Parks Department, local government, dog owners, and other members of the community cooperate. The run has World's Fair-style benches, an elegant wrought-iron fence and a water fountain. The run's new surface—soft crushed granite—is easy to clean and maintain. And it's soft on dogs' paws. For information or to become a member of Riverside Dog Owners Group—the very active lobby group that oversees this run—visit www.riverside-dog.com.
Location: Riverside Park Central Promenade at West 105th Street
Under foot: Crushed granite
Features: Water fountain, small-dog area, poop bag dispensers, benches, trees. In summer months, there's a dog-friendly outdoor café right across the promenade from this run.
In charge: John Herrold, 212-222-0040 or johnfh@concentric.net
Manager: Riverside Park Dog Owners Group, c/o Riverside Park Fund, 475 Riverside Drive, Suite 249, New York, NY 10115. 212-222-7516

Dog Run 87 Organized fund-raising by the community resulted in a renovation that enlarged the

run, provided much-needed drainage, and a new fence. There is a spacious separate area for dogs who are small or antisocial. Word has it that a water fountain is on the way.
Location: Riverside Park at West 87th Street
Under foot: Crushed granite
In charge: Shelly Friedland and Michael Zorek, dogrun87@aol.com
Manager: Riverside Park Fund, 475 Riverside Drive, Suite 249, New York, NY 10115. 212-870-3070

Riverside Park 72nd Street "South Slope" Off-leash Play Field For many years now, Friends and Lovers Of Riverside Area Life (FLORAL) has worked to get approval for a permanent run at the 73rd Street Track Infield. Approval was given—and then rescinded. Instead, FLORAL was told it could make this temporary run at 72nd Street permanent. However, FLORAL continues to work on final approvals and funding with the City. For a detailed look at the political intrigue involved, and to help out, visit FLORAL's Web site at www.rspfloral.org.
Temporary Location: Riverside Park at West 72nd Street
Under foot: Dirt and hay
Features: Several benches, poop bags, poop scoopers, hanging flower pots, water source.
In charge: Jeffrey Zahn, 212-580-6932 or info@rspfloral.com
Manager: FLORAL, c/o Riverside Park Fund, 475 Riverside Drive, Suite 249, New York, NY 10115. 212-870-3070

Bull Moose Dog Run (a.k.a., Teddy's Dog Run) After a major renovation, this dog run, in the shadow of the Museum of Natural History, re-opened in late 2000 to rave reviews.
Location: West 81st St. at Columbus Ave.
Under foot: Pea-gravel
Features: Water faucets, a separate area for small dogs
In charge: Richard Gordon, 212-580-2065 or rmg4dogs@aol.com
Manager: The Friends of Museum Park Dog Run, Box 412, Planetarium Station. New York, NY 10024.

Upper East Side

Carl's Dog Run This is a well-maintained dog run in a lovely park. Past the main run, towards the river, is a second run for small dogs. A stone's throw from Gracie Mansion, this smaller run has a superb view of the East River and the 59th Street Bridge.

Location: Carl Shurz Park, East 86th Street at East End Avenue
Under foot: Pea gravel
Features: Benches, poop scoops
In charge: Susan Bernstein, 212-288-3304.
Manager: Carl Schurz Park Dog Run Committe, 217 East 85th St., P.O. Box 116, New York, NY 10028.

East 60 Pavilion Esplanade This sparse, unofficial dog run is, according to one user, "the best kept secret around." And the dog owners who come here would like to keep it that way. "If you ever go to the Beekman Place dog run you'll see why we don't want any exposure," another user told Urbanhound.com, sotto voce. "The dog walkers there bring in eight to ten dogs and they make a mess of the place!"

Whatever. Dog walkers or no, the run at Peter Detmold Park (see below) has a lot more going for it than this strip of concrete does. But if you do visit this run, beware the gap in the railing by the river: a small dog could slip through and be in for a 70-foot drop.
Location: East 60th Street and East River, directly over FDR Drive
Under foot: Concrete
Features: A bench, poop bags, lights, water faucets

Midtown East

Peter Detmold Park A lovely, well-maintained run with plenty of space—lots of trees, nice benches, historical lamps. But the FDR Drive makes it noisy and the winds coming across the river can be fierce.
Location: East 49th Street, at FDR Drive. Behind Beekman Place.
Under foot: Concrete tile, dirt, and occasional patches of grass
Features: Benches, poop bags, trees, lamps
In charge: Geri Can Rees, gvr@prodigy.net
Manager: Peter Detmold Park—Animals Run Free (PDP-ARF, Inc.) c/o Maranyc, 120 East 56th Street, New York, NY 10022

Robert Moses Park Hardly worthy of its road-builder namesake, this dog run is just a tiny, narrow strip of pavement. Nonetheless, people who use the run regularly tell us the park's friendly community of dogs and their owners make up for the lack of amenities.

Location: East 41st Street, at First Avenue
Under foot: Concrete
Features: None

Hell's Kitchen/Clinton

Hell's Kitchen Dog Run This charming members-only dog run sits on land borrowed from the Metropolitan Transportation Authority. Perched on a strip below an overpass and above a tunnel, it's easy to miss, so take note: it's on the southeast corner of West 39th and 10th Ave. You need a key to get in. Membership costs $15 a year ("check or money order ONLY" warns a sign at the run). There are around 150 members.
Location: West 39th Street at 10th Avenue
Under foot: Wood chips
Features: Chairs, umbrellas, small plastic pool for dogs, a fenced-in flower garden, lights
Manager: Hell's Kitchen Neighborhood Association, 212-957-3667

DeWitt Clinton Park This once-shabby dog run is being upgraded thanks to the efforts of the newly formed Friends of DeWitt Clinton dog owners group. In mid-2000, a new fence and a double-gated entrance were installed. Plus, the run now has a water supply. There's more to come.
Location: West 52nd and 11th Ave.
Under foot: Concrete
Features: Benches, historical lamps
In charge: Esther Willard, fodcdr@hotmail.com

Chelsea

West Chelsea Dog Run The original Chelsea dog run, at West 22nd Street and 11th Avenue, was closed when construction of the new Chelsea Waterside Park began. This new dog run—located in a triangle bordered by 11th Avenue, 24th Street and the West Side Highway—opened in October 2000 after much lobbying and wrangling by the West Chelsea Dog Owners Association. "Our Dog Park represents the first time a dog play area has been designed into a city park from the outset," reads the Association's Web site at www.bitsworld.com/dogrun. "In that sense, it represents an acknowledgement, on the part of the city and the state, that dogs do exist, that there are a lot of them in this neighborhood, and that they need a place to call their own."

New York's First Dog Run

Dog Runs are one of the great social experiments of modern New York; a tenuous compromise between dog owners, dog phobics, police, and the Parks Department.

The city's first dog run opened in 1990 in Tomkins Square Park in Manhattan's East Village. There had been riots in the park between cops, squatters, and the homeless. Afterwards, the park was closed. When it reopened, we dog owners were granted a patch of land, in the hope that we'd help keep the park safe.

The catch: we had to maintain the run on our own. We had to keep the place clean, raise money for repairs, prevent fights (not just between dogs, but among their owners too), find homes for the streams of dogs dumped at the run, and save the trees. And all this without precedent, for we were the only dog run in the city.

The founder of our run, Monay Germaine, ran a tight ship. She established formal rules and created a financial structure, but when she retired, an informal bunch of us took charge. We're idiosyncratic, which is a nice way of saying we rule by chaos. We've remained resistant to an organized dog-owners' group, and none of us has titles, for example. Among us is a group of senior citizens who want official badges designating them to enforce dog run rules. Then there's the old-time East Villager who insists her pit bull should be allowed in the run—even though he's attacked several dogs and one human.

For all of our disorganization, we're a tight-knit community. Our Halloween Parade has been a smashing success. We keep communal listings of local dog-friendly bars, restaurants and stores. And my friend Elizabeth and I even started an occasional dog-run newsletter, The Scoop. Like all experimental societies, we've created our own conventions: we refer to one another by our first names followed by our dog's names. At the dog run, I'm Carol (Jolly).

Along the way, we've made fast friends—both human and hound. My dog Jolly adores a dog named Shadow. When they spot each other at the run, they wriggle with excitement. And yes, our dog run has become something of a singles scene. As many of us have discovered, however, dating a fellow dog-run user is nearly as foolhardy as dating someone at work: when it's over, you're stuck seeing your ex every day.

Carol Vinzant, Tompkins Square Dog Run

Under foot: Concrete
Location: 11th Avenue and West 24th Street
Features: Trees, hilly terrain, and street lamps
In charge: Keith Gardner, dogrun@bitsworld.com

Gramercy/Flatiron/Union Square

James' Dog Run Named "Best Place to Ogle Others' Dogs" by the Village Voice, this is one of urbanhound.com's favorite dog runs. Recently renovated, this run is rarely crowded, always clean, and the dog owners here keep to themselves. One drag: there's no water outlet. One warning: until the Madison Square Park renovation is completed, don't be surprised to see a rat or two scurrying past you.
Location: Madison Square Park, East 24th Street at Fifth Avenue
Under foot: Pea gravel
Features: Poop bags, benches, trees
Manager: Friends of James' Dog Run, PO Box 1119, Madison Square Station, New York, NY 10159.

Union Square Dog Run A newly formed group has taken charge of this small run—and not a moment too soon: despite its popularity, the Union Square Dog Run suffers from serious neglect. Renovation plans calls for installing proper drainage and an elegant iron fence, as well as new benches and tables, and even some landscaping. But before an overhaul can take place, money is much needed (at least $25,000). To help out, contact the people listed below.
Location: Union Square, Broadway at 15th Street and Union Square West
Under foot: Crushed stone
Features: Benches, two picnic table, poop scoopers
In charge: Lisa Max, 212-242-1414 or Lmax28@aol.com, and Hatun Aytug, 212-228-2251.
Manager: Friends of Union Square Dog Run, c/o Gary Hymowitz 22 West 15th St., New York, NY 10011.

West Village

Washington Square Dog Run One of the best-known in the city, in one of the most popular parks, this dog run is showing signs of wear. On nice weekends it can get so crowded you may lose your dog in the crowd. That said, the Washington Square Dog Run Association is one of the city's most active: it organizes fund-raisers, raises money from local retailers, puts out an annual calendar featuring the dogs of Washington Square, and publishes an occasional magazine called *Dog Run*.

Location: Washington Square Park, West 4th Street at Thompson Street
Under foot: Pea gravel
Features: Benches, trees, water hose, water bowls, poop scoopers
In charge: Wayne Amendola,
Manager: Washington Square Dog Run Association

West Village DOG Run West Village Dog Owners Group (WVDOG) was founded in the early 1990s to promote local off-leash recreation for dogs. Since then, without any public funding, WVDOG has built, insured and maintained dog runs on scraps of unused private and public land. Originally located at Pier 52, WVDOG Run moved to 10th Avenue and 15th Street, then landed here on Little West 12th. This run is kept locked: to get a key, you must be a member. Membership, which costs $40 a year, is open to anyone who wants to join, but because space is limited to around three hundred families there's often a waiting list. Membership information is available on WVDOG's Web site at www.wvdog.org

Location: Little West 12th Street between Washington Street and 10th Avenue
Under foot: Asphalt
Features: Eight benches, a water hose, drinking bowls, awnings
In charge: Tracy Sides, 212-807-0093 or wvdog1@aol.com
Manager: West Village Dog Owners Group, 41 Bethune Street, New York, NY 10014

Mercer-Houston Dog Run Located in the shadow of NYU housing, across the street from the Angelica Film Center, this small, nicely maintained dog run is only open to members. To request an application, write to the Mercer-Houston Dog Run Association (visit their Web site at www.frr.com/dogrun.htm) and be prepared to wait: the run is limited to 300 members. Members, who must live in Community Board District 2, pay $50 a year.

Location: West Houston Street at Mercer Street, northwest corner
Under foot: Asphalt
Features: Four benches, a water hose, a dog bowl, plastic pool for dogs (in the summer)
Manager: Mercer-Houston Dog Run Association Inc, 51 Macdougal Street, #101, New York, NY 10012

East Village

Tompkins Square Dog Run Established in 1990 (see page 56), this was the first dog run in New York City, and it's still one of the best and the biggest. Some people complain that Tompkins attracts aggressive dogs, but everyone agrees that the run has one of the tightest communities of dog owners. Tompkins hosts an annual Halloween party for dogs, costumes and all. On the second Saturday of every month, volunteers gather to clean up the run. And to cover the cost of looking after dogs that are abandoned in the East Village, Tompkins Dog Run collects money for a fund called First Run Reserve Fund (run by Monay Germaine, 212-979-6014).

Location: East 9th Street at Avenue B

Under foot: Wood chips

Features: Benches and picnic tables, water, a dog memorial statue (brass tags nailed into the remains of an old tree commemorate dogs lost or gone to heaven)

In charge: Carol Vinzant, 212-979-5327 or cvinzant@pipeline.com

Manager: East Village Parks Conservancy, PO Box 138, Peter Stuyvesant Station, New York, NY, 10009

Soho/Tribeca

Tribeca Dog Run This clean little run is located on P.S. 234 property. Though it is not kept locked, this is a membership run: applications are available at the dog run and the fee is $50 a year (if you can't afford the fee, you may volunteer your time instead).

Location: Warren Street, between Greenwich Street and West Street

Under foot: Asphalt

Features: Water hose, plastic wading pool for dogs (in the summer), benches, and an awning

In charge: M.J. Bettenhausen, 212-732-9657

Manager: Dog Owners of Tribeca, 310 1/2 Greenwich Street, New York, NY, 10013.

Lower East Side/South Street Seaport

FishBridge Park This small dog run is in a charming park hidden just south of the Brooklyn Bridge, near the South Street Seaport. The park's superb Web site at www.fishbridge.org explains how local officials and community activists turned this "rat-infested garbage dump into an urban oasis of blooming roses, golden cosmos, and soaring morning glories."

Location: Dover Street, at Pearl Street

Under foot: Textured concrete tiles

Features: Water hose, wading pool (summer only), benches, lock-box for toys, lockbox with newspapers for picking up after your hound.
In charge: Gary Fagin, 212-267-5316 or garyfagin@mindspring.com
Manager: South-Water-Front Neighborhood Assoc., P.O. Box 279, Peck Slip Station, New York, NY 10272

<u>Financial District/Battery Park City</u>
Battery Park City In early 2000, a group of about 450 BPC dog owners got together, created the Battery Park City Dogs association, and demanded more rights for their hounds. The results were immediate: not only are the existing two dog runs being better maintained, but plans are now underway for new dogs runs, one in an area known as "Pumphouse Plaza" (near the Gateway Plaza apartment complex) and another in the northern part of BPC. Despite these gains, however, dog owners in BPC face much opposition from residents who would prefer to see dogs banned altogether. For details, visit Battery Park City Dogs' Web site at http://BPCdogs.org.
Location: There are two runs here: one at West Thames Street between Little West Street and Battery Place; the other at River Terrace, near Murray Street.
Under foot: Concrete
Features: Nice view of the Statue of Liberty, but not much else
In charge: BPC Dogs' Jeff Galloway, jeff.galloway@rundog.com and Paula Galloway, paula@rundog.com or 212-837-6629
Manager: Battery Park City Parks Conservancy, Two South End Ave., New York, NY 10280. 212-267-9700

BROOKLYN

<u>Brooklyn Heights</u>
Palmetto Playground This small run opened in October 1999. It's popular and well-maintained.
Location: Columbia Place and State Street, in a corner by the Brooklyn-Queens Expressway.
Under foot: Well-compressed earth
Features: A supply of water, four benches, one park light
In charge: Joe Merz, 718-855-8996 or willowfunk@aol.com

Hillside Dog Park Until late 1999, this largely deserted, triangular two-and-a-half acre piece of land was used as an unofficial dog run. Then, after a dog who dashed into the street was killed by a car, the Parks Department fenced the entire space. This in turn sharply increased use of the

land by dog owners, whose presence improved safety. Along the way, the enclosed area has become more appealing to local residents without dogs. And now Hillside Dog Park faces opposition from folks who want the dog run downsized to provide space for other activities. In response, the grassroots Friends of Hillside Dog Park was formed to mobilize local dog owners and raise money to upgrade the run. To join, add your name online at http://groups.yahoo.com/group/hillsidedogs or call 718-404-3901 x9471.
Location: Columbia Heights and Middagh Street
Under foot: Wood chips
Features: Not much other than some nice trees, but benches and a water supply are planned.
In charge: Muffet Jones, Friend of Hillside Dog Park, mjones11201@yahoo.com.

Carroll Gardens
DiMattina Park Located at an abandoned basketball court, this dog run re-opened in June 2001 after extensive renovation. The dog run has been re-built, a new surface has been added along with a water source, benches and a double entrance gate
Location: Hicks and Rapelye Street
Under foot: Concrete
Features: Seven trees, three benches, poop bags, lights, water supply
In charge: Craig Hammerman, craighammerman@aol.com or James Aridas
718-625-1484 or penguin325@aol.com

Bay Ridge
Owl's Head Park Opened in late 2000, the Owl's Head dog run is a joint venture between the Parks Department and a new volunteer group called Friends & Neighbors of Owl's Head Park. The run is around 150-feet long and 40-feet wide and it's in one of the city's most beautiful parks.
Location: 68th Street and Shore Road
Under foot: Grass
Features: Doggie bags and a tree. Benches are on order.
In charge: Bernadette Hoban, Friends & Neighbors of Owl's Head Park,
718-745-4218 or bdh528@aol.com.

Dyker Heights
Dyker Beach Park Located in one of the city's great parks, in the shadow of the Verrazano Bridge, this is not an official dog run. It exists thanks to the members of the Dyker Beach Golf

Course who have allowed off-leash dogs to use the area as long as the poop is cleaned up. However, as it seems the poop ain't been cleaned up after all (!), the future of this run may be on shaky ground. Be smart: clean up after your dog! One local resident, Evangelina Exarhoulias, is working to make this a permanent and official dog run. For more information, or to lend a hand to the effort, email her at tsahpinaki@yahoo.com

Location: Street and 7th Ave

Under foot: Grass

Features: Lots of room to run

Manhattan Beach

Shore Boulevard Dog Run This informal dog run isn't fancy—and it can get real muddy in rain—but it's used enthusiastically by local dog owners who are strictly banned from the neighborhood's public beach. If you come by car, be warned that parking on the streets is difficult year round, and forbidden outright on weekends from May 15 to September 15.

Location: Shore Blvd. and Kensington St., just outside Kingsborough Community College.

Under foot: Grass and dirt

Features: A nice view of the ocean

In charge: Manhattan Beach Community Group's Dana Borell, Manbeachcg@aol.com.

QUEENS

Flushing

Cunningham Park After a few years as an unofficial dog-gathering spot, this run became an official dog run in 2000. Despite being in a park that spans 358 acres, this dog run is small. Nevertheless, users tell us "the people and dogs are very nice."

Location: Horace Harding Expwy and Grand Central Pkwy

Forest Hills

Flushing Meadow Park Separated from the lake in Flushing Meadow Park by the Grand Central Parkway (a walkway connects them), this dog run is big, popular and well-maintained.

Location: Between 64th Rd and 64th Ave, along the Grand Central Pkwy.

Under foot: Wood chips

Features: Pretty trees and plenty of benches

Woodside

Doughboy Park This small run sits on the side of a hill in a quiet part of Queens. The park is well cared for and clean, perhaps too clean: you get the feeling this place just isn't used by dogs.
Location: Doughboy Park, Woodside Ave and 55th Street
Under foot: Dirt and pebbles
Features: A trash can and a chain link fence—in other words, not much

THE BRONX

Riverdale

John's Dog Run The main activity in this run appears to be digging. So, let you dog have some fun digging up the already beaten plot while you enjoy the view.
Location: Ewen Park, Riverdale to Johnson Avenues, south of West 232nd St. Down the steps in the clearing on the right.
Under foot: Dirt, stones, a little grass
Features: A beautiful view and some plastic lawn furniture.

Frank's Dog Run This run is small, badly maintained and enclosed by a flimsy fence. Unless it's your only choice for an off-leash experience, stay away.
Location: Frank S. Hackett Park, Riverdale Ave., 245th Street, and Henry Hudson Pkwy. South of 245th St., follow path up the hill and around to the right.
Under foot: Dirt, stones, sticks
Features: None

Seton Park Of moderate width, but a very long run that may give your dog a chance to actually run.
Location: West 235th St. & Independence Ave. West of Independence on 235th, near the Spuyten Duyvil Library.
Under foot: Mostly dirt, with some grass around the fringes of the pen

Van Cortlandt There are two good-sized dog runs in this huge (1,146 acres) park: one is a basic dog run; the other is a canine-agility playground, a first for the city, but beginning to show signs of wear. Visit the park's Web site at www.vancortlandt.org
Location: Van Cortlandt Park, West 252nd St. & Broadway, enter on the path on 252nd on follow it about 100 feet to the left.

Under foot: Well-trodden grass and earth
Features: The agility course includes a teeter-totter, hurdles, a ladder, three chutes, and a hanging tire.
In charge: Friend of Van Cortlandt Park, c/o Van Cortlandt Park Golf House, Bronx, NY 10471, 718-601-1460 or FriendVCP@aol.com
Manager: Linda Dockeray, Administrator for Van Cortlandt and Pelham Bay Parks, 718-430-1890

Pelham Bay

Pelham Bay Dog Park Pelham Bay dog owners would like to raise money to upgrade this small run. They'd like new benches, a source of water, and more space.
Location: Middletown Rd. & Stadium Ave. The run is about 300 feet northwest of the parking lot.
Under foot: Pebbles
Features: Benches
In charge: Janice Coco, c/o Friends of Pelham Bay Park, One Bronx River Parkway, Bronx, NY, 10462, 718-430-1890.
Manager: Linda Dockeray, Administrator for Van Cortlandt and Pelham Bay Parks, 718-430-1890

Norwood

Williamsbridge Oval Dog Run This popular dog run, just south of Woodlawn Cemetery, is part of the sprawling Williamsbridge recreational area.
Location: On the northern end of Williamsbridge Oval, a block south of the Gun Hill Road entrance.
In charge: Williamsbridge Oval Recreation Center, 718-543-8672

STATEN ISLAND

As this book was going to press, we learned that the city's parks commissioner had approved Staten Island's first dog run. It will be located at Wolfe's Pond Park on Raritan Bay. For information, visit the Web site of the Dog Owners Group of Staten Island at http://community.silive.com/cc/DOGSI. Or email the group's founder, Anna Hall, at cgctester@webtv.net.

How to Start a Dog Run

This is a summary of Urbanhound.com's detailed guide to starting a dog run written by Jeffrey Zahn, co-founder and president of the New York Council of Dog Owner Groups (www.nycdog.org), a powerful alliance that lobbies for off-leash recreation around the city.

Start a Dog Owners' Group Begin by mobilizing local dog owners. Circulate a petition in your neighborhood to collect a few hundred names, addresses, phone numbers and e-mail addresses. Then register your group with the coordinator of volunteer efforts at the Department of Parks and Recreation (call 212-360-1310 or visit www.ci.nyc.ny.us/html/ dpr/home.html).

Pick a Spot Almost any open space could work as a dog run. Identify more than one site and list pros and cons for each. Space on private land requires the owner's permission (located through your Community Board). Even privately owned sites may need public and government approval.

Write a Proposal and Draw up a Plan Outline the benefits of a dog run to the community at large stating how and by whom it will be maintained, and include a sample list of dog-run rules. Explain why your chosen site is ideal, but also include the pros and cons of other options. Include a rough budget and funding plan. Create a simple drawing showing how your run will fit in the surrounding area and include its basic components: fence line, water location, entrance, and surface choice (wood chips, pea gravel or crushed granite are the most popular).

Find the Funds A decent dog run—with basic drainage, surfacing, a sturdy fence and gates, benches, and a source of water—will cost at least $50,000 to $75,000. Then there's maintenance which runs around $3,000 to $5,000 a year in a public park, and far more in a private space (where you may need to pay for insurance and garbage collection). Once you're approved the Parks Department will help you develop a budget and construction plan. If you're not working with the Parks Department, get help from NYCDOG (e-mail info@nycdog.com or visit www.nycdog.org).

City Council members may have discretionary funds they can allocate to a dog run. The Parks Department often puts up partial funding for construction, (but not for maintenance—dog owners cover that expense). And you can raise money from local dog owners, local merchants (especially pet-related), and companies that make pet products.

Work the Spheres of Influence Many people get a say in whether or not your dog run gets built:

The owner of the property. If your proposed dog run is in a park, you will have to grapple with the Department of Parks and Recreation. Be prepared: the Parks Department will likely want to give you not only less space, but also a less desirable location than you want. Write a letter stating your plan to the administrator of your park, and send a copy to your Borough Commissioner and the Commissioner of the Parks Department. Include a request for a meeting. Follow up by phone. In the case of a privately owned site, contact the owner directly.

The Community Board. Go to monthly Community Board meetings, learn how the board functions and identify members who seem likely to be sympathetic (or hostile).

Local elected officials. City Council members, State Assembly members, and State Senators are receptive to appeals from large neighborhood groups, so contact them as soon as your petition numbers start adding up. To find them, go to the New York Public Interest Group's "Who Represents Me" Web page at www.nypirg.org or call 212-349-6460.

Other local groups. Contact Business Improvements Districts, block associations, schools, bird watchers, and neighboring residential and commercial buildings in your area. These groups will likely be against your dog run, especially if it's sprung on them or "threatens" a space they use.

Get Approved Officially, to build your run you need only the approval of the site's owner but it's almost impossible to move ahead without approval from your Community Board. As the Community Board is a lightning rod for your opponents, be ready for complaints about unsanitary conditions, noise, odors, aesthetics, and more. Some suggestions:

- Start a public relations campaign. Contact neighborhood newspapers, and use flyers, a newsletter or a Web site to educate the community.
- Have your supporters attend (and speak at) Community Board meetings. Call on NYCDOG to help in your testimony. Encourage local veterinarians and other supportive community leaders to speak at these meetings. Celebrities can be extremely helpful too.
- Start a letter-writing and phone-calling campaign well ahead of public approval meetings. Target the Parks Department, elected officials, and ranking Community Board members.

Keep Up The Good Work Once the dog run is built, keep your dog owners' group active for fundraising and clean-ups. Have regular meetings with the Parks Departments and community officials to keep everyone involved and upbeat.

City Parks

New York City has 27,000 acres of parkland so, wherever you live, chances are there is at least a small park near you. By law, all dogs must be on a leash no longer than six feet at all times in city parks, except in official, enclosed dog runs. That said, some parks operate under an unofficial rule established under Parks Commissioner Henry Stern which allows dogs to be off leash during the "courtesy hours" of 9 P.M. to 9 A.M. (or, in Prospect Park, 5 P.M. to 9 A.M.). Unfortunately, these off-leash hours are technically against the law—they're a "courtesy" granted by the Parks Department, which is to say they depend on the Parks Commissioner's whim.

Leaders of New York's canine community have asked the Parks Department for a firm stance on this issue—ideally, to make the off-leash courtesy hours official (and thus legal)—but so far, nothing has changed.

Here we've listed local parks where dogs romp off-leash during "courtesy hours." With the exception of Manhattan's Riverside Park, parks with dog runs (see pages 50-64) do not permit off-leash activity outside their runs. Warning: park rangers are increasingly vigilant about enforcing leash laws. A first offense will get you a $100 fine per dog. And fines double for each subsequent offense, up to a maximum of $800 per dog!

If you're looking for information on public beaches, see "Outdoor Swimming" in Chapter Four, page 82.

MANHATTAN

Central Park Over the years, various groups have tried to establish dog runs in Central Park. But both the Parks Department and the Central Park Conservancy, the not-for-profit group that maintains the Park, oppose dog runs because, they say, dog runs are not in keeping with Frederick Law Olmsted and Calvert Vaux's original 1858 design for the park (and rollerblade and bike paths are?).

In the meantime, dogs romp off-leash before 9 A.M. and after 9 P.M. Many dogs quietly run off leash at other hours too, which accounts for the tension between dog owners and the Park Enforcement Patrol, who are cracking down on dogs off leash. Dog owners say they've been harassed, intimidated, and even handcuffed by overzealous enforcement officers. Terry Fonville, president of the Riverside Dog Owners Group, has set up a task force to collect evidence of harassment by the PEP (to contact Terry, e-mail twfonville@earthlink.net).

Central Park PAWS, an advisory group formed in early 1999, is trying to improve communications between dog owners and park officials. PAWS (http://www.centralparkpaws.org) has put together a dog-owner's guide to Central Park that, sadly, is not much more than endless regula-

Central Park: My Backyard

I think of Central Park as my backyard. And, as my best companion, William, a yellow Lab, knows, it's a heavenly place for dogs.

Some areas of the Park are off limits to dogs, both on and off leash. In other areas, such as Cedar Hill or the Ramble, dogs have to be on leash at all times. But in much of the park—just about anywhere you don't see a posted sign stating otherwise—dogs can play off leash between 9 P.M. and 9 A.M.

Every morning, William and I set off for the Park. Racing to meet his friends, William is always in the lead. Our favorite place to walk is the Great Lawn oval path in the center of the park behind the Metropolitan Museum of Art. Although the Great Lawn itself is off limits to dogs at all times, the path around the lawn is a superb place for an off-leash morning walk. Early each morning, until 9 A.M., the Great Lawn oval and most of the adjacent lawns are packed with frolicking dogs enjoying the off-leash privilege granted by the parks commissioner.

After 9 A.M., when William has to be on leash, he and I take long walks in other dog-friendly parts of the park: around the Reservoir on the bridle path, through the Ramble, or around the lake to the Bethesda Fountain. So when my suburban friends tell me they feel sorry for my city dog, William and I tell them they're crazy. We have an 843-acre backyard and we love it!

Susan Washburn Buckley, Central Park PAWS

tions, including a list of the park's 13 areas where dogs are forbidden (the Woodlands, Ramble, Sheep Meadow, Strawberry Fields, East Lawn, among others). For a copy of the free guide call 212-360-2728.

PAWS is also working with the Central Park Conservancy to have canine watering holes attached to 13 human fountains throughout the park. Currently, there're just two dog fountains in the park, one at the East 90th Street entrance, the other northwest of the Great Lawn oval. PAWS can be reached through Ed Benson of the Central Park Conservancy at 212-360-1422.

By the way, at East Drive and 67th Street a bronze statue is devoted to a hound: Balto, the Wonder Dog—a Siberian Husky who in 1925 led a team of sled dogs through a blizzard to deliver the fresh serum that saved the people of Nome, Alaska, from a diphtheria epidemic. A plaque at the base of Balto's statue reads, "Dedicated to the indomitable spirit of the sled dogs that relayed anti-toxins 660 miles over rough ice, across treacherous waters, through Arctic blizzards from Nenana to the relief of stricken Nome in the Winter of 1925." What better mascot for an urban hound?

Riverside Park The Upper West Side's Riverside Park is the only park with dog runs that allows unleashed dogs outside those runs. That said, the areas where dogs are allowed off-leash are so restrictive that many dog owners consider the park's rules draconian. Nevertheless, the rules must be followed here. Based on anecdotal evidence, Urbanhound.com estimates that more tickets are issued to unleashed dogs in this park than in any other, so listen up.

Leash or no leash, dogs are never allowed in:

- Playgrounds
- Ball fields
- Gardens
- Landscape restoration areas
- The 72nd Street running track
- South Lawn (73rd to 75th Streets)
- The 91st Street Hill
- Sakura Park (122nd Street)j

Dogs are permitted, but must always be leashed on:

- The promenade from 83rd to 91st Streets
- The lawn from 101st to 105th Streets
- Within five blocks of any dog run

For more information contact Terry Fonville of the Riverside Dog Owners Group at 212-222-7516 or visit the group's Web site at www.riversidedog.com.

Stuyvesant Square This small, formally designed park spans both sides of Second Avenue, from 15th to 17th Streets. For many years, two dozen or more unleashed dogs and their owners gathered each morning before 9 A.M., and in the evenings too, in the cobbled oval area near 15th Street on the west side of Second Avenue.

But in April 2001, the Parks Department announced that off-leash "courtesy hours" had been rescinded here. In response, a group of local dog people have been trying to convince local politicians and Parks officials to reinstate off-leash. As this book was going to press, the park was still off limits to unleashed dogs.

A resolution does not seem likely. In May 2001, *The New York Observer* quoted the parks commissioner saying: "'We're pro-dog. We allow them off-leash when we can.'" The article added, "'But Stuyvesant Park,' he said, 'just isn't a place where they can: the park's too small, and it causes too many problems.'" For the latest on the off-leash squabble in this park, contact Simon Kahn of the Stuyvesant Park Steering Committee at simonkahn@hotmail.com.

BROOKLYN

Prospect Park When it comes to dogs, the beautiful Prospect Park is the most enlightened park in the city. Prospect Park's off-leash rules are liberal. There are as many dog fountains as there are human fountains. And between 7 A.M. and 9 A.M. on the first Saturday of every month (rain or shine) a "Coffee Bark" is held in the Long Meadow, behind the Picnic House (enter Prospect Park West and 4th Street, go left around Picnic House). Coffee, Dizzy's muffins, and dog biscuits are served.

Coffee Bark is just one of many events sponsored by the Fellowship for the Interests of Dogs and their Owners (FIDO), a group of dog owners dedicated to promoting off-leash activity at Prospect Park. For more information on FIDO, the city's most proactive group of dog owners, visit www.fidobrooklyn.com or call 718-404-3903 x2640.

As well, if you're a serious Brooklyn-based dog person, consider joining Off Leash's Brooklyn DogChat, the city's top dog-centric e-mail discussion group (officially devoted to Brooklyn dogs, DogChat is a wonderful resource for all the city's dog owners). To sign up, go to Off Leash's Web site at www.offleash.com.

Here are the main rules regarding canines at Prospect Park:

- In winter (November 1 through March 31), dogs must be on leash between 9 A.M. and 5 P.M. In summer (April 1 through October 31), dogs must be on leash between 9 A.M. and 9 P.M.;
- At all other times dogs may be off leash only in the Long Meadow, the Nethermead, and the Peninsula Meadow;
- On weekdays during winter and summer, dogs may be off leash in the Nethermead after 5 P.M.;
- Dogs are not allowed in playgrounds;
- Dogs are not allowed on the bridle paths;
- Dogs are not allowed on ball fields when games are in progress.

Fort Greene Park Fort Greene dog owners are well-organized and working hard to make this 30-acre historic park as dog-friendly as Prospect Park. If you live in the area, consider joining the Fort Greene Park Users and Pets Society (PUPS). Apart from improving communication between park officials and dog owners, PUPS hosts an annual hound costume contest at Halloween, organizes park clean-up days, publishes a calendar, and has its own Web site at www.fortgreenepups.org. To join PUPS, contact Kath Hansen at wenley@mindspring.com. For general information about Fort Greene Park, visit www.fortgreenepark.org.

McCarren Park On the border of Williamsburg and Greenpoint, the lovely McCarren Park has long observed off-leash "courtesy" hours between 9 P.M. and 9 A.M. But in April 2001, in response to complaints from a member of the Police Athletic League, off-leash hours were rescinded. Outraged, neighborhood dog owners have formed the Williamsburg and Greenpoint Dog Owners Group (WAGDOG) to fight back. As this book was going to press, WAGDOG had met with the Police Athletic League, the 94th Precinct Police Department, Community Board 1 and the Parks Department to propose that courtesy hours be reinstated. No word yet on whether the effort has been a success. For more information, contact WAGDOG member Noam Mor at noammor@earthlink.net.

QUEENS

Alley Pond Park With 635 acres of woodlands, meadows, fresh and salt water marshes, Alley Pond Park in northeast Queens, near Nassau County, is one of the best places in the city to let a dog run off leash. Every morning before 9 A.M., a group of dogs and their owners gather at the upper level of the park, at the corner of Union Turnpike and Winchester Boulevard. For more information, contact Judy Scudari, a dedicated dog person who works with the not-for-profit Alley Pond Environmental Center, 718-229-4000.

4 houndactivities

HAVING FUN WITH YOUR DOG

Every year there are more and more events for dogs and dog people in New York City. Here we list the best-known events, organized by the time of year they take place. If you'd like to know about current canine events in the city, including lectures, walkathons, parties, and gatherings, sign up for Urbanhound.com's monthly newsletter at www.urbanhound.com.

Gatherings & Events

YEAR-ROUND: COFFEE BARK, PROSPECT PARK, BROOKLYN

Between 7 A.M. and 9 A.M. on the first Saturday of every month (rain or shine) a "Coffee Bark" is held in Prospect Park's Long Meadow, behind the Picnic House (enter the park at Prospect Park West and 4th Street, go left around Picnic House). Coffee, Dizzy's muffins and dog biscuits are served. Coffee Bark is sponsored by Fellowship In the Interest of Dog Owners (FIDO). For details, visit www.fidobrooklyn.com or call 718-404-3903, x2640.

YEAR-ROUND: CENTRAL PARK PUG PALS, CENTRAL PARK, MANHATTAN

As far as we know, only one breed of dog has earned the distinction of having a section of Central Park (unofficially) named for it. Pug Hill is just behind the statue of Alice in Wonderland, inside Central Park at East 74th Street. Every weekend at 12:30 P.M., and occasionally on weekday evenings, members of the Central Park Pug Pals gather here for a romp. Afterwards, they sometimes recharge with a visit to Pug Bros. Popcorn, a snack shop on Columbus Avenue between 72nd and 73rd Streets.

APRIL: DACHSHUND SPRING FIESTA, WASHINGTON SQUARE PARK, MANHATTAN

Legend has it that Adrian Milton founded the Dachshund Friendship Club because his Dachsie Damon, distraught over the loss of his twin brother, needed companionship. Damon got what he was looking for: as many as 500 Dachshunds have been known to show up for the Club's semi-annual gatherings, held each October and April in Greenwich Village's Washington Square Park. Sometimes, as a sign of devotion to their stumpy hounds, Oktoberfest attendees sing The Dachs Song, which begins simply, "There's no other dog like a Dachshund." (The complete lyrics are on the Internet at www.cygnus.uwa.edu.au/~opalowl/Song.html.)

For more information, contact the Dachshund Friendship Club, c/o Adrian Milton, 245 E. 11th St., New York, NY 10003. To subscribe to the club's newsletter send a check for $12 to Adrian.

MAY: DOGS WALK AGAINST CANCER, RIVERSIDE PARK, MANHATTAN

Thousands of dogs and their owners participate in this walkathon held each May in Riverside Park to raise funds for the American Cancer Society and the Animal Medical Center's cancer clinic. For more information, call 212-237-3872 or visit www.dogswalk.com.

JUNE: PUPNIK, PROSPECT PARK, BROOKLYN

This annual potluck picnic for dogs and their people is held on a weekday evening in late June in the Nethermead. The event includes games and contests in such competitive categories as Dog-Owner Lookalike, Best Kisser, and Best Treat-Catcher. For information, contact FIDO at 718-404-3903 x2640 or visit www.fidobrooklyn.com.

JULY: BROADWAY BARKS!, SHUBERT ALLEY, MANHATTAN

Since 1999, actors Bernadette Peters and Mary Tyler Moore have hosted Broadway Barks! to raise money for FIDONYC, their animal welfare organization. The July event, which features many celebrities, their dogs, and their fans, is intended to raise awareness of homeless dogs in New York City shelters. For more information, visit www.fidonyc.org.

FALL: BARC PARADE AND DOG SHOW, WILLIAMSBURG, BROOKLYN

Each fall, the non-profit Brooklyn Animal Resource Coalition (BARC) hosts a canine parade in Williamsburg to raise money for homeless pets and to celebrate the Brooklyn dog. With around a thousand humans and their canine companions, splendid homemade parade floats, colorful themes (e.g., a celebration of the '70s), a microchipping clinic, and a wonderful dog show, the BARC parade is one of the coolest dog events around. Plus there are prizes awarded in such categories as Sweetest Temperament of Gruffest Looking Dog, Owner-Dog Lookalike, Most Talented Puppy, Best Dressed, and Best Butt. For more information call BARC at 718-486-7489 or visit their Web site at www.barcshelter.org.

OCTOBER: BLESSING OF THE ANIMALS

Each October, on St. Francis of Assisi Feast Day, churches all over the city open their doors to pets. The largest and most elaborate such gathering takes place at Manhattan's Cathedral of St.

John the Divine, on Amsterdam Avenue at 112th Street (212-316-7400), an enormous space that can easily host hundreds of pets and their owners, joined by elephants, camels, pigs and other animals from zoos and circuses, for a special service and blessing. Note: dogs are welcome year-round at some parishes, including Manhattan's St. Clement's Episcopal Church at 423 West 46th Street, between Ninth and Tenth Avenues (212-246-7277) and the Church of the Holy Trinity at 316 East 88th Street between First and Second Avenues (212-289-4100).

OCTOBER: ITALIAN GREYHOUND PLAYDATE, MANHATTAN

Once or twice a year, usually in October, Heleyn Frumin, an Italian Greyhound aficionado, hosts a gathering of the delicate breed in a Manhattan park. For information contact Heleyn at 212-534-1922 or heleyn@earthlink.net.

OCTOBER: WOOFSTOCK, CENTRAL PARK, MANHATTAN

This annual event, officially known as the ASPCA Dog Walk, is held in October at Central Park's Rumsey Playfield and raises money for stray and abandoned dogs. More than a walkathon, Woofstock is a dog-themed carnival, with pet "channelers" and photographers; a canine Olympics; demonstrations by working dogs and stunt dogs; and appearances by celebrity hounds. For more information, contact the ASPCA at 212-876-7700 or visit www.aspca.org.

OCTOBER: DACHSHUND OKTOBERFEST, WASHINGTON SQUARE PARK, MANHATTAN

See entry for Dachshund Spring Fiesta, page 73.

OCTOBER: HALLOWEEN HOWLS

The city's first official canine Halloween costume party took place at Tompkins Square Dog Run in Manhattan's East Village many years ago. Now, there are dozens of Halloween events for hounds all around the city.

Dog Run Halloween Events: The best-known parties and costume contests are at Manhattan dog runs and include those hosted by Tompkins Square (in 2000, top honors went to a Corgie disguised as a Hoover vacuum cleaner); FLORAL (at Riverside's West 72nd Street Run); Bull Moose Dog Run at West 81st Street (2000's top prize went to a Pug named Pearl whose head was decorated with an immense paper maché oyster shell); and Carl's Dog Run (in Carl Schurz Park, East 86th Street). But new parties are popping up all the time. One popular new event in Brooklyn is the Great PUPkin Halloween Costume Contest in Fort Greene Park (for information, visit www.fortgreenepups.org).

French Bulldog Halloween Parade: If you own a Frenchie, join members of the Greenwich Village French Bulldog Association who wear black capes and march up Sixth Avenue in The Village Halloween Parade each year. For more information, visit www.gvfba.com or email snort@gvfba.com.

Empire Diner's Annual Canine Halloween Costume Contest: This event is said to be "a huge blow-out party every year," "the talk of Chelsea for weeks afterwards," and "lots of silliness." With the tables outside this famous diner (210 Tenth Ave., Manhattan) cleared away, a canine costume parade and contest takes place; awards are presented.

DECEMBER: BARK THE HERALD ANGELS SING, PROSPECT PARK, BROOKLYN

This long-standing holiday tradition in held on a Saturday a couple of weeks before Christmas from 8 A.M. to 10 A.M. in the Long Meadow and features caroling, cookies, and chestnuts roasted on an open fire. For information, contact FIDO at 718-404-3903, x2640 or visit www.fidobrooklyn.com.

Sports and Games

If you and your dog are tired of playing fetch, read on. There are plenty of canine activities in and around the city. To play dog sports at a competitive level, you'll have to drive to clubs and events outside the city. But if recreation is all you want, there are more and more options within city limits.

On the forefront of canine activities in New York is Manhattan's Doggy Village at 227 East 44th Street, which is positioning itself as a kind of Canine Chelsea Piers, offering classes in agility, competitive obedience, tricks, Frisbee, flyball, and rally obedience. Call 212-213-4288 for more information (Biscuit & Bath's Doggy Village is a membership club, but you don't have to join to take classes).

To learn just about everything there is to know about dog sports, visit the superb Dog Play Web site at www.dog-play.com.

RECREATIONAL AGILITY

Agility involves teaching your dog to race through an obstacle course (tunnels, hanging tires, hurdles, elevated planks, chutes, weave poles). Almost any dog can try agility, but to master this event a dog has to be fast, fit, alert and responsive to commands. Herding breeds tend to excel at agility.

Non-competitive agility classes are offered at:

Send that Dog to Camp

What with dog daycare centers, swimming pools and Halloween howls, life for the urbanhound has improved immensely. Still, we wish there were even more things for dogs and their people to do that offer real fun—like summer camp! Here are two for both week-long and one-day jaunts.

Camp Gone To The Dogs, 802-387-5673. www.camp-gone-tothe-dogs.com
If you loved summer camp as a kid, Camp Gone To The Dogs is for you and your hound. Started in 1990 by Honey Loring, Camp Gone To The Dogs offers three one-week summer holidays in Vermont for dogs and their humans. Every day is packed with such classes and activities as agility, herding, rally obedience, puppy training, freestyle dancing (!), clicker training, flyball, tracking, and swimming. Some of the area's top dog trainers teach here. Camper hounds (as many as 350 dogs of all ages and levels) can do as much or as little as they like. Aside from the physical activities, there's plenty of socializing. Fees, which include housing, classes, training, and meals, range from $800 to $1,200, depending on the session you attend and the accommodation you choose.

Pet Aways, 212-420-7638. www.pet-aways.com
In May 2001, having lost her job as design manager at an Internet company, Helene Czech decided to start Pets Away, a company devoted to short getaways for hounds and their humans. As this book was going to press, Pets Away was just starting to offer daylong excursions to Bear Mountain in New Jersey's Harriman State Park and to the Robert Moses State Park dog-friendly beach on Fire Island. Included in the price ($145 and $155, respectively) is transportation to and from the parks by minivan, a croissant and coffee for the outbound ride, snacks and water bottles for dogs and humans, a picnic lunch, dog towels, poop bags, and, on the Robert Moses trip, beach umbrellas.

All About Dogs, 210 East 23rd Street (between 2nd and 3rd Aves.), 212-481-2656. The space here is very small, but classes are casual and intimate (normally around six dogs/people show up). Rather than sign up for a full course, you can drop in when you'd like and pay as you go. Each one-hour session is $25.

Biscuits & Bath's Doggy Village, 227 East 44th Street (2nd and 3rd Aves.), 212-692-2323. Classes, which run weekly for six weeks, are taught by Andrea Arden's Manhattan Dog Training and take place in a good-sized course set up on artificial grass. The course costs $300. (You don't have to be a Doggy Village member to sign up.)

ASPCA, 424 East 92nd Street (1st and York Aves), 212-876-7700 x 4423. There are three levels of classes here: beginner, novice, and advanced. Classes run weekly for seven weeks and cost $230 (with a discount for dogs adopted from the ASPCA).

COMPETITIVE AGILITY

Aside from the local clubs listed below (one in Staten Island, the others all within an hour of the city), names of other, lesser-known clubs are available from the American Kennel Club at www.akc.org and the United Kennel Club at www.ukcdogs.com.

One good local resource is Debra Jane Seltzer of Brooklyn's Park Slope whose dogs Ruffian (a Chihuahua) and Gripper (a mixed-breed) are accomplished agility competitors. Visit her Web site at www.netcolony.com/pets/agilitynut/4gd.html for wonderful photos, information on the sport, and useful links.

The Dog Obedience Club of South Nassau, 197 Maple Avenue, Rockville Center, NY. 516-766-9740

Fast Pawz, 139 Kiswick Street, Midland Beach, Staten Island, NY. 718-987-6744

Long Island Agility, 33 Route 110 (North of Jericho Turnpike), Huntington, NY. 516-427-5672 or 516-234-4762. http://pages.prodigy.com/FGKX00A/lia.htm

Port Chester Obedience Training Club, 230 Ferris Avenue, White Plains, NY. 914-946-0308. www.pcotc.org/agility.htm

Skyline Agility Club, Garnerville, NY. Contact Ruth Bryden in New Jersey, 201-664-2151. www.geocities.com/Petsburgh/Haven/7789/index.html

St. Hubert's, 22 Prospect Street, Madison, NJ. 973-377-0116. www.sthuberts.org/whatwedo/

Staten Island Companion Dog Training Club, 1315B Travis Avenue, Staten Island, NY. 718-761-8048. www.geocities.com/sicdtc

Dog-Friendly New York

When it comes to an appreciation for all things dog, New York ain't Paris (sadly). Our dogs are banned from restaurants, from most buildings, and they're not permitted in many stores. Still, more and more places welcome hounds.

At Manhattan's Paragon Sporting Goods, for example, we were told that dogs are "encouraged." Bed Bath & Beyond has shopping carts lined with dog beds. A growing number of local hardware stores, wine shops and shoemakers keep Milk Bones behind the counter. Manhattan's venerable Strand Books happily lets you and your dog to browse the stacks. And, so dog-friendly is The Corner Bookstore on the Upper East Side, that it hosts an annual Canine Buffet.

For all this progress, however, the city's ban on dogs in restaurants (other than service and police dogs) is here to stay. Grey Dog's Cafe in Manhattan's West Village, a cramped, laid-back spot with delicious soups and sandwiches, is the only restaurant we know of that actually allows dogs inside (we're not sure how they get away with it, but we're sure glad they do). However, in summer, plenty of restaurants with sidewalk seating will accommodate dogs—some even cater to canine customers by offering bowls of water and liver treats. For the scoop on the most urban-hound-friendly outdoor restaurants and cafes in your neighborhood, go to Urbanhound.com's message board and click on a topic called "Dog-Friendly New York." Here are just a few favorites among the many listed:

- Barking Dog Luncheonette on Manhattan's Upper East Side (with an outdoor canine watering trough);
- Boat Basin Cafe at West 79th Street in Manhattan's Riverside Park;
- Bubby's in Manhattan's Tribeca;
- Caffe Cafe in Bay Ridge, Brooklyn;
- Cargo Cafe, Staten Island (two blocks from where the dog-friendly ferry docks);
- Fred's on Manhattan's Upper West Side (named after the owner's black Lab);
- Naidre's in Park Slope, Brooklyn
- Pastis in Manhattan's Meatpacking district (which stocks water bowls of various sizes)

THERAPY DOGS

If your dog is sweet-natured, sociable, unflappable and obedient, he'd make a wonderful therapy dog, amusing children in hospital wards and cheering up the infirm at hospices and senior centers. Studies suggest that dogs help lower people's blood pressure, ease stress, and reduce depression. Volunteers say that bringing their dogs to hospitals is tremendously rewarding.

To participate, dogs and their owners have to be certified through a therapy dog training program. The best known program in the city is the Good Dog Foundation, which has a six-to-eight-week course and coordinates visits (call 888-859-9992, or email GoodDogFoundation@yahoo.com). The ASPCA and the national Delta Society offer a less intensive program through Pet Partners (call 425-226-7357, or visit the Delta Society Web site at www.deltasociety.org).

CANINE GOOD CITIZENS

If your dog is obedient, and responds well to commands, you may want to work toward earning the AKC's Canine Good Citizen certificate—a test that demonstrates your dog's fine manners (and is much appreciated by landlords and co-op boards). For more information on the Good Citizen Award, visit this page on the AKC Web site: www.akc.org/love/cgc/index.cfm.

COMPETITIVE OBEDIENCE AND RALLY OBEDIENCE

If your dog still hasn't learned the "down" command, competitive obedience is not for you: it is exacting, and covers a seemingly endless number of commands and complex tasks. Rally obedience, a new sport, combines response to commands with speed.

Because the American Kennel Club dominates obedience events, many of them are restricted to purebred dogs (see www.akc.org/dic/events/obedtrack/obtrack.cfm). For mixed-breed dogs, events are organized by the United Kennel Club (www.ukcdogs.com) and The American Mixed Breed Obedience Registration (www.amborusa.org).

For lots of information on competitive obedience, visit www.k9web.com/dog-faqs/activities/obedience.html. For more about rally obedience, visit www.geocities.com/dogtrain.geo/ rally.htm.

With the exception of Long Island Agility, all the dog clubs mentioned under the competitive agility section, page 78, also offer classes and sponsor competitions in competitive obedience. Apart from the Staten Island Training Club, however, the only place in the city that offers competitive and rally obedience classes is Doggy Village (see contact info under recreational agility, page 77).

CANINE FRISBEE

Probably because we lack the required space, New Yorkers are not big canine Frisbee enthusiasts. Nevertheless, the sport (also known as Flying Disc Dog) is taken very seriously in other parts of the country. At the competitive level, canine Frisbee is much more than good exercise: it requires tremendous skill and speed. Events include a freestyle component as well as a structured course that measures distance and tests accuracy. This sport tends to be dominated by Border Collies (though a Whippet was one of the most famous champions of all time). To view excellent Frisbee training video clips, visit www.dogchow.com/incred/tricks.asp.

The Yankee Flyers Dog and Disc Club, based in Connecticut, is the only club in the New York region devoted to canine Frisbee. Founded and run by Gail Mirabella, a three-time canine Frisbee world finalist and a member of the Purina Incredible Dog Team, the club organizes events and holds clinics around the country. Contact Gail at mirabg@pfizer.com or 860-859-9853. Another good local source is Bob Warwick, a member of the Yankee Flyers Dog club who maintains a terrific Web site devoted to his champion Frisbee player, a Labrador named Rudy: www.netlabs.net/hp/lew/rudy/. Rudy's Web site includes Frisbee training tips, photos, and a list of Frisbee events in the Tri-State area.

Even for observers, Frisbee competitions are great fun. To learn about the handful of competitive events that make their way to New York, visit the Web site of Rudy (see above) or Sky-Hounz, organizers of the largest disc dog competitions, at www.skyhoundz.com.

TRACKING

If your dog follows his nose, he may love tracking, a sport that involves tracing a human scent along courses that vary in length. To learn about the sport of tracking, visit Daniel Tratnack's site at http://personal.cfw.com/~dtratnac/main/titlepg.htm

Two clubs in the area host tracking events and offer classes too. The Hudson Valley Tracking Club is based in Garrison, NY, about 85 miles north of the city. For information, call or e-mail Stephanie Crawford at 607-755-1996 or SACVLF@aol.com. Port Chester Obedience Training Club is in White Plains, NY, and can be reached at 914-946-0308 or via its Web site at www.pcotc.org/tracking.htm.

LURE COURSING

If your dog is a sight hound (Afghan Hound, Basenji, Borzoi, Greyhound, Ibizan Hound, Irish Wolfhound, Pharaoh Hound, Rhodesian Ridgeback, Saluki, Scottish Deerhound, or Whippet), chances are she'll love lure coursing. This sport involves chasing a plastic rabbit around a track. Dogs are judged for speed, endurance, agility, and enthusiasm.

For more information on lure coursing, check out "How to Get Started in Lure Coursing," at www.greyhoundadoption.org/lurecoursing.htm or visit the Web site of the American Sighthound Field Association at www.asfa.org. As well, visit the Web site of Haley and Niagra, two Brooklyn Greyhounds who love the sport at www.thegreyhounds.com.

EARTHDOG TRIALS

Terriers and dachshunds were bred to capture badgers, rats, and other small animals, and this sport allows them to experience the thrill of the hunt, without actually harming a living creature. Dogs learn to follow an animal's scent into a lair and alert their owners to the presence of a caged rat. To learn more about earthdog trials in the New York area, visit the American Working Terrier Association Web site at www.dirt-dog.com/awta/index.shtml.

INDOOR SWIMMING

In the last few years, two swimming pools for dogs have opened in New York City. Both are largely used for canine hydrotherapy, but allow recreational swimming—though, in our opinion, neither pool is all that appealing.

Biscuits and Bath's Doggy Village, 227 East 44th St. (between 2nd and 3rd Aves). An annual swim membership costs $100, and each 30-minute swim costs $30. Call 212-692-2323.

Bonnie's K9 Swim Center, 136 9th Avenue (19th St.) A 25-minute swim costs $25; 55 minutes is $55. Call 212-414-2500 or visit www.k9-swimtherapy.com.

OUTDOOR SWIMMING

New York has no shortage of spots for canine dips, but there are hazards involved. Among them: contaminated water, $100 fines for swimming in a city park, tickets for being on most beaches, and aggressive swans (in spring 2000, a swan in Central Park killed a Jack Russell Terrier that belonged to designer Donna Karan's daughter Gabby).

Officially, only one beach in the area allows dogs all year round:

Robert Moses Field 5 at the Fire Island National Seashore This gorgeous mile-long strip of beach is about an hour from the city by car (without traffic). To get there from the Long Island Expressway, take exit 53 South; follow that to Exit 40 South and watch the signs for Robert Moses

Park. When you're crossing the big bridge right before the island, you can see a lighthouse to the left. That's where you're going: Field 5. Between April and November there's a $5 entrance fee per car; between Memorial Day and Labor Day it's $7. Warning the tide can be strong here and dogs are supposed to be on leash at all times (the fine is $25; police patrol the beach in SUVs). Also, if hanging out with naked men and women disturbs you, stay away—This beach is open to nudists. For more information, call 631-289-4810 or visit www.nps.gov/fiis.

Intrepid dog owners have alerted Urbanhound.com to the beaches listed below—but keep in mind that none of these spots is officially open to dogs, at least not year-round. So if you suddenly start getting ticketed by the police, don't say you weren't warned. The best way to avoid trouble is to go during the off season, or early in the morning.

Jamaica Bay, Gateway National Recreation Area, Brooklyn & Queens The section of the Gateway National Recreation Area that surrounds Jamaica Bay has several nice beaches. Plum Beach is just off Shore Pkwy., near Sheepshead Bay, Brooklyn. A little further along Shore Pkwy is Floyd Bennet Field, another spot with good access to the water. Then there's Fort Tilden, a 317-acre park toward the end of the Rockaway Peninsula in Queens. A former US Army base, Fort Tilden has one of the last natural sand dune systems in the city. For more information call 718-338-3688 or visit www.nps.gov/gate/ or www.nps.gov/gate/homepage/jb-bp.htm. For information on Rockaway only, visit www.rockaway-online.com.

Gravesend Bay Beaches, Coney Island, Brooklyn At the westernmost tip of Coney Island, near Seagate, lie a few lovely, quiet beaches that are open to the public. But these are not official public beaches with lifeguards and signs. "They are just there," a local told Urbanhound.com. "And a fine secret they are."

Great Kills Park, Staten Island The place for swimming here is about halfway down the southeastern coast of the island. For information, visit www.SI-Web.com/Recreation/GreatKills.html.

Watch Hill, Fire Island There's a nice sandy beach here, with big waves and, away from the shore, a beautiful nature trail. To get here, take the ferry from Patchogue on Long Island, about sixty miles out of the city. For more information, call 516-289-4810 or visit www.nps.gov/fiis/. Ferry schedules are available at 516-475-1665 or www.davisparkferry.com.

5 

houndtravel

HOW TO SCHLEP YOUR DOG AROUND TOWN AND BEYOND

With a little effort, you can take your dog just about anywhere. In most cases, however, getting around town depends on the kindness of cabbies, train conductors and bus drivers; so behave! If all else fails, call a pet taxi (see page 87 for listings). As for airline travel, it can be dangerous for dogs, so ask yourself if your hound wouldn't be just as happy, or happier, staying at home with a good caretaker.

Public Transportation

Before you run to catch the train with your dog, double-check the rules listed below. Restrictions on canines are often open to interpretation—they seem to change day by day, and often depend on who answers the phone. Good luck. (Note: none of the restrictions below apply to guide dogs, who, by law, are allowed just about everywhere.)

MTA Subways and Buses, 718-330-1234. www.mta.nyc.ny.us/nyct
Dogs in kennels or bags are allowed on the city's subways and buses. That said, the rules state "no big dogs." Unfortunately, there's no official definition of a "big dog," which is to say that the conductor's discretion decides whether a dog gets on or not. So be smart: travel with your hound during off-peak hours. One urbanhounder tells us she successfully travels by subway with her dog in a shopping cart. Another favors using the original L.L. Bean zipper tote, size extra large.

Long Island Railroad, 718-558-8228. www.mta.nyc.ny.us/lirr
Same rule as MTA subways and buses (see above).

Metro-North Railroad, 212-532-4900. www.mnr.org/mnr
Dogs are allowed as long as they do not, in the words of a Metro-North spokeswoman, "become offensive to your fellow commuters." Unless your dog is tiny, it's best to travel during off-peak hours. Restrain your dog, either by leash or kennel. As well, Metro-North recommends that dog owners arrive early to clear their dog with the conductor (they "appreciate that"). For the most part, we hear only praise for the kindness Metro-North shows its canine passengers.

Staten Island Ferry, 718-390-5253. www.ci.nyc.ny.us/html/dot/html/get_around/ferry/statfery.html
The official rule regarding hounds on the ferry is that there is no official rule. In most cases, dogs are allowed on board, as long as they are leashed, well-behaved, and remain outside on deck. The ferry's deckhands have the right to reject any dog.

New York Waterways, 800-533-3779. www.nywaterway.com
Dogs in kennels and bags, or wearing muzzles, are allowed on these private interborough ferries. Depending on the size of your dog, and the day or mood of the deckhands, you may be required to stand on deck away from the seated passengers.

PATH Trains, 800-234-7284 www.panynj.gov/path
All dogs in bags or kennels are allowed on PATH trains.

New Jersey Transit, 800-772-2222. www.njtransit.com
Dogs in kennels or bags are allowed on these trains.

Hampton Jitney, 800-936-0440. www.hamptonjitney.com
The Jitney allows dogs in carriers small enough to fit under your seat or on your lap. There's a $10 charge for pets.

Amtrak, 800-872-7245 www.amtrak.com
The rule is simple: no dogs, ever (with the exception of guide dogs, of course).

Greyhound, 800-231-2222. www.greyhound.com
Don't let the name fool you—Greyhound forbids all dogs, except guide dogs.

Taxis, Cars, and Limos

NEW YORK CITY TAXIS AND LIMOUSINES, 212-676-1000. www.ci.nyc.ny.us/html/tlc/
Taxi and limo drivers aren't obliged to transport your dog—but many will. The smaller your hound, the better your chances. Be polite: ask the driver if he wouldn't mind; reassure him that your dog is clean, well-mannered and quiet. Bring along a towel to protect the seat. Tip well. For a small additional fee, most limousine or livery-cab companies will let you bring along your dog as long as you give notice when making a reservation.

RENTAL CARS

If you call the headquarters of the major rental car companies they'll tell you they charge no additional fee for pets. But, curiously, local offices of Hertz and Avis, among others, do impose a fee of as much as $75 for cars returned with any dog hair. They claim vacuuming dog hair takes extra effort (and cleaning up after slobs who leave behind ketchup stains doesn't?). Either way, we've never met a dog person who's paid these charges: New Yorkers simply keep their dogs out of sight when they pick up and drop off a rental, and, if their dog sheds, they get rid of the evidence.

PET TAXIS

As noted above, most limo or livery-cab companies allow pets (usually for an additional charge). But in certain cases you may need a pet taxi. Unlike a cab, pet taxis are equipped to handle emergencies (they carry such equipment as stretchers, muzzles, and gloves) and have room for big dogs. Also, they'll take an unaccompanied dog to and from a kennel, groomer, summer home, dog show or an airport. One company, Pet Taxi (page 88), even has a summer shuttle to the Hamptons.

This list includes the better-known pet taxis in the city. Before hiring a pet taxi you should be sure they have air conditioning, clean and well-ventilated crates or safety harnesses. Depending on how far you're sending your dog, you may also want to know that the taxi company belongs to the Animal Transportation Association or the Independent Pet and Animal Transportation Association International (for a list of members, visit www.ipata.com). These associations require members to comply with federal regulations regarding handling animals.

Manhattan

Pet Chauffeur, 212-696-9744. www.petride.com

David Lang started Pet Chauffeur in 1996. He now has six vehicles (four minivans, one cargo van, and a station wagon), all of which are equipped with kennels and, for emergencies, stretchers. In Manhattan, rates range from $25 to $35 (there's a surcharge for a trip outside of regular hours, 7 A.M. to 9:30 P.M.). One way to LaGuardia Airport is $59, plus tolls; Newark and JFK each cost $75. There are fixed rates to most points near the city—a ride to East Hampton, for example, is $275—but Pet Chauffeur will travel just about anywhere for roughly $40 an hour (with a four-hour minimum), plus gas, tolls, food and lodging. Expect to pay $1,400 to have your dog driven to Miami, as one New Yorker did. Pet Chauffeur is a member of the Animal Transportation Association.

Paw Mobile, 212-594-7087 or 917-734-2779. www.pawmobile.com
Roger Spear, who started Paw Mobile in 1998, drives dogs around the city in his minivan. He does not use crates; instead dogs are secured with leashes attached to the van's floor. In Manhattan, rates are $20 to $30, depending on distance (a surcharge is added to trips outside of regular hours, 8 A.M. to 7 P.M., Monday through Saturday). A ride to LaGuardia is $65, plus tolls; JFK and Newark airports are each $70. To points in the outer boroughs and Long Island, Paw Mobile charges $35 an hour (even if your dog is only going one way, hours are calculated on a round-trip basis). Outside the state, prices climb to $40 a hour. Paw Mobile's van is equipped with a pet stretcher. Emergency calls that require a dog to be carried out of your apartment in a stretcher and rushed to hospital start at about $75.

Pet Taxi, 212-755-1757. www.epettaxi.com
Pet Taxi, which has five minivans, was started by Larry Reilly in 1995. Pet Taxi will transport a dog anywhere in the country; rates are calculated based on distance. In Manhattan, rates range from $20 to $35. A ride to LaGuardia is $56, plus tolls; to JFK and Newark, $66. In the summer of 2001, Pet Taxi started a shuttle service to transport dogs to the Hamptons: it follows the exact route of the Hampton Jitney and cost around $50 one way.
Pet Taxi, a member of the Independent Pet and Animal Transportation Association International, also offers emergency services: for $85 and up, depending on the pick-up and drop-off point, an injured dog will be picked up in a stretcher, muzzled if necessary, carried out of your building, and rushed to the hospital. Emergency response times average around 20 minutes.

Petex, 212-685-1173.
Gail Pierangelino is the woman behind Petex, a small pet taxi service with one cargo van. She charges between $20 and $25 for most trips within Manhattan. One way to LaGuardia Airport is $58, plus tolls; Newark and JFK and Newark run about $68.

Queens
Carol's Ark, 718-278-4677. www.carolsarkpettransportation.com
Based in Astoria, Carol's Ark is primarily a pet-supply store and a groomer, but owner Carol Panagio also offers a pet transportation service, mainly handling dogs that travel by airline cargo. She also chauffeurs pets on long-distance trips. She has charged $3,500, for example, to drive a dog to Missouri.

Coping With Car Sickness

"Is there anything I can do for my dog who always gets car sick? I've tried Dramamine about an hour before a trip—and no food for at least 5 hours before—but the poor thing still gets sick. Any suggestions?" **Betsy Brevitz, DVM, answers:**

Dramamine and no food (water is O.K.) for 6 to 8 hours before a trip works very well for many dogs with car sickness, but since your dog isn't one of them, here are some other things to try:

Exercise first: Before getting in the car, walk or play with your dog until she's ready for a nap.

Give her a safe haven: A crate or carrier is the safest, calmest place for a dog to ride. Racing from lap to window makes dogs anxious, and anxiety makes car sickness worse.

Move her up front: Like people, dogs with car sickness feel better if they can sit in the front seat and look out. Keep it cool in the car, and if you're not using the air conditioner, open the windows a few inches so she gets lots of fresh air. (Be safe: use a car safety harness for dogs; or, for a small dog, a towel-lined crate or carrier.)

Make it short: If your dog gets sick after 30 minutes, give her some pleasant car experiences to help overcome the bad ones: take her on a 15-minute drive to a park or a friend's house; then walk or play with her for 15 minutes; then drive home. (Don't give her any Dramamine, but do withhold food for at least 4 hours beforehand.) Do this a couple of times a week. The idea is to end the car ride before she gets sick. If 15 minutes is too long, try 10, or even 5 minutes. Similarly, when you take a longer car trip, you might try stopping and taking a short walk every 20 minutes or so.

Give it time: Young dogs sometimes outgrow car sickness, just as children do.

Give her a snack: I've read that some dogs may feel less car sick if they eat a light snack an hour or two before the trip. I don't know anyone who's done this, but if you're feeling brave, you might try it. Just be sure to bring a roll of paper towels!

Let her be a homebody: If she continues to be miserable in the car, consider leaving her at home with a pet sitter when you hit the open road.

Move up to a stronger drug: If you've tried the other tips listed here and are still having problems, talk to your vet about using acepromazine, a prescription veterinary drug that is sometimes used for car sickness. The drawbacks: "ace" will make your dog groggy; and getting the dose right can be difficult, because it affects different dogs differently. To see how it affects your dog, I'd suggest testing the recommended dose one day when you'll be home. If it knocks her out for 12 hours, and your car trip is only 4 hours long, you'll know to use half the dose for your trip.

Air Travel

Domestic airlines seem to be working harder to annoy people who travel with their dogs. In the old days—that is, until around mid-2000—you could bring small dogs on board, and check bigger dogs as luggage. Now American and Delta, among others, refuse dogs as checked baggage between May and September, while United and Continental ban them year round. Instead, they require that you ship your dog as cargo.

What's the difference? The airlines claim that animals shipped as cargo are better cared for—but as far as we can tell, the change is largely semantic. What it means for you is that the cost of bringing your dog on holiday has increased from around $50 to as much as $500, each way. For that reason, and because airline travel can be scary and even dangerous for some dogs, some New Yorkers prefer to have their dogs transported by car (see "Pet Taxis," page 87).

Read on for specific rules by airline (we only list the major carriers who operate out of New York). Also, see the box on page 92 for tips on how to fly with your dog. All airlines require that your dog travel with a health certificate issued by your vet no more than 30 days before departure (or 10 days, depending on the airline). To travel in temperatures below 45°, you also need a letter from your vet saying your dog can handle the cold. Generally, all dogs are forbidden from flying in temperatures below 20° or over 85°. And dogs must be at least eight weeks old. Foreign carriers, by the way, still permit dogs as checked baggage.

The US Department of Agriculture has a useful online brochure called "Traveling With Your Pet" available at www.aphis.usda.gov/oa/pubs/petravel.html.

Air Canada. 888-247-2262. www.aircanada.ca

We include Air Canada in this list of domestic airlines because it's one of the most dog-friendly carriers and, if you're desperate, it may make sense to fly through Canada to get to a US destination. This airline even sells airline-approved kennels at the airport.

About the only restriction on pets is that they're not allowed as checked baggage between November 1 and March 31 on CL65 and BAe146 aircraft—two small planes without a heated cargo hold. But neither of these models flies on major routes out of New York. Also, there are limits on the number of checked pets per flight, so be sure to reserve a spot. The fees for dogs is $50 (Can$65). The maximum size for carryon kennels is 9 x 15.5 x 21.5 inches.

American Airlines. 800-433-7300. www.aa.com
Dogs that fit comfortably under the seat can be brought on board anytime for $75 each way (14 x 23 x 9 inches is the size limit). Otherwise, for the same fee, dogs can travel during the winter as checked luggage.

However, between May 15 and September 15, your dog has to travel as cargo. If the combined weight of dog and kennel is less than 70 pounds, you can send your dog via Priority Parcel. Otherwise, you're stuck using Express Air Service, which requires dropping your dog off at the cargo terminal at least two hours before departure and waiting at least two hours for your dog to show up after you land on the other end. Both Priority Parcel and Express Air cost around $200 or more each way, depending on weight, size, and destination.

Continental. 800-575-3335. www.continental.com
Dogs that fit comfortably under the seat can be brought on board for $75 each way (14 x 22 x 9 inches is the size limit). Otherwise, all pets traveling on Continental are only accepted as cargo through the carrier's QuickPak Live Animal Program. The cost is $169 to $299 (plus a fuel surcharge of 2 1⁄2 cents per pound) depending on destination, weight, and kennel size.

Delta. 888-SEND-PET (888-736-3738). www.delta.com/airlogistics
Dogs that fit in a crate no larger than 21 x 13 x 9 inches can travel under your seat. Otherwise, pets can be shipped as checked luggage for $75—except between May 15 and September 15, when they must be sent as cargo using Delta Pets First cargo service. Depending on the size and weight of your dog and his kennel, cargo costs range from $150 to $750 in the continental U.S., and up to $1,300 for trips involving Alaska or Hawaii.

Northwest. 800-225-2525. www.nwa.com
This airline is one of the few majors that still allows dogs as checked luggage all year round (as long as, combined with their kennel, they weigh no more than 150 pounds). On the downside, the cost for checking your dog is high: between $139 and $299 each way, depending on size and weight. For $75, dogs that weigh 15 pounds or less can be stored under the seat in front of you (crates must be no bigger than 9" x 14" x 22").

Tips On Flying With Hounds

It can't be said often enough: traveling by cargo poses dangers for dogs. So use common sense: be especially cautious if your dog is old, unhealthy, or is a pug-nosed breed. If you have a choice, travel by car or by train. At the very least, observe these pointers:

- Fly a reputable airline;
- Unless you absolutely have no choice, only take a direct flight. If you must change flights, be sure you can collect and then re-check your dog at the layover airport. Try to give yourself a long enough layover to take him out for a walk;
- In the summer, travel early or late in the day to avoid heat; in winter, travel mid-day to avoid severe cold. (This has nothing to do with the temperature in the cargo compartment, which is pressurized and kept between 50 and 70 degrees by law, but with temperatures in exposed loading areas);
- To avoid dangerous delays and confusion, don't travel during peak holiday times;
- Make sure your dog's collar and ID tags are sturdy;
- Use a top-quality airline-approved crate with enough room for your dog to turn around in;
- Cover your crate, using stickers or paint or permanent marker, with notices that say: "HI! My name is XX. Please be NICE to me. Thanks!" and "I'm traveling from XX to XX on Flight # XX" and "My Parent's name is XXX. Phone: XXX. Cell: XXX." The more stuff that calls attention to the crate the better;
- Carry a photograph of your dog that you can use to help find him if you're separated;
- Get to the airport a half hour earlier than usual, check in, but don't let them take your dog

United. 800-241-6522. www.united.com
Small dogs can travel with you in the cabin for $75 each way if they fit comfortably in a kennel under the seat (22 x 14 x 9-inches). Otherwise, dogs are not allowed as checked luggage. United only accepts dogs shipped as cargo by a commercial shipping company approved by the airline. Costs for sending your dog via cargo range from $300 to $500 each way.

away until the last moment (usually 30 minutes before departure). Once you've checked in, take your dog outside for a walk and to let him pee/poop.

- Be ABSOLUTELY certain that the door of the kennel is SECURE, really secure—but not locked, as it may need to be opened in case of emergency. Just above the door, write: "DO NOT open this door without the permission of owner or a licensed veterinarian!"
- On a short flight, don't give your dog food or water for six hours before the flight (generally, dogs are fine without water for 12 hours, but ask your vet).
- Don't leave your dog until a baggage handler actually comes to collect him. Give the baggage handler a $5 tip. Ask him to please be sure the dogs is O.K.: we don't know if this helps, but it makes us feel better.
- Be sure not to leave anything in the crate that your dog can rip to shreds, might get sick from, or choke on. A hollow white bone or a Kong stuffed with peanut butter may help keep him calm.
- Don't give your dog sedatives unless you have to, and only then on the advice of your vet. Sedatives make it difficult for your dog to adjust to temperature changes and turbulence, and they may impede his breathing. 
- At the gate, if you can look out the window and watch baggage being boarded, watch for your dog. If you can't see him being loaded, wait until all the other passengers have boarded then ask the gate attendant to radio the baggage area to make sure your dog has been loaded. Refuse to board unless they confirm that your dog in on the plane.
- As you board the plane, stick your head around the corner toward the pilots, (whose door is usually ajar) and say, very politely, " I just wanted to let you know my dog is on this flight, in cargo. It's his first time flying so I'd really appreciate your making sure he's O.K. and double-checking that he's in the right compartment."

US Airways. 800-428-4322. www.usairways.com
We love U.S. Airways because they not only accept dogs as checked baggage all year round, but they also keep prices reasonable. Whether you bring your dog onboard (12 x 17 x 8 inches high is the size restriction) or check your dog as luggage (maximum weight: 100 pounds), the cost is $75 each way.

6

houndmanners

TEACHING YOUR DOG TO BEHAVE

Everyone hates badly behaved dogs. They nip, jerk the leash, jump on strangers, chew furniture, run away, pee on Persian carpets, and yap and yap and yap. Lack of exercise, a poor diet and health trouble are often to blame for bad behavior. Then there's obedience training, or, rather, a lack of it. Every dog, even the tiniest, needs at least basic training. And not only for the obvious reasons—training stimulates a dog's mind, prevents boredom, and strengthens the relationship between human and hound.

How to Train Your Dog

You can learn to train your dog by consulting books and videos—if you're motivated to do it yourself. For the rest of us, classes are the way to go. There are places that will take your dog, train him for you, and send him back when the job is done. We don't recommend that approach. Just as your dog has to learn to respond to commands, so too you need to learn how to give commands correctly and consistently. Besides, obedience training is not a one-time event—it requires constant reinforcement. In group classes with six to eight participants, your dog will learn to respond to your commands even while being distracted by other dogs. Classes also help dogs develop social skills, let you exchange notes with other dog owners, and they're reasonably priced. If you prefer more individualized attention, or if your dog is aggressive or especially difficult to train, work with a private trainer.

Many New York dog trainers, including those listed in this chapter, offer both private and group classes, from puppy preschool to advanced obedience. Once you've made it through the basics, you may want to work toward earning the AKC's Canine Good Citizen certificate, a test that demonstrates your dog's fine manners (and is gratefully appreciated by landlords and co-op boards). For more information on the Good Citizen Award, visit this page on the AKC Web site: www.akc.org/love/cgc/index.cfm. Dogs that excel at obedience often make good therapy dogs (see Chapter Four, page 80, for more information).

TRAINING TRENDS

Every dog responds differently to training: what works for one may not work for another. In the old days, dogs that behaved badly were hit with a rolled-up newspaper, smacked under the chin, zapped by an electric shock collar, or worse. Now, influenced by pioneers like Ian Dunbar and

Karen Pryor, the top dog trainers embrace "positive-reinforcement" or "reward-based" training, which favors teaching dogs through rewards rather than punishment. The idea is grounded in Pavlov's experiments. If good behavior is consistently rewarded (with treats or praise), a dog will be motivated to behave well. Punishment is said to simply make a dog fearful. A version of positive reinforcement training is "clicker training," a method that advocates the use of a handheld clicker when rewarding a dog for good behavior (to learn more about clicker training and reward-based training, check out the books and videos we list beginning on page 102).

Despite the opposition to punishing dogs, some of the best trainers still believe in "corrections," quick snaps of a chain-slip when a dog does not respond to a command. Other reward-based trainers, however, think corrections are, at best, unnecessary and ineffective. As for pronged training collars, they've become so controversial that if you use one you'll probably be told off by strangers in the streets. As an alternative, many trainers now favor nylon head collars, such as a Halti or Gentle Leader (to the uninitiated, these look rather like a muzzle).

Our attitude is this: learn as much as you can about various training methods and products, then use those that work best for you and your dog.

TOP DOG TRAINERS

We list some of the best-known dog trainers here in alphabetical order. We include the borough where these trainers are based, but almost all of them will travel anywhere in the city for private lessons and a few offer group classes in more than one borough. Some trainers only give private lessons; others offer both group and private classes. A few have their own classroom; others borrow or rent space in a church, a park, or a local pet store. Group classes generally run for six to nine weeks, are limited to eight dogs, and range in price from around $110 to $300. Private classes of 60 to 90 minutes generally cost about $100 to $150, but prices can rise quickly depending on where you live and how much work your dog needs.

Don't limit yourself to our list: there are many other worthy trainers and obedience classes in the city. Ask around. Your vet, breeder, shelter and other dog owners can all offer recommendations. If you adopted your dog from a shelter, there's a good chance your shelter offers low-cost training classes (they may even be included in your adoption fee). The ASPCA Behavior Helpline, at 212-876-7700 x4357, provides referrals to trainers. Another good resource is the Association of Pet Dog Trainers (APDT), a membership group of trainers who participate in continuing education. For names of APDT members in your area, call 800-PET-DOGS (800-738-3647) or visit the association's Web site at www.apdt.com.

Training Options

Training Option	Works Well For	Not Advised For
DO-IT-YOURSELF TRAINING USING BOOKS AND VIDEOS	■ Owners with motivation and discipline ■ Owners on a tight budget ■ Puppies and dogs that learn quickly and easily ■ Dogs without behavior problems	■ Owners who need hands-on guidance and encouragement ■ Dogs that are hard to teach, stubborn or aggressive ■ Dogs with behavior problems
GROUP TRAINING CLASS	■ Puppies and dogs who need socialization ■ Owners who want to meet other dog owners ■ Owners on a budget	■ Aggressive dogs ■ Dogs with serious behavior problems
PRIVATE TRAINER	■ Dogs with problems that might not be addressed in a group class ■ Aggressive dogs ■ Owners who want a trainer to come to their home, like one-on-one attention, or can't commit to a class schedule	■ Owners on a budget ■ Puppies (who need socialization)

All About Dogs: Jane Kopelman
210 East 23rd Street (between 2nd and 3rd Aves), Manhattan. 212-481-2656.
Puppy Class, Basic Obedience, and Continuing Education/Canine Good Citizen. Group classes run six weeks and cost $250. Private lessons are also available. Jane, a former behavior counselor at the ASPCA, is experienced in training dogs adopted from shelters and she specializes in helping aggressive dogs. She volunteers with Training Wheels, a shelter outreach program that uses early intervention to helps keep families and their pets together.

ASPCA Center for Behavioral Therapy
424 East 92nd Street (1st and York Aves), Manhattan. 212-876-7700, x4423. www.aspca.org
Puppy Kindergarten, Basic Obedience, Canine Good Citizen/Advanced Beginner. Classes run seven weeks and cost $230 (there's a discount for dogs adopted at the ASPCA). All instructors are members of The Association of Pet Dog Trainers and have many years of training and behavior consultation experience.

City Dog: Liz Gordon
Manhattan, 212-255-3618
Beginning Obedience, Competitive Obedience. Group classes run nine weeks and cost $325. A fixture in Chelsea since 1976, City Dog recently lost its space, but will continue to offer group classes around Manhattan.

Dogs in the Hood: Sue Nastasi
Manhattan, 212-595-3353. www.canisphoto.com/training.htm
Sue offers private puppy and adult dog training lessons anywhere in the city. She's been training dogs since 1997 and believes in promoting friendly, well-mannered, and gentle dogs through caring leadership. Sue also teaches group classes with Manhattan Dog Training (see page 99), and therapy dog training and certification through the Good Dog Foundation.

The Educated Puppy and Dogs, Too: Barbara Giella, Ph.D.
Church of Gethsemane (10th and 11th Streets), Park Slope, Brooklyn. 718-788-3602.
www.educatedpuppy.com
Puppy Kindergarten/Beginners, Intermediate/AKC Canine Good Citizen, Advanced Obedience. Group classes, which meet in the church's social hall and enclosed garden, run for six to eight weeks and costs $150 to $300, depending on the level. Private lessons are available anywhere in the city. Barbara, a trainer since the mid-1980s, emphasizes positive reinforcement, problem prevention, and owner education. She uses clicker training.

Empire of the Dog: Denise Herman
Williamsburg, Brooklyn. 917-723-5233. www.empireofthedog.com
Denise specializes in small dogs (in particular, fear and barking problems). She uses reward-based and clicker training. She offers private classes and teaches group lessons with Manhattan Dog Training (see page 99).

Follow My Lead: Phyllis Couvares and Peggy Spencer
Universalist Church, Central Park West at 76th Street, Manhattan. 212-873-5511
Beginner, intermediate, and advanced obedience. Group classes, which take place at the church and in nearby parks, run seven weeks and cost $285. Private lessons are also available. Phyllis and Peggy have about fifty years training experience between them. Peggy specializes in problem solving; Phyllis on problem prevention, especially with puppies. Both focus on teaching owners how dogs learn.

Tyril Frith
Brooklyn. 718-252-8501. www.tyrilfrith.com
Tyril, a trainer with over thirty years experience, has built a reputation as the man to handle dogs with serious aggression problems, but he works with all kinds of dogs and teaches all levels of obedience. He offers private lessons only.

Happy Tails Family Dog Training: Deb Manheim
718-788-3898
Puppy Kindergarten, Basic Obedience, Advanced Basic Obedience. Group classes run eight weeks and cost $250. Private behavior consultations and training lessons are also available. Deb focuses on reward-based training.

Manhattan Dog Training: Andrea Arden
Biscuits & Bath's Doggy Village, 227 East 44th St (2nd and 3rd Aves) and the New York Dog Spa and Hotel, 145 West 18th St. (6th and 7th Aves), Manhattan. 212-213-4288. www.manhattandogtraining.com
Puppy Class, Adolescent/Adult Class, Basic Clicker Training, Obedience for Small Dogs, Advanced Obedience, and Behavior Problem Solving. Group classes run six weeks and cost $300. Private lessons are also available. An advocate of reward-based training, Andrea, who is Urbanhound.com's training advice columnist, has written three books on dog training. She's also the principal trainer for the Good Dog Foundation, a New York based animal assisted therapy program.

Red Dog Training: Elaine Buchsbaum
Manhattan. 212-534-1290. www.reddogtraining.com
Elaine, a trainer with ten years experience, sees herself as a "relationship counselor" for dogs and owners. She works to teach owners how to take charge. She offers private lessons, trains thera-

Heel! Teaching Your Dog to Walk Properly on a Leash

A dog likes nothing better than to go for a walk; so it's not surprising so many dogs get excited and pull on the leash. And since your dog is discovering new sights and smells with each step he takes, you are essentially competing for his attention. If you get upset and jerk the leash, you aren't likely to solve the problem; in fact, that often makes matters worse. While some dogs respond to collar corrections, most dogs eventually get desensitized to the correction, which means you end up jerking harder and getting no result.

These are the essential ingredients of enjoyable dog walking: the dog walks close to your side (or heels) when requested; he sits when you stop; and at other times he ranges and sniffs without exerting undue tension on the leash. But a dog must understand that the walk won't continue until he walks nicely.

Here's how to "explain" good behavior to your dog. Stand still with your dog on leash, ignoring all his antics and simply wait for him to sit. It doesn't matter if he jumps, barks, or pulls on

py dogs, and she teaches group classes with Manhattan Dog Training (see above).

Vancouver Dog Training: Pat McGregor
Upper West Side, Manhattan. 212-877-7116
Basic Obedience, Pet Therapy Training. Group classes—which meet at various indoor and outdoor locations on the Upper West Side—run 10 weeks, and cost $375 (they include one private session). Pat encourages owners to view exercise and socialization as integral to a dog's behavior.

Walk This Way Canine Behavior Therapy: Renee Payne
Manhattan, 212-260-8423. www.doggiecouch.com

leash. He is just working out all the ploys he can think of to get you moving. Eventually your dog will sit, if only for an instant. The moment he sits, say "Good dog" and offer a piece of kibble (or some other delicious treat). Then take one step, stand still and wait for him to sit again.

The single step will reactivate your dog. This time though, he is likely to take less time to sit. Once he does, same as before, go through the good-dog-kibble-step routine. After just ten or so repeats of this, you will find your dog will sit the instant you stop.

Now try taking two steps before stopping for the dog to sit. Then go for three steps. You'll find your dog becomes surprisingly attentive and does not pull on leash. Instead your dog eagerly anticipates each standstill so he can sit to claim another piece of kibble and then move forward.

Now take five steps in each sequence and then eight, ten, twenty and so on. You will soon find your dog walks calmly and attentively by your side, and sits promptly and eagerly whenever you stop—we call this walking on leash. And you've trained your dog to do it without a single correction and by only uttering the lovely words "Good dog!"

Now comes the real pay off. Alternate periods of walking on leash (signaled by a suitable request to "Heel" or "Keep close" or "By my side") with periods when you allow him to range on leash and sniff (signaled by a suitable instruction to "Go on" or "Go sniff"). But do not allow your dog to tighten the leash when ranging. If he does, simply stand still until he sits by your side. This will accustom your dog to sitting close when you stand still at the curb or as someone passes by.

Andrea Arden, Manhattan Dog Training

Puppy Preschool, Basic Obedience, Advanced Obedience. Group classes, which are held at various locations in Brooklyn and Manhattan, run six weeks and cost $249. Private classes are also available. Renee, who has been training dogs for three years, often works with aggressive dogs and with dogs suffering from separation anxiety.

Who's Walking Who: Stacy Alldredge
Manhattan 212-414-1551
Basic Obedience, Intermediate Obedience. Stacy holds classes at the Petco on Union Square, offering one of the best deals in New York: classes run seven weeks and cost $107 (basic) or $175 (intermediate) per course. However, as we were writing this book, Stacy was planning to open her

? Is This the Right Trainer for Me?

There are dozens and dozens of good dog trainers in New York, each with his or her own style. So before you commit to a particular trainer, ask to sit in on a class (without your dog). Whether you're considering private or group classes, you'll want to first see the trainer at work. Consider:

- Are the classes small enough to allow for individual attention?
- Do the dogs and their owners seem to be having fun?
- Does the trainer explain and demonstrate techniques clearly?
- Does she or he answer questions helpfully?
- Does the trainer use methods of discipline that make you uncomfortable?
- Does she or he offer different solutions depending on the dog and human?
- If you have children, are they welcome to attend?
- Is proof of vaccination required for all dogs in the class? (it should be.)

own space; so check with her for the new address and prices. Stacy has worked in animal shelters and as a veterinary technician, and also offers private classes and nutritional counseling. Aside from basic obedience, she works with dogs that suffer from aggression, separation anxiety, obsessive compulsive behaviors, and fear.

Training Resources

Whether you take an obedience class, work with a private trainer, or train your dog on your own, the books and videos listed below will help you understand how dogs learn, and the best ways to teach them. These resources, listed in alphabetical order by title, are those most often recommended by the city's top dog trainers and by Urbanhound.com members. Prices may vary. The Web sites www.dogwise.com and www.dogbooks.com are two outstanding sources for dog books and videos.

BOOKS

The Art of Raising a Puppy, the Monks of New Skete (Little Brown & Co, 1991)

The Monks of New Skete have been breeding and training German Shepherds in upstate New York for decades. But even while many dog owners rave about this best-selling book, it remains controversial because it promotes certain discipline practices (including "the shakedown") considered outdated. As one message posted on Urbanhound.com notes: "I like parts of the Monks of New Skete books, but these folks advocate the use of choke chains and collar corrections. Aren't we over that yet?" Hardcover, 274 pages, $19. The monks are also the authors of *How to Be Your Dog's Best Friend*, which was published in 1978.

The Culture Clash, Jean Donaldson (James & Kenneth Publishers, 1996)

The book most recommended by dog trainers, *The Culture Clash* aims to educate people about why dogs behave the way they do. Donaldson shows how our unrealistic expectations of dogs are counterproductive, and how an approach grounded in an understanding of the species can make training far more effective. Paperback, 224 pages, $14.

Dog-Friendly Dog Training, by Andrea Arden (Howell Book House, 2000)

This simple, accesible book, with charming illustrations by Tracy Dockray, is a great introduction to positive training methods. It includes a useful explanation of how reward-based training works, plus practical guidance on house-training, basic manners, and dealing with behavior problems. Paperback, 160 pages, $14.

Don't Shoot The Dog: The New Art of Teaching and Training, Karen Pryor (Bantam Books, 1999)

A book about how to shape the behavior of dogs and the other animals in your life (including people!). Pryor, a former dolphin trainer and the creator of clicker training, explains the principles behind behavior modification. This is mostly a book of theory (for more practical guides to clicker training, visit Pryor's Web site at www.dontshootthedog.com). Paperback, 202 pages, $10.

How to Teach a New Dog Old Tricks, Ian Dunbar (James & Kenneth Publishers, 1998)

Dunbar is the father of reward-based training, and this is the classic work on fun, postitive training methods. It is a comprehensive and practical guide to basic obedience, behavior modification and troubleshooting for puppies and older dogs. Paperback, 192 pages, $18.

VIDEOS

Training The Companion Dog, Ian Dunbar (James & Kenneth Publishers, 800-784-5531)
This four-volume set, adapted from a BBC series, features master reward-trainer Ian Dunbar at work. The set costs $89.95, or $25 per 60-minute tape: Vol.1, Socialization and Beginning Obedience; Vol. 2, Behavior Problems and Household Etiquette; Vol. 3, Working on Leash and Heeling; Vol.4, Recalls and Stays.

Take a Bow . . . Wow! Fun and Functional Dog Tricks, Sheri Lippman and Virginia Broitman, 800-BOW-WOW2 (800-269-9692) or www.takeabowwow.com
A 30-minute video that teaches how to use clicker training to teach tricks including opening and closing doors, waving, fetching, and carrying things.

Puppy Love: Raise Your Dog the Clicker Way, Karen Pryor with Carolyn Clark, 800-47-CLICK (800-472-5425) or www.clickertraining.com
How to use the clicker training method to teach your puppy or older dog. Covers housetraining, basic manners, and tricks. Includes a clicker.

7

houndcare

FINDING PEOPLE AND PLACES TO CARE FOR YOUR DOG

"Is it unfair to get a dog if I'm at the office all day?" is a question we get asked all the time. The best answer: It depends. It depends on the age, personality and energy level of your dog. It depends on how many hours you work. But one thing is certain: like most humans, dogs don't like being alone. If you must leave your dog for ten hours at a time, find him a playmate, hire a dog walker or take him to daycare. If you travel for business, find someone nearby who boards dogs. For help, read on.

Dog Walkers

Accustomed to spending $4 for a cup of coffee with foamed milk, many New Yorkers no longer view dog walkers as an indulgence. That explains why there are so many dog walkers—and why we're hearing more stories about scam artists. Earlier this year, for example, a popular dog walker on Manhattan's Upper West Side was caught, on videotape, popping his head into a client's apartment, checking that they weren't home, then quickly leaving without walking the dog. In another case, more sloppy than criminal, a dog walker switched one dog for another, leaving the wrong dog in the wrong apartment.

Remember: dog walkers are not regulated. Most big dog-walking services are insured and their employees bonded, but that doesn't guarantee your dog will be well looked after. So use good judgement and common sense when hiring a walker. Compare walking services to independent dog walkers. Ask around. Chat up dog walkers you see at the dog run. Get suggestions from your vet, obedience trainer, or neighborhood pet-supply store. Visit Urbanhound.com's services and supplies directory (www.urbanhound.com/houndServices/ directory.asp). Do your research.

Private walks are terrific, but expensive (between $15 and $30). Group, or pack walks of up to eight dogs are cheaper (around $10), but your dog may spend half his time going to other dogs' apartment buildings for pickups. If you live near a dog run, a third option is a playgroup, a bunch of dogs that get taken together to a nearby run for an hour or more each day.

Remember, you're not just hiring someone to look after your dog, you're also giving that person the keys to your house. Once you've found a potential dog walker, ask her lots of questions, listen carefully, watch her around your dog, and follow your gut instinct. Call one or two of her current clients—you may discover that she's dependable, but slow-moving and better suited to walking a pocket dog than your excitable Boxer.

Dog-Walking Companies

There are hundreds of dog walkers in this city. A recommendation from a friend, vet or trainer is the best way to find a good one, but you can also contact some of the established dog-walking companies. Here are a few to start with. We admit we're biased towards walkers with useful and informative Web pages. And remember that these are commercial establishments, meaning this list does not—and could not—include the many wonderful independent dog walkers in New York.

For the names of other Brooklyn dog walkers, including individuals, visit the Offleash Web site: www.offleash.com. For names of still more dog walkers, check out the following organizations, whose Web sites can be searched by zip code:

- Pet Sitters International at 800-268-SITS or www.petsit.com;
- The National Association of Professional Petsitters at 800-296-PETS or www.petsitters.org.

Membership in these organizations, by the way, is not a guarantee of quality; it simply means a walker or sitter has paid a fee to join, and has agreed to abide by certain standards or ethical codes. Finally, there's the Pet Sitters Yellow Pages, which carries listings of any dog walkers and sitters who pays a fee of $6: www.petsitters.com/states/nyork.html.

Many dog walkers are also dog sitters, who will also care for your dog if you're away for a day or two, or longer (for long-term boarding facilities, see page 118). Having a pet sitter stay at your place will probably run you about $60 a day. If your dog stays at the sitter's home or facility, figure on paying between $30 to $40 a day.

MANHATTAN

Animal Associates: Richard Gordon, 212-580-2065 or Rmg4dogs@aol.com
Individual walks: 30 minutes, $15; one hour, $25. Limited to between 75th and 96th Streets on the Upper West Side.

Biscuits & Bath, 212-737-2345
Individual walks: 30 minutes, $15. Playgroups in Central Park or Doggy Village: one hour, $25. Additional dogs from the same household are $10 each. Limited to between 20th and 90th Streets.

Central Bark West, 917-856-7955
www.centralbarkwest.net
Individual walks: 30 minutes, $10 to $15; one hour, $15 to $20 (depending on the number of walks per week). Group walks: 30 minutes, $7 to $9; one hour, $10 to $15

Essential Info For Your Dog's Caretaker

Before you leave your dog in the care of a walker, sitter or kennel, put together a cheat sheet that includes all the information listed here. Give one copy to your dog's caretaker and post another on your fridge.

- Dog's name, age, and breed
- Owner's name
- Owner's contact info (home phone, work phone, cell phone, email)
- Alternate contact person
- Vet (name, phone and address)
- After-hours emergency clinic of choice
- ASPCA Animal Poison Control Center, 888-426-4435
- NYC dog license number
- Tattoo or microchip number
- Relevant medical history
- Feeding instructions
- Special care instructions

The Dog House, 212-665-4320
www.thedoghousenyc.com
Individual walks: one hour, $20. Playgroups: two hours, $26. Limited to the Upper West Side.

Mensch Petsitters: Robin Taher, 212-831-6137
http://members.nbci.com/menschpetsit/housesit.html
Individual walks: 30 minutes, $15. Limited to the Upper East Side.

Pet Mates, 212-414-5158
www.petmates.com
Individual walks: 30 minutes, $14; 45 minutes, $17; one hour, $21

Pet Aways, 212-470-7638

www.pet-aways.com
Individual walks: 15 minutes, $15; 30 minutes, $22; one hour, $32. Additional dogs from the same household are $6 each. Group walks: 30 minutes, $15; one hour, $25. Limited to the East Side.

Puddles Pet Service, 212-410-7338
www.puddles.com
Individual walks: 30 minutes, $18; 45 minutes, $24: one hour, $30

Three Dog Knight: Avi Molad, 212-724-1379
Individual walks: 30 minutes, $25; one hour, $35. Group walks (4 dogs max): 30 minutes, $15; one hour, $25.

Two Dogs and a Goat, 212-631-1157
http://twodogsandagoat.com
Individual walks: 30 minutes, $16.25. There's also a branch in Sag Harbor.

Village Pet Care, 800-426-9439.
www.villagepetcare.com
Individual walks: 30 minutes, $12; 45 minutes, $14.50; one hour, $17

Walkee Doggie, 212-925-8100.
www.walkeedoggie.com
Individual walks: one hour, $25. Group walks (3 dogs max): one hour, $14. Limited to Lower East Side, Tribeca, and Soho.

BROOKLYN

Critter Sitter: Michele Finley, 718-768-0372
Individual walks: 30 minutes, $10 to $12. Limited to Park Slope.

Four Paws Dog Walking, 718-852-6359
http://home.earthlink.net/~doggiewalker/index.htm
Individual walks: 30 minutes, $10 ($12 for puppies) or $15 for two dogs of the same household. Limited to Carroll Gardens and Cobble Hill.

Tailwaggers, 718-834-5985
Group walk: 30 minutes, $10. Playgroups in Prospect Park, $15.
Limited to Carroll Gardens, Cobble Hill, and Park Slope.

QUEENS

Carol's Ark: Carol Panagio, 718-278-4677.
Individual walks: 20 minutes, $15. Limited to Astoria.

Daycare Centers

When the media wants to demonstrate how slavishly New Yorkers indulge their dogs, they point to dog day care. Let them mock, we say. Dog day-care centers are one of the best things to have happen to dogs in this city—especially those whose owners work 12-hour days.

Day-care centers range from the basic (one open room) to the elaborate (indoor grass, on-staff vets, and Web cams that let owners check up on their hounds). Prices run from $15 to $32 a day. In picking a day-care center, consider these issues:

- **Location** Can you get there easily?
- **Hours** Pick-up and drop-off times can be restrictive
- **Walks** Some facilities take their dogs out three times a day; others never do
- **Water** At some places, to slow the flow of pee, water is severely restricted
- **Outdoor Space** Some centers have lovely yards and roof decks
- **Quiet Space** Is there a comfortable place for your dog to rest?
- **Cleanliness** Daycare centers should be reasonably clean, if not spotless
- **Cost** Do you get discounts for frequent use?
- **Restrictions** They should insist on proofs of vaccination and turn away aggressive dogs
- **Safety** Find out what they do when a dog is injured or sick. Ask how they prevent fights. Consider if there's any way to evacuate in case of a fire.

Before your dog goes to day care, make sure he is up-to-date on all his vaccinations, including kennel cough, or bordatella, which is spread by dogs in close quarters. It's also wise to use a monthly flea preventive, such as Frontline or Program.

TOP DAYCARE PROVIDERS

New dog daycare centers open all the time, so don't limit yourself to our list: there may be other

Dog Walkers: Big Company or Free Agent?

Type of dog walker	Advantages	Disadvantages
SERVICE	■ Likely to be insured and bonded ■ As a registered business, it's more likely to offer recourse if you have a problem ■ If your regular walker can't make it, there's a back-up ■ May be trained to handle emergencies	■ More likely to be impersonal, with less individual attention to your dog ■ More likely to only offer group walks-or be more expensive for private walks ■ You may get many different walkers
INDEPENDENT	■ You'll always get the person you screened ■ More likely to form a long-term close bond with your dog ■ More apt to adjust her schedule or walk to suit your dog ■ May be less expensive	■ Probably isn't insured or bonded ■ Isn't likely to have a back-up when she calls in sick ■ Offers little recourse in the case of a problem

great spots we've overlooked. Many of the places we list here also offer over-night boarding, which makes them an excellent resource if you have to leave town at the last minutes, or will only be gone for a day or two. If you're leaving for more than a few days, however, you're better off sending your dog to a place that specializes in longer-term boarding (see page 118) Long-term kennels are cheaper and they usually have lots more outdoor and indoor space than a daycare center.

MANHATTAN

Upper East Side

Run Spot Run, 415 East 91st Street (between First and York Aves.), 212-996-6666.

Can I Sue My Dog Walker?

"While in the care of a dog walking service, my Golden Retriever ripped apart and swallowed a tennis ball. Because some of the pieces got lodged in her stomach, she had to undergo $2,500 worth of surgery. Can the dog walker be held liable for negligence?"
Attorney Darryl Vernon, of Vernon & Ginsberg, answers:

Under the law, dog walkers can probably be required to show "reasonable care" in their work—which could mean that if they do not prevent your dog from ingesting something dangerous, they (or the dog-walking service they work for) may be liable.

That said, the circumstances of such a case are crucial. It is possible that the dog walker couldn't reasonably do anything to prevent your dog from swallowing a tennis ball. If you do attempt to sue, remember that New York courts treat pets as if they were personal property (much like a TV, dogs are only worth what you paid for them) and so you're not likely to recover anything for pain and suffering. If you hope to recover your medical costs, gather as much evidence as possible, including witnesses and such experts as veterinarians to prove damages and liability.

www.runspotrun.com
There's over 5,000 square feet of romping room here, plenty of space to divide dogs by size and temperament into three areas.
Hours: 7 A.M. to 10 P.M. every day
Cost: $15 to $19 a day, depending on size of dog. Regulars get a small discount.

Biscuits and Bath Doggy Gym, 1535 First Avenue (80th Street), 212-794-3600
This fancy place has AstroTurf dog runs with bridges and hoops to amuse your dog. As well, for dogs trying to nap, there's a separate area called Lullaby Village. Dogs are separated by size and walked every two to three hours. For an extra fee, a jitney service picks up and delivers dogs.
Hours: 7 A.M. to 7 P.M. every day
Cost: A members-only facility. Membership costs $250 the first year; $150 a year thereafter. On top of that, day care costs $30 to $35 a day. Hourly rates are available.

Sutton Dog Parlour, Kennel and Playcare Center, 311 East 60th Street (1st and 2nd Aves), 212-355-2850
www.suttonpets.com,
A gated roof deck overlooking Second Avenue has wading pools, slides, and obstacle courses. Small dogs are kept in their own corner of the yard. In cold weather or rain, dogs stay inside, where they can climb over beds, futons and couches.
Hours: Weekdays, 8 A.M. to 7 P.M.; Saturday, 8 A.M. to 7 P.M.; Sunday, 9 A.M. to 6 P.M.
Cost: $20 to $25 a day.

Upper West Side

Camp Canine, 46 West 73rd Street (Central Park West and Columbus), 212-787-DOGS.
This center has three good-sized rooms, each devoted to a different size of dog. Dogs are taken for walks outside, but only for an additional fee.
Hours: 7 A.M. to 9 P.M. every day
Cost: $21 to $28 a day.

Sit, Stay, Play, 140 West 67th Street (Broadway and Amsterdam), 212-712-9535
Small, but clean and friendly, this facility is right below Animal General's new vet office. Dogs are walked several times a day. Because there is only one main room for dogs, small dogs are kept in the employee lunchroom.
Hours: Weekdays 7:30 A.M. to 8:00 P.M.; weekends from 8 A.M. to 4 P.M.
Cost: $24 a day, during weekdays (on weekends, a boarding rate of $40 is charged). There are discounts for regulars.

Midtown

Biscuits and Bath's Doggy Village, 227 E. 44th St. (2nd and 3rd Aves), 212-692-2323
This former carriage house has five big floors carpeted with AstroTurf and hanging tires, a seesaw and hoops. The décor, with its white picket fences, is very Shabby Chic. There's a vet on site, and grooming and training are also available. For an extra fee, a jitney service picks up and delivers dogs.
Hours: 7 A.M. to 11 P.M. every day
Cost: A members-only facility. Membership costs $250 for a year, or $175 for six months. On top of that, daycare costs $30 to $35 a day, plus $5 if your dog stays past 7 P.M. The hourly rates is $8, with a two-hour minimum.

Chelsea

Paws Inn, 189 Ninth Avenue (21st and 22nd Streets), 212-645-7297. www.pawsinn.com

Dogs who stay here get taken outside four times a day; either on walks, or to the facility's fenced-in "Woof Deck." Paws Inn offers boarding and grooming too.

Hours: 7 A.M. to 10 P.M. daily

Cost: $24 a day; $13 for a half day.

New York Dog Spa and Hotel, 145 West 18th Street (6th and 7th Aves), 212-243-1199. www.nydogspa.com

A clean, modern space where dogs are divided into several small areas based on size and temperament. Lack of natural light is one complaint we hear. Dog Spa will pick up and deliver your dog, for a fee. Grooming, training and even massage are available.

Hours*:* 7 A.M. to 10 P.M. every day

Cost*:* $26 to $32 a day.

Murray Hill

Little Red Pet Shop, 202 East 25th Street (2nd & 3rd Aves.), 212-481-6131

Once a pet-supply store, Little Red is now a small daycare facility that handles no more than ten dogs at a time.

Hours*:* 7:30 A.M. to 6:30 P.M. every day

Cost*:* $25 per day, with discounts for frequent guests.

Greenwich Village

Bed & Biscuit: Shelley Davis, Washington Square Park area. 212-475-6064. www.bednbiscuit.com

Shelley cares for no more than a handful of dogs at a time in her Greenwich Village apartment. Sensitive to special dietary needs, she's proud that she serves only organic treats (and homemade chicken soup). She will work on housebreaking puppies and boards dogs too, for $50 a night.

Hours*:* 8 A.M. to 8 P.M. every day

Cost*:* $25 for up to ten hours; thereafter $5 a hour.

Questions For Prospective Dog Walkers

- How many dogs do you walk at a time? (Anything more than four seems excessive to us.)
- Do you visit a dog run during the walk? (Some dogs love them; other hate them.)
- Do you have a dog? (Yes is a good answer.)
- What do you do in extreme weather? (Most dogs can't handle long walks in severe heat or cold.)
- If you pick up other dogs on the way, what will you do with my dog? (A dog should never be left unattended, e.g. tied up outside a building)
- Have you ever had to deal with an emergency while walking a dog? If so, what did you do? If not, what would you do?
- Can someone fill in for you if you're out sick?
- Do you provide any additional services, such as boarding?
- How long have you been in business?
- Can you provide two current clients as references? (Always call references.)

<u>Lower East Side</u>

Personalized Pet Care by Alice, 90 Ludlow Street (Broome & Delancey Streets), 212-228-7894 www.doggiediva.com

Alice has 6,000 square feet of indoor space, plus another 4,000 square feet outside. She also offers boarding and grooming.

Hours*:* Weekdays, 6:30 A.M. to 10:00 P.M.; weekends, 8:00 A.M. to 9:00 P.M.

Cost*:* $25 a day

<u>Soho</u>

Alternative Pet Care, 33 Howard Street (Broadway and Lafayette), 212-941-5083

This place has two floors and many couches for dogs to lounge on. Dogs are walked three times a day. Grooming is also available.

Hours: 6 A.M. to 10 P.M. every day

Cost: $22.50 a day; $15 a half day

Tribeca

The Wagging Tail, 354 1/2 Greenwich Street (Harrison and Franklin Streets), 212-285-4900.
www.thewaggingtail.com

This 3,000-square-foot facility faces the street and gets plenty of natural light. A Web cam lets owners check up on their pets via the Internet. Wagging Tail will pick up and drop off your dog for an extra fee. They also offer overnight boarding.

Hours: 7 A.M. to 10 P.M. every day

Cost: $19.95 to $24.95 a day.

BROOKLYN

Williamsburg

Dog Abby, 60 Metropolitan Avenue (Kent and Wythe), 718-387-7767.
www.dogabby.com

Dog Abby has indoor and outdoor play areas, with a wading pool outside during summer months. A Web cam lets owners check up on their pets via the Internet. Boarding for dogs and cats is also available.

Hours: Weekdays, 8:00 A.M. to 7:30 P.M.; Saturday, 9:00 A.M. to 5:00 P.M.; Sunday, closed.

Cost: $25 a day. Small discounts available to regulars.

Dog and Company, North 11th Street, 718-302-3955 or 888-DOG-7097

This daycare center is housed in a 3,000-square-foot former carriage house. Dogs get to hang out on futon couches and are taken for several walks a day. Daycare fees include pick-up and delivery from Manhattan and Brooklyn.

Hours: Weekdays, 7 A.M. to 8 P.M.

Cost: $30 a day, or $27 for regulars (includes pick-up and delivery)

Carroll Gardens

Woofs & Whiskers, 59 Summit Street (Columbia and Van Brunt Streets), 718-237-0298.
www.woofsnwhiskers.com

Space inside is somewhat cramped, but the best thing about Woofs & Whiskers is the 7,000-square-foot outdoor run.

Hours: Monday to Thursday, 8 A.M. to 6 P.M. Depending on demand, may be open on other days as well.

Rates: $20 a day

The Dog Walkers' Manifesto

We wish that all our clients would:

- Keep emergency numbers updated and conspicuously posted, including vet, office, cell phone, and beeper numbers;
- Keep equipment and supplies, including leashes, collars, treats, food, medication, poop bags, and accident cleaners—in consistent and convenient locations;
- Make sure collars are in good condition, fit properly, and carry proper identification.
- Alert us to changes in their dog's condition, including medical problems;
- Write clearly or type all notes, and keep pen and paper handy so we can leave notes if necessary;
- Never ask us to run non-dog related errands, like returning videos or picking up dry cleaning;
- Inform us of the presence of workmen, guests, and cleaners—and advise them we will be there to walk the dog;
- Warn us if any of their neighbors have "issues" with their dog, or if there are problems in the building we need to know about;
- Keep locks and gates in good working order. If locks are changed, give us the new key immediately;
- Make sure the alarm is turned off if we do not have the code;
- Provide a dog towel for rainy days;
- Give us adequate notice of schedule changes and vacations;
- Not talk down to us (we are doing this because we love animals, not because we are too stupid or unskilled to have a "real" job).
- Pay in a timely fashion.
- Tip us, especially around the holidays (it shows that you appreciate the care we give your dog).

Composed by a group of full-time dog walkers in Park Slope, Brooklyn

Kennels

To find a kennel, ask friends or your vet for suggestions. See our list here. And visit the Web site of the American Boarding Kennels Association at www.abka.com, which includes a list of member kennels by state. (For a kennel to be accredited by the ABKA, it must meet a lengthy list of criteria and pass an on-site inspection.)

Because many kennels are outside the city, and because dogs are often picked up and delivered, dog owners rarely inspect kennels in person. That's a mistake. We've heard horror stories about kennels that were thought to be wonderful places until dog owners learned otherwise.

Take the time to visit a kennel, preferably unannounced, and ask yourself: Does the staff seem competent and friendly? Do they interact regularly with dogs? Are the facilities clean and comfortable? Are they adequately heated, ventilated, and lit? Do dogs have individual food and water bowls? Are dogs kept in caged kennels or in one open area? If they're kept in individual cages, how often are they free to roam inside and out? How often do dogs hang out with one another?

Ask the kennel to provide you with the names of two or three customers as references. Ask if a proof of vaccination is required (it should be). Other good questions: What happens if a dog is injured or becomes ill? How much is charged for pickup and delivery from the city? How many walks a day do dogs get? Do they bathe dogs in their care?

TOP KENNELS

These are some of the best-known boarding kennels in the New York City region. When available, we've included comments from city dog owners who have used these places.

Almost Home Kennels
174 Pudding Street, Putnam Valley, NY 10579. 845-528-3000
www.almosthomekennels.com
Distance from the city by car: Between 60 and 90 minutes
Rates: $27.50 a day.
Livery information: Pickup and drop-off available in Manhattan, Monday to Thursday, noon to 2 P.M. Above 59th Street, $50, below 59th Street, $60, one way.

Barkingham Palace
26 Davis Avenue, Port Washington, NY 11050. 516-944-5757

www.barkinghampalace.com
Distance from the city by car: About 45 minutes
Rates*:* $17 to $50 a day, depending on how large a space your dog is kept in, and whether he's kept together with other dogs or alone.
Livery information: No pickup service

Best Friends Pet Resort
269 Red Schoolhouse Road, Chestnut Ridge, NY 10977. 914-371-4000
825 Route 22 West, North Plainfield, NJ 07060. 908-822-9200
www.bestfriendspetcare.com
This national chain has two branches close to the city.
Distance from the city by car: About an hour
Rates*:* $21 a day in North Plainfield; $26 a day in Chestnut Ridge
Livery information: No pickup service

Country Estates Kennels
4838 Arthur Kill Road, Staten Island, NY 10309. 718-356-3933
Distance from the city by car: About an hour from Manhattan (it's located at the far end of Staten Island).
Rates*:* $20 to $25 a day, depending on the size of the dog
Livery information: Pickup and delivery is $45 to $100 each way, depending on location
Urbanhounder comment: "An excellent boarding kennel. . . . I have used their services for three occasions for my three greyhounds and they were well cared for."

Grace Lane Kennels
46 Grace Lane, Ossining, NY 10562. 888-PET-CAMP
www.gracelane.com
Distance from the city by car: About 30 minutes
Rates*:* $23 to $25 a day
Livery information: Pick-up and delivery in Brooklyn and Manhattan is free during scheduled pickup times on Tuesdays and Thursdays. At other times: $75 each way.
Urbanhounder comment: "I've been using them for 10 years. If you have more than one dog, they can be boarded in the same room. Each dog room leads to an individual run to which the

dog has constant access during the day when the weather is nice. They medicate, if necessary, at no cost. My dogs are in good shape, physically and emotionally, when I pick them up."

Rondout Valley
4628 Route 209, Accord, NY 12404. 914-687-4406
www.suesternberg.com/02boarding.html
Distance from the city by car: 2½ to 3 hours
Rates: $20 a day
Livery information: Limited pickup and drop-off service, $75 each way.
Urbanhounder comments: "I used Rondout to board my two small dogs. . . . They came back in great shape and well-groomed. They're Pekinese and need to get near a brush on a regular basis." And "Rondout Valley is run by Sue Sternberg who has a superb reputation not only for caring for her charges, but in understanding canine behavior in general. She is very active in shelter and kennel education and management."

Rye Country Boarding Kennels
21 Nursery Lane, Rye, NY 10580. 914-967-4577
Distance from the city by car: About 45 minutes
Rates: $14 to $20 a day
Livery information: Weekday afternoon pickup and drop-off service for Manhattan only, $20 each way.
Urbanhounder comment: "The kennels are clean and roomy and well-tended. Each kennel has a run and the dogs are let out 3 times per day. I've boarded my dogs there for 20 years, and they have always come back healthy and happy."

Woods End Kennels
66 Woods End Road, Putnam Valley, NY 10579. 877-325-4042
www.woodsendkennels.com
Distance from the city by car: About 90 minutes
Rates: $25 to $28 a day, depending on accommodation (there are "luxury suites" for toy dogs). Plus extra fees for special playtime, medication delivery, and so on.
Livery information: Weekday afternoon pickup and drop-off service for Manhattan only, $20 each way.

8 

houndhealth

KEEPING YOUR CITY DOG HEALTHY

This chapter, though far from a complete guide to your dog's health, addresses the essential health issues for New York City dogs, from exposure to rat poison and West Nile Virus, to pet health insurance and veterinarians who make house calls. For plenty more hound-health information, visit Urbanhound.com, where Dr. Betsy Brevitz, a graduate of Tufts University School of Veterinary Medicine and Urbanhound.com's resident veterinarian, has posted answers to hundreds of questions from city-dog people.

City Health Issues

There are particular dangers that only a city dog encounters. Here, in alphabetical order, are the ones to be most concerned about:

DE-ICING SALT

Salt on cracked foot pads can sting like crazy, and snow clumps between the pads hurt too. If the snow and salt bother your dog's feet, you may want to invest in some waterproof dog boots (the most popular brand, Muttluks, sells for around $30). Some people have reported success with Musher's Secret, a wax that is rubbed onto a dog's pads and between the toes before going outside. The wax apparently helps seal cracks in the pads, thereby protecting against the sting of salt. Using petroleum jelly as a salt barrier doesn't seem to work as well (though some people swear it's just as good as Musher's Secret and cheaper). Just remember never to doctor your dog's feet with any salve or moisturizer that isn't safe to eat, because lick it off he will.

Even if your dog's feet don't seem sore after a winter walk, it's a good idea to rinse them with plain warm water and dry them as soon as you get home. This will keep your dog from licking the chemicals off his feet and will also melt any painful ice or snow buildup between his toes. Finally, be sure to keep the hair between your dog's paws as short as possible: less hair means fewer painful clumps of snow.

If you can talk your building manager into the extra expense, or if you de-ice your own walkway, there are "paw-safe" ice melters on the market that work well and don't sting (one popular brand is called Safe Paw).

LEPTOSPIROSIS

In the summer and fall of 2000, New Yorkers worried that a leptospirosis epidemic had hit. The disease, known as lepto or swamp fever, killed two Brooklyn dogs and sickened a few others in the city.

What is lepto? It's a bacterial disease transmitted by the urine of infected animals, often rats, but also by raccoons, skunks, squirrels, opossums, livestock, and other animals. Although the disease is rare, lepto bacteria are fairly common: the U.S. Centers for Disease Control and Prevention estimates that half the nation's rat population carries lepto bacteria. The bacteria can infect people, but that's unusual. In New York City, only two suspected human cases of lepto have been reported in recent years (one in 1989 and one in 1996). For detailed information about lepto, visit Urbanhound.com's health pages.

In the meantime, here are suggested precautions against lepto:

- Don't let your dog chase rats or roam in rat-infested areas.
- Don't let your dog drink from, wade in, or swim in ponds or stagnant pools of water.
- Discuss with your vet whether your dog should be vaccinated against lepto, given his environmental and medical history. Lepto vaccines do not offer absolute protection, but they reduce the chances of infection.
- Remember that you can get lepto from an infected dog: wear gloves when cleaning up urine from a sick dog (consult a physician if you become ill after contact with an animal that might have lepto).
- Don't leave food for animals outdoors. You're likely to be feeding rats as well.
- Report blocked drains or other areas of stagnant water to the city via its Web site at www.nyc.gov/html/doh/html/wnv/wnvwater.html or by calling 877-968-4692.
- Report rat infestations to New York's Pest Control Services Division via its Web site at www.nyc.gov/html/doh/html/pest/pestrat.html or by calling 212-442-9666.

LYME DISEASE

Transmitted by deer ticks, Lyme disease has become more common in the northeast as urban sprawl spreads to wooded areas. Ticks are especially numerous and active during the transition months into and out of cold weather, such as October/November and March/April. So those are the times to be extra watchful and to use anti-tick products, such as a spot-on, spray, or collar. Ask your vet which one's best for your dog.

If you go hiking and find your dog covered with ticks, get them off as soon as possible: ticks need to be attached and feeding for 24 hours in order to transmit Lyme Disease. The easiest way to remove ticks is to use tweezers or a "tick picker" (a brand called Ticked Off is good).

After removing as many ticks as you can find, put a Preventic collar on your dog right away—the collar will help remove any ticks you might have missed. Note that a flea collar won't work. You must use an anti-tick collar with the active ingredient Amitraz.

How do you know if your dog has Lyme Disease? Symptoms include loss of energy, fever, and sometimes lameness or swollen joints. Your best bet is to monitor your dog's energy, appetite, and behavior for a month or so after you go hiking, and take her to the vet if she seems out of sorts.

PUPPY WARTS

Because city dogs spend so much time in dog runs, they're more likely to transmit viruses and diseases, both big and small. If you notice a few wart-like growths around your puppy's mouth, they're probably puppy warts, which come from a virus that is easily passed from dog to dog when they're play-fighting (no, humans can't catch the virus—it's dog-specific). It may take a few weeks, but the warts eventually disappear as the puppy builds up an immunity to the virus. Puppy warts don't need to be removed or treated unless they make eating uncomfortable or become irritated from rubbing against the dog's teeth.

RATS

Just about every New York dog has played with a dead rat at least once, and some have played with live rats as well. There are a few things to worry about here. One, the possibility that the rat could transmit leptospirosis (see page 123); and secondly, that your dog may injest rat poison, which is as toxic to dogs as it is to rodents. Watch for notices about rat poison in parks, and consider keeping your dog on-leash if rat poison was put out recently. If there's a chance your dog may have eaten rat poison, take your dog to your vet for a blood test (for more on rat poison, see page 140).

WEST NILE VIRUS

West Nile Virus, which is transmitted by mosquitoes, can lead to West Nile Encephalitis, an inflammation of the brain. The virus first showed up in the U.S. in 1999; by the end of 2000, there had

Where to Get Help at 4 A.M.

Animal Medical Center
510 East 62nd Street (between York Ave. and the FDR), Manhattan. 212-838-8100
Open 24/7

Brooklyn Veterinary Emergency Service
453 Bay Ridge Avenue (between 4th and 5th Aves), Brooklyn. 718-748-5180
Open 8 P.M. to 9 A.M., Monday through Friday, and around the clock on weekends from Saturday at 4 P.M. to Monday at 9 A.M.

been 79 cases of severe disease in New Yorkers, including eight deaths.

So, can West Nile affect dogs? Potentially yes, but the infection in dogs tends to be brief and mild. Often they have no symptoms at all. The West Nile virus does not multiply in a dog's bloodstream the way it does in birds' bloodstreams, so a mosquito cannot transmit the disease from a dog to a person or other animal.

Mosquitoes are believed to be the only insect vector for West Nile virus in this area. According to the national Centers for Disease Control and Prevention (CDC) Web site (www.cdc.gov/ncidod/dvbid/westnile/q&a.htm), "Ticks infected with West Nile virus have been found in Asia and Africa . . . However, there is no information to suggest that ticks played any role in the New York area outbreak."

The New York City Department of Health has posted a fact sheet on West Nile virus in cats and dogs at www.ci.nyc.ny.us/html/doh/html/wnv/wnvfaq13.html.

WINTER STREET SHOCKS

Every winter there are reports of dogs in New York being shocked by walking in areas where underground electric wires have shorted out: the combination of salt, wet snow, and an electric current can lead to one nasty jolt. There's no sure way to prevent this, but in winter it is a good idea to steer your dog around metal grates, plates, and lamp posts as best you can. If your dog does get zapped, be sure to report the incident to Con Edison by calling 212-683-0862. Typically Con Ed will send someone over right away to correct the short.

Finding a Good Vet

There are many, many vets in NYC (see Urbanhound Yellow Pages, page 186) and you may have several to choose from in your neighborhood. Talk to other dog owners and post a request for recommendations on Urbanhound.com's message boards. In making your selection, consider:

- **Proximity to your home.** If you don't have a car, getting any dog other than a pocket dog to the vet is a pain in the neck. New York cab drivers often refuse to stop for people with dogs.
- **Size of the practice.** Some vets practice on their own, others have partners. A larger practice probably has longer hours and other vets you can see when yours is not available.
- **Cost.** What are the vet's rates for standard procedures like an annual checkup and vaccines? New Yorkers face some of the country's highest veterinary bills, but even here prices vary.
- **Availability.** Is the practice open on weekends or evenings? What if you have an after-hours emergency? If you call with a question, how long does it take the vet to get back to you?
- **Specialties.** Does the vet have any specialties? If your dog is old, has a particular health problem, or her breed is prone to a certain condition, find a vet with the right experience.
- **Services.** Does the practice allow prompt walk-in service for regular maintenance like clipping nails or emptying anal glands, or do you need an appointment? What's the charge for these walk-in services? Does the practice charge separately for these services during a regular office visit? How much?
- **Credentials.** Where did the vet go to school? Is he or she a member of any professional associations? Do you have the sense that she tries to stay in the loop?
- **Comfort level.** When you call the office, is the receptionist helpful and knowledgeable? Is the office clean, and does it run smoothly? Do you feel comfortable talking to the vet and asking questions? Does he explain things to you thoroughly and patiently? Does he do his best to put your dog at ease? (Some dogs may be nervous at the vet no matter what.)
- **Attitude.** Does the vet approach treatment with an eye to alternatives? More and more, dog owners have become concerned about excessive vaccination schedules, overuse of antibiotics, flea preventives and other drugs. Is the vet open to discussing the options? Does she care?

Low-Cost Health Care

A standard annual exam at a Manhattan vet, including vaccines and an annual supply of heartworm medication, can easily run $250. Neutering or spaying costs between $200 and $300. If the thought of paying those prices gets your knickers in a twist, check out the clinics listed here: they offer top-notch vet care at below-market rates.

The ASPCA Bergh Memorial Animal Hospital, 424 East 92nd Street (between 1st Ave and York), Manhattan. 212-876-7700 x4200.
www.aspca.org
Annual exams costs $40 with an appointment, $50 for drop-ins.
Neutering is $55; spaying is $65 (dog over 50 pounds pay slightly more).

Bide-a-Wee Clinic, 410 East 38th Street (1st Ave and the FDR), Manhattan. 212-532-5884.
www.bideawee.org
Annual exam cost $32.50, plus $15 for each vaccine. In July and August, neutering and spaying is free to all New York City dogs or cats. During the rest of the year, rates start at $30 for dogs under 30 pounds, and increase with the weight of the dog.

Fund for Animals' Have-A-Heart Spay & Neuter Clinic, 355 West 52nd Street (8th and 9th Aves.), Manhattan. 212-977-6877
www.fund.org/sanctuaries/n2_clinic.asp
Routine care is not offered, but low-cost spaying and neutering is.
The fee is $35; discounts for people in need.

The Humane Society of New York, 306 East 59th Street (1st and 2nd Aves.), Manhattan. 212-752-4840.
www.humanesocietyny.org
Annual exam is $25, plus $15 for each vaccine. Neutering and spaying starts at $30 for dogs under 30 pounds; price increases with the weight of the dog.

Muffin's Pet Connection, 718-833-7988,
http://www.muffins.org/
This non-profit animal welfare group offers spay or discount neuter certificates that can be used at 69 New York-area vets. Cost is $42 for neuter, $62 for spay; price may be higher for pets over 30 pounds.

The Animal Medical Center

Everyone knows that New York has some of the world's best hospitals for humans. But few are aware that the city also boasts one of the most famous hospitals for hounds and animals of all types: the nonprofit Animal Medical Center on Manhattan's Upper East Side (510 East 62nd Street; 212-838-8100).

The largest private animal hospital in the country, the AMC, open 24 hours a day, every day, is the place to go if your dog needs emergency care or if he's being treated for a serious illness. Endoscopy, brain surgery, MRIs, CT scans, ultrasound, reconstructive knee surgery, chemotherapy, radiation treatment, dialysis, skin grafting, and on and on—there's almost no procedure that AMC can't do. On staff are 80 vets with 28 different specialties.

Don't go to the AMC for warm and fuzzy routine care: this hospital is chaotic, intense, and packed with sick animals and exhausted humans. As well, there's not much sympathy for those who can't pay the AMC's high prices: before your dog is rolled into the operating room, you'll be required to pay at least half the estimated fee up-front. Expect that fee to be big. Hip replacement costs around $3,200. A cataract removal is $1,500 per eye. Root canal is $1,000. Kidney dialysis? $55,000 a year. If you earn less than $32,000 a year, or are a senior citizen on a fixed income you may qualify for free or discounted care. Knowing that one day you may depend on the AMC to save your dog's life is reason enough to sign up now for pet health insurance (see page 130).

Vets Who Make House Calls

For dogs that are too sick or too old, or for owners who can't or don't want to leave home, there are vets who make house calls. Mobile vets offer full physical exams, including vaccinations and blood tests. Some travel in a van stocked with supplies and bring along a veterinary technician for assistance; others simply show up with a well-stocked doctor's bag. All mobile vets are affiliated with an animal hospital.

Vets who make house calls point to added benefits other than convenience: visiting patients' homes lets them spot trouble (a toxic plant or a dangerous terrace), allows them more time for examination, and makes the process less stressful for animals and their owners. The downside is cost: house-calls are at least 20 percent more expensive than office visits. Most of these vets charge a flat house call fee, plus an additional fee for the exam. It's more economical if you have more than one pet, since you'll only be charged the house call fee once per visit. As with non-mobile vets, vaccines, medications, and treatments are extra.

The vets listed here, all licensed with the State of New York Board of Veterinary Medicine, specialize in house calls. Not listed here are the many city veterinary hospitals that will dispatch a vet to your house if you ask.

Dr. Amy Attas, 212-581-PETS
Dr. Attas has been practicing since 1987 and making house calls since 1992. Many of her patients are geriatric pets.
Hospital Affiliation: Center for Veterinary Care, 236 East 75th Street, Manhattan.
Traveling Vet Technician: Yes
Service Area: Manhattan
Cost: house call fee: $140, includes exam for one pet. Additional exams: $70 per pet

Dr. Lewis H. Berman, 212-832-8417
Because Dr. Berman has five vets who work with him, his practice can make house calls at any hour, and on a moment's notice. After hours, a technician will always answer and a vet is always on call. However, Dr. Berman will only make house calls to patients whom he has already seen in his hospital.
Hospital Affiliation: Park East Animal Hospital, 52 East 64th Street, Manhattan
Traveling Vet Technician: Yes
Service Area: Citywide
Cost: house call fee: $140, includes exam for one pet. Additional exams: $70 per pet.

Dr. Charles Kaufman & Dr. Kenneth Jaffe, 718-373-0240
www.mobilevet.baweb.com
Drs. Kaufman and Jaffe started Mobile Veterinary Unit, which is devoted to house calls, in 1975. They also run their own veterinary hospital in Brooklyn.
Hospital Affiliation: Their own, Mobile Vet, 94 Avenue U, Bensonhurst, Brooklyn
Traveling Vet Technician: No

Service Area: Brooklyn, Queens and Staten Island
Cost: house call fee: $75, includes exam for one pet. Additional exams: $25 per pet.

Dr. George Korin, 212-838-2569
Dr. Korin has been practicing since 1985 and making house calls since 1990. Clients say Korin is timely, professional, extremely caring, an overall benefit to their dogs' health.
Hospital Affiliations: East Side Animal Hospital, 321 East 52nd Street, Manhattan and West Chelsea Veterinary Hospital, 203 10th Avenue, Manhattan
Traveling Vet Technician: Yes
Service Area: Manhattan, between Tribeca and 96th Street; Brooklyn, from Greenpoint to Williamsburg.
Cost: house call fee: $75. Exam: $65 per pet.

Dr. Eric Maddon, 718-494-4497
Dr. Maddon's been making house calls since the mid-1990s, after more and more of his clients requested the service. Maddon allows his patients to page him anytime of day or night.
Hospital Affiliation: Veterinary Medical Center of Brooklyn, 5010 Kings Highway, Brooklyn.
Service Area: Brooklyn, Queens, and Staten Island.
Traveling Vet technician: Yes
Cost: house call fee: $50. Exam: $20 per pet.

Dr. Tom Parker, 718-832-8130
Dr. Parker, who works part-time at the Cobble Hill Animal Clinic, has made house calls 1991.
Hospital Affiliation: Cobble Hill Animal Clinic, 173 Court Street, Brooklyn
Traveling Technician: Yes
Service Area: Brooklyn
Cost: house call Fee: $75. Exam: $15 per pet.

Pet Health Insurance

New Yorkers face among the country's highest veterinary bills. Should you take out pet health insurance? We think so. We've heard too many stories of pet owners held ransom at the animal hospital—forced on the spot to decide whether to spend $6,000—or to euthanize their dog.

In this section we look at all the major pet insurance plans (and one veterinary discount savings plan). We compare cost, policies, coverage, and even the fine print. To make it easier to compare policies, we asked each firm how we'd be covered if Sweetie, our old Labrador Retriever, had her hip replaced at Manhattan's famous Animal Medical Center, where the procedure would likely cost $2,500.

Use this section as a starting point for your own research. Consider your needs. If you have a puppy, you can save hundreds of dollars in the first year alone with a plan that covers vaccines and spaying or neutering. For an older dog, look for plans that cover dental care, prescription medications, and such diagnostic tests as ultrasound and EKG. If your dog has a chronic or recurring condition, carefully check the "pre-existing problem" clauses.

Remember that details included here may have changed since this book went to press. When you speak to an insurance company, double-check exactly what is covered. Three common exclusions are hereditary defects, routine dental care, and heart-worm prevention.

Veterinary Pet Insurance, 800-872-7387
www.petinsurance.com
VPI is the biggest and the oldest pet health insurance company around (in business since 1982). It offers lots of options, which means you can pretty much customize a plan to suit your dog. The downside? Costs rise fast as soon as your dog starts to show signs of age. Policies are fairly confusing, with numerous clauses and exceptions and plenty of small print. And, the limits on how much you can collect for procedures seem arbitrary.

Size: 127,500 dogs (and 22,500 cats) covered nationwide

Covered: Accident and injury coverage includes exams, diagnostic tests, surgeries, hospitalization, prescriptions, anesthesia and follow-up exams when necessary. Also includes acupuncture and chiropractic work.

Not Covered: Pre-existing conditions (unless the dog has not needed treatment for the problem in at least six months), congenital problems, hereditary defects, breeding problems and behavioral issues. Also not covered: elective procedures, boarding, grooming, food, parasite treatment, vitamins and supplements, orthodontics and routine teeth cleaning.

Payout: Deductible is $40 per incident. After that, VPI pays 80 percent of the first $180, then 100 percent of the remainder.

Standard Plans:

- The Gold Plan covers accidents and injuries up to pre-set amounts (for example: up to $1,056 for back surgery; $1,109 for a pacemaker). Costs depend on age and breed of dog (for exam-

Why Should I Fix My Dog?

New York City law now requires that just about all dogs adopted from shelters or bought at pet stores be spayed or neutered. Even if your dog doesn't fall under this law you should have your dog "fixed" by the time he or she is eight months old. The only people with a good excuse for not doing this are those who show dogs or breed dogs professionally.

It's a fact: dogs that are fixed make better pets. Neutered dogs are less likely to start a fight at the dog run, less likely to run away, and less inclined to mark their territory by peeing on everything in sight, including your great aunt's flower pot. Also, neutering eliminates the risk of testicular cancer and reduces the risk of prostate infections and cancers. As for spaying, it eliminates the headache of having a dog in heat twice a year. Not only do dogs in heat have messy vaginal discharges, but they must be confined for at least three weeks during heat to prevent provoking male dogs. Spaying also dramatically reduces the risk of health problems including breast cancer. (By the way: myths aside, dogs that are fixed don't suffer sexual frustration—they simply haven't a clue as to what they're missing.)

If you adopt from one of the big local shelters, your dog will probably be fixed for free, or for far less than a regular vet charges. Smaller shelters may have discounted rates with a local vet. If you're not offered a discount, consider using one of the low-cost clinics listed on page 127. Also, two national toll-free hotlines offer discount certificates for, or referrals to, low-cost spay and neuter services: Spay USA (800-248-SPAY or www.spayusa.org) and Friends of Animals (800-321-PETS or www.friendsofanimals.org).

ple, a Golden Retriever puppy will run you $109 a year; a five-year-old Labrador Retriever costs $157). Maximum payout is $2,500 an incident; $9,000 a year.

- The Advantage Plus Plan is the same as the Gold Plan, but the preset amounts are higher ($1,825 for back surgery; $1,785 for a pacemaker). The Golden Retriever puppy will cost $191; the five-year-old Lab, $281. Maximum pay-out is $4,500 an incident; $14,000 a year.

Optional Coverage:

- Vaccination and Routine Care Coverage includes one annual physical exam, all vaccinations, testing, prescription flea control, routine dental or comprehensive health screen (includes blood test, urinalysis and EKG). It also covers spaying or neutering, and the cost of implanting an ID microchip. This optional coverage costs an additional $99 a year.
- Cancer Endorsement Coverage doubles coverage for cancer treatment. Under the Gold Plan, for an additional $14 to $29 a year, cancer coverage tops out at $5,000 a year. With the Advantage Plus Plan, for another $34 to $71 a year, you get up to $9,000 a year in reimbursements for cancer treatment.

How Sweetie Would Fare: Not well. Though cases are evaluated individually, VPI probably wouldn't cover her hip replacement because in Labs, bad joints are considered a hereditary defect.

Premier Pet Insurance, 877-774-2273
www.ppins.com
Founded in 1997, Premier has built a good reputation in a short period of time. Coverage is thorough, the policies are easy to understand, and the company's Web site is user-friendly. We also like that there are no preset prices for procedures, so even if your vet charges Manhattan prices, you always get 80 percent reimbursed (after deductible and up to the annual limits, of course). One big downside: no coverage for congenital defects, and insuring old dogs can get very expensive—if they're covered at all.

Size: Several thousand dogs in 46 states. (Premier still hasn't made it to Louisiana, Montana, Nebraska and Virginia.)

Covered: Illnesses and injuries, spaying and neutering, vaccines, surgery, hospitalization, prescriptions. Routine checkups and dental care are covered in more expensive plans. Also covered: diagnostic tests, follow-up visits as needed, and anesthesia. Dogs with pre-existing injuries or illnesses can get coverage if at least 90 days have passed since they last needed treatment.

Not Covered: Congenital defects, chiropractic care, acupuncture, holistic and experimental treatments, treatment of behavioral problems, boarding and grooming. (Newly insured dogs must be less than nine years old.)

Payout: Deductible is $100 a year. After that, Premier pays 80 percent per claim.

Standard Plans:

- PremierBasic covers up to $1,500 per incident and up to $7,500 a year. Routine care (medical and dental checkups, vaccinations and the like) is not covered. Cost is $120 a year for dogs up to nine years old, $150 for dogs nine to 11, and $180 for dogs 12 and up. Certain breeds (Dalmatians and Great Danes, for example) may cost more.

- PremierPlus covers up to $3,500 per incident and up to $10,000 a year. Most routine care is covered (with the exception of routine dental care). Cost is $230 a year for dogs up to nine, $287.50 for dogs nine to 11, and $345 for dogs 12 and up.
- PremierUltimate covers up to $5,000 per incident and up to $12,000 a year. Routine care (including dental check ups) and additional exams (a visit to the vet to treat a back injury, for instance) are covered. Cost is $362 a year for dogs up to nine, $452.50 for dogs nine to 11 and $543 for dogs 12 and older.

Optional Coverage: None

How Sweetie Would Fare: Premier sometimes covers hip replacement surgery for dogs who develop hip trouble late in life, so they may cover our Lab's operation. If so, Premier would cover at least $1,500 of the $2,500 cost, depending on our policy. But if Sweetie's bad hips are diagnosed as a "congenital anomaly," we're out of luck.

Preferred PetHealth Plus, 888 424-4644

www.pethealthplus.com

Coverage of hereditary and congenital conditions is a big plus. And we like the fact that Preferred doesn't pay claims based on a confusing fee schedule. What we don't like is the low lifetime (as opposed to an annual) limit: how long is $5,000 going to last?

Size: About 3,375 dogs and 1,125 cats covered nationwide

Covered: Surgery, hospitalization, prescriptions, examinations, lab fees, x-rays and diagnostic tests. Congenital and hereditary diseases are covered (for an additional premium), as are cancer treatment and holistic procedures. Pre-existing conditions are covered for an additional premium.

Not Covered: Elective procedures, such as spaying or neutering, routine dental checkups, experimental treatments, behavioral therapy, breeding, food and grooming.

Payout: For bills of $200 or less, there is a $40 copayment; Preferred pays the balance. Otherwise, after a deductible of $200 a year, Preferred covers 80 percent.

Standard Plans:

There's just one basic plan. It covers up to $2,500 a year, or $5,000 over a lifetime. Premiums range from $105 to $198 a year, depending on breed and age (a five-year-old Collie would cost $165).

Optional Coverage:

- Extended Coverage Endorsement covers half the cost (up to a maximum of $25 or $50 per claim, depending on the procedure) of spaying or neutering, annual check-ups, and non-surgical emergency care (such as treating a broken leg after an accident). It costs an additional $35 a year.

- Coverage of Pre-Existing Conditions adds another 50 percent to a standard premium. The five-year-old Collie would cost $247.50 (up from $165).
- Coverage to Extend Lifetime Limit adds another 10 percent to a standard premium. It increases the lifetime coverage from $5,000 to $10,000.

How Sweetie Would Fare: Finally! An insurance company that agrees pay for her hip replacement. On medical bills of $2,500, Preferred would reimburse $1,840.

Pet Assure, 888 789-7387
www.petassure.com

Pet Assure is not an insurance company; it's a health-care savings plan for pets that lets you save money without the hassle of filing insurance claims. If you visit the vet more than once or twice a year, the plan pretty much pays for itself. But if your dog gets really sick or needs serious surgery, a regular insurance plan is probably better (assuming your dog's problem is not exempt from coverage). Also, to be eligible for Pet Assure savings you need to use a vet who participates in the program.

Size: Nationwide, Pet Assure has about 16,500 canine members and more than a thousand participating vets (around 35 in New York City).

Covered: Just about everything, including chronic, hereditary and congenital problems. As well, routine checkups, dental care, surgery, prescription medicine and holistic therapy.

Not Covered: Non-prescription flea medications, food, routine boarding and grooming (although, in participating stores, Pet Assure does offer discounts of 10 to 15 percent on some of these items).

Payout: If your vet is part of the Pet Assure network, you get an on-the-spot 25 percent discount on all veterinary care.

Standard Plans: To join costs $99 a year per dog, or $129 a year for two or more dogs.

Optional Coverage: None

How Sweetie Would Fare: Not badly. Of her $2,500 bill for hip replacement surgery, Pet Assure would get us a $625 discount. (We wouldn't be able to use the Animal Medical Center however; it's not part of Pet Assure's network.)

Petshealth Insurance 877 592-7387

Petshealth covers just about everything, which is great (though we'd be happier if alternative medical treatments such as acupuncture and chiropractic work were included). The policy options offer adequate but limited choice. For example, there is no coverage of congenital problems, some of the plans are very expensive (especially if you have older dogs), and dogs must be under nine years old to join. Also, we're disappointed and surprised that this company does not have a Web site.

Size: About 5,600 cats and dogs covered in 40 states. Not available in Alaska, Arkansas, Hawaii, Idaho, Louisiana, Montana, Nebraska, Nevada, Virginia, and Washington.

Covered: Prescription medicine, diagnostic tests, x-rays, surgery, spaying or neutering, anesthesia, hospital stays. Dogs with pre-existing conditions can get coverage if they have been healthy for at least 90 days. Coverage of dogs with terminal illnesses like cancer are decided on a case-by-case basis (depending on how long it's been since your dog's last recurrence).

Not Covered: Congenital problems, non-prescription flea medications, non-routine dental care, alternative treatments like acupuncture. Annual checkups, routine dental care and vaccinations are only covered under the more expensive plans.

Payout: After a $100 deductible, Petshealth pays 80 percent.

Standard Plans:

- Basic Care covers up to $1,500 per incident; up to $8,000 a year. It costs between $120 and $144 a year, depending on breed. Dogs nine and older pay up to 50 percent more.
- Value Care covers up to $3,500 per incident; up to $11,000 a year. It includes an annual checkup and vaccinations. Cost is $230 to $276 a year, depending on breed. Dogs nine and older pay an extra 25 to 50 percent.
- Choice Care covers up to $5,000 per incident; up to $13,000 a year. It includes an annual checkup, vaccinations, flea treatment and routine dental care. Cost is $362 to $434 a year, depending on breed. Dogs nine and older pay an extra 25 to 50 percent.

Optional Coverage: None

How Sweetie Would Fare*:* As long as her hips aren't deemed a "congenital anomaly," her hip replacement would probably be covered by Petshealth. On fees of $2,500, the plan would cover at least $1,500 (the exact amount depends on your plan).

Poisons!

Dogs stick their noses in everything. They'll eat anything. That's why you have to dog-proof your house. In high enough doses, just about anything can poison your hound. In this section, Dr. Betsy

Brevitz, Urbanhound.com's on-site veterinarian, lists common household toxins that are harmful to dogs (for more information on the subject, visit this Web page: www.urbanhound.com/hound Health/poison.html).

If you think your dog may have ingested something toxic, call your vet or an emergency veterinary clinic immediately. The information here is not a substitute for personal medical attention: it's an educational resource. The ASPCA National Animal Poison Control Center at 888-426-4435 is another terrific resource (the charge is $45 per case). But you should always call your vet first so your dog can be treated right away. Remember that vomiting should be induced only in certain situations, so call your vet before trying any treatment at home.

ANTIFREEZE

For an animal, antifreeze is one of the most toxic substances imaginable. It smells and tastes sweet, which explains why dogs (and cats) are drawn to it. But once it's swallowed by your hound, antifreeze starts shutting down the kidneys almost immediately. If caught within a few hours, antifreeze poisoning sometimes can be treated successfully by administering 4-methylpyrazole or ethanol intravenously for several days. Call your vet immediately if you think your dog (or cat) has ingested antifreeze. To avoid the problem, don't let your dog lick spots or drink from puddles on the streets!

CHOCOLATE

This is one toxin that is not as deadly as many dog owners think. That said, it's not a good idea to feed your hound Hershey Kisses or Oreos. Chocolate contains theobromine and caffeine, both of which at certain doses can cause tremors, heart arrhythmias, and seizures. Because of its high fat content, chocolate also can trigger a painful bout of pancreatitis.

Unsweetened baking chocolate is most dangerous because it contains ten times the level of theobromine and caffeine than milk chocolate. The toxic dose of unsweetened chocolate is about 3 ounces (three squares) for a 20-pound dog, about 6 ounces for a 40-pound dog, and about 9 ounces for a 60-pound dog. In practical terms, this means that if your 80-pound Lab eats half a chocolate cake, he is less likely to have heart arrhythmias and seizures than he is to vomit and have diarrhea.

COFFEE, ALCOHOL AND TOBACCO

It should go without saying that coffee, bourbon, and cigars aren't good for dogs. Caffeine can cause tremors, heart arrhythmias, and seizures; alcohol can cause weakness, depression, and staggering; and tobacco can cause drooling, vomiting, weakness, and coma. All of these effects depend on the dose and the dog, of course, so if your dog has eaten a pack of Camels, don't panic—but do call your vet.

FLEA PRODUCTS

Almost all flea products can be toxic if they are not used the way they're meant to be. Cats are especially sensitive to many of the compounds found in flea products, but dogs and puppies can run into problems too. Treating your dog several days in a row with a dip that's meant to be used only once every two weeks, spraying your dog with a product that's meant for furniture and rugs, or using sprays, dips, and spot-ons all at the same time could poison your dog's nervous system. So read the directions carefully. Make sure you have the right dose for your dog's weight and age. Don't apply flea products more often than needed. Double-check to see if they can be used in combination with other products.

GARBAGE

Dogs love garbage. They're attracted to rotten food. The problem is that certain molds and bacteria in spoiled food produce toxins. If your dog gets into the trash and soon starts shaking, vomiting, and having diarrhea, he may have garbage poisoning. Other signs include tremors, seizures, weakness, or collapse. If he seems very ill, call your vet right away. Treatment for shock (IV fluids, medication) may be warranted.

HOUSEHOLD CLEANERS

Toilet bowl cleaners, drain openers, bleach, detergent, and Pine-Sol are just a few of the cleaning products that can cause problems. Do not let your dog drink out of the toilet. Do not leave a bucket of cleaning solution unattended—your dog might stick his nose into it or taste it. Keep dogs off floors that are wet with cleaning solutions. Keep cleaning products closed and put them away safely when you're not using them.

HOUSEPLANTS

Don't assume that any plant is okay for a dog to eat. After all, even plants that are not defined as toxic, such as green grass, can still cause vomiting, hives, or other problems. Some of the most toxic and potentially fatal plants are sago palm, castor bean plant, rosary plant, Chinese lantern, ornamental pepper, azalea, rhododendron, and yew. Dumb cane (dieffenbachia), philodendron, caladium, and begonias can cause swelling and hives in the mouth and throat. Bulbs (tulip, amaryllis, crocus, daffodil, and so on) can cause GI (gastrointestinal) irritation. Though they're not usually deadly, mistletoe and poinsettias can make animals sick. Be safe: keep all houseplants out of your dog's reach.

LEAD AND ZINC

Lead poisoning is a threat to animals as well as to children. Dogs will sometimes eat paint chips or chew on painted woodwork or linoleum. The main sources of zinc poisoning are post-1982 pennies, which are 97 percent zinc; some screws and bolts, including those used in some old pet carriers; and zinc oxide ointment. Some puppies will play with and chew on coins and other metal objects, so be sure to keep such things out of reach. Symptoms can include GI signs (vomiting, diarrhea, abdominal pain), anemia, or neurologic signs (depression, blindness, circling, shaking).

MACADAMIA NUTS

Surprisingly, macadamia nuts can cause weakness or paralysis in dogs. The exact substance that triggers the reaction is unknown. Usually, a dog will develop weakness or paralysis in the hind legs within about 24 hours of eating macadamia nuts, then gradually regain strength over several days. The toxic dose is very small—as little as one ounce of nuts for a 20-pound dog—so never leave macadamia nuts where a dog (or cat) can reach them.

MOTHBALLS

Some dogs are attracted to mothballs. The toxicity of mothballs depends on how many are eaten and how big and healthy your dog is. They contain either naphthalene or paradichlorobenzene, which in high doses can cause hemolytic anemia or convulsions.

PAIN RELIEVERS

Humans take over-the-counter pain killers and headache remedies so routinely that you may assume they're safe for dogs. They're not. Never give a dog ibuprofen (Motrin, Advil), naproxen (Aleve), or acetaminophen (Tylenol)—not even a child's dose is safe. These pain relievers can cause severe, even fatal, stomach ulcers and kidney damage in dogs. Buffered or enteric-coated aspirin (Bufferin, Ecotrin) can sometimes be used for arthritis pain in dogs. But aspirin shouldn't be given to a dog that is already on a prescription pain reliever, like Rimadyl or Etogesic. Finally, if you do give your dog aspirin, don't self-prescribe it: ask your veterinarian what the proper dose and frequency is for your dog.

OTHER MEDICINE

Dogs can chew open childproof bottles, gnaw on tubes of ointment, and knock pills off of counters, so keep all medications—your dog's as well as your own—well out of reach. Heart medications, antidepressants, and Sudafed (pseudoephedrine) are just a few of the drugs that can cause problems. Less common but extremely toxic to dogs are Efudex (fluorouracil) and Dovonex (calcipotriene)—two prescription skin creams—and isoniazid, an oral medication for tuberculosis. If you suspect your dog has gotten into any medication, even one that was prescribed for him, call your vet right away.

RAT POISON

Rat poison is just as tasty and just as toxic to dogs as it is to rats. Rodent poison often contains coumarin, which can lead to fatal internal bleeding. The good news: if you catch it early, coumarin poisoning usually responds well to treatment. How can you tell if your hound has swallowed rat poison? Unfortunately, you won't notice symptoms (bruises, nosebleeds, sore joints, bloody vomit, or blood in the feces) until your dog is already in trouble. So if you think your dog has eaten mouse or rat poison, don't wait for signs; see your veterinarian right away.

When you move into a new apartment or house, don't let your dog explore until you've checked carefully for rodent poison. Be sure to look around the radiators and the fridge: exterminators love to stash mouse and bug baits there. Get rid of roach and ant baits too. The plastic or metal containers could get stuck in a dog's stomach or intestines. And some of them contain insecticides that cause vomiting, tremors, or weakness.

Alternative Medicine

Does alternative medicine work? Scientific studies have yet to answer that question, but dog owners are voting with their pocketbooks. Almost a third of pet owners say they've used some form of alternative treatment on their animals. Virtually every (human) alternative medical practice, from acupuncture to Bach flower remedies, has been tried on dogs. Even the American Veterinary Medical Association, the guardian of traditional veterinary education and practice, has acknowledged alternative medicine by publishing guidelines for its use in animals. If you're interested in alternative medicine for your hound, be sure to read Dr. Betsy Brevitz's advice in the box on page 142, "Before Trying Alternative Care . . ."

Here we list the most popular alternative treatments and suggest ways to find practitioners. For more information on alternative veterinary medicine, go to Urbanhound.com's Hound Health section. Another excellent resource is the Complementary and Alternative Veterinary Medicine Web site at www.altvetmed.com. It includes the American Holistic Veterinary Medical Association's directory of alternative veterinarian practitioners, listed by state and by area of specialty (the direct link is www.altvetmed.com/ahvmadir.html). For recommendations by phone, call the AHVMA at 410-569-0795.

Acupuncture: Acupuncture has been shown to increase blood circulation and the release of natural painkilling substances by the body. For that reason, it can be helpful in the management of chronic pain in dogs, such as that from arthritis. The International Veterinary Acupuncture Society (IVAS), founded in 1974, trains and certifies veterinary acupuncturists. The society's Web site at www.ivas.org includes a list of IVAS-certified acupuncturists by state.

Chiropractic: Veterinary chiropractic has caught on especially for horses, whose backs must withstand enormous stresses, but it is also used on dogs and other animals for back pain, lameness, neurologic problems, and rehabilitation following injuries. The American Veterinary Chiropractic Association, founded in 1989, trains veterinary chiropractors. The association provides a directory of members on its Web site at www.animalchiro.com, though at the moment there is only one vet listed in New York City.

Homeopathy: Developed by the German physician Samuel Hahnemann in the early 1800s, homeopathy uses the principle of "like cures like." Symptoms are seen as the body's attempt to overcome an illness, and that reaction is stimulated rather than suppressed by giving minuscule amounts of substances that in larger doses would cause the same signs. The Academy of Veterinary Homeopathy trains and certifies veterinary homeopaths. For a directory of homeopathic practitioners visit the academy's Web site at www.acadvethom.org.

Massage and Physical Therapy (including Hydrotherapy): Various forms of healing touch, physical therapy, hydrotherapy (see below), and massage are practiced on dogs. They can be helpful for rehabilitation from broken bones and other injuries; after back, hip, or knee surgery; and for arthritis.

To learn about rehabilitation and physical therapy in animals, visit Professor David Levine's Web site at the University of Tennessee: www.utc.edu/~dlevine. For referrals to animal physical therapists, talk to your vet or a veterinary surgeon. Two places in New York City offer canine hydrotherapy:

Before You Try Alternative Care . . .

Get a traditional veterinary diagnosis. You should have as much information about your dog's ailment as possible before making decisions about treatment. Talk to your vet, do tests if necessary to arrive at a diagnosis, and then discuss the traditional treatment options. Alternative-medicine practitioners will also use the results of diagnostic tests such as x-rays, blood chemistry profiles, or bacterial cultures to help determine a treatment plan.

Tell your vet that you'd like to take a holistic approach. If your vet knows you'd prefer not to give your dog antibiotics, for example, he or she might recommend medicated baths and a switch to a hypoallergenic diet for treating a skin infection, or time in a steamy bathroom and lots of fluids for a case of kennel cough.

Don't stop medications without talking to your vet. Talk to your vet if you plan to switch from traditional medications to an alternative therapy. He or she can advise you on how to make the transition and tell you what danger signs to watch for when tapering off medication.

Ask your vet to recommend alternative-medicine practitioners. Many mainstream vets know colleagues who practice alternative medicine. Your vet may also have other clients who can recommend alternative practitioners.

Ask alternative-medicine practitioners about their background. Look for someone who has training and experience with the species of animal you're looking to treat. You want a chiropractor who understands a dog's musculoskeletal system, and an herbalist who knows which formulas are safe and effective for which species. Many different veterinary associations offer training and certification in alternative medicine practices. But remember that membership in a group is not an endorsement of an individual's skills. Talk to the practitioners to make sure you feel comfortable with their experience.

Ask the alternative-medicine practitioner what results you can expect. Like prescription medicines, every alternative therapy will not work for every dog. The practitioner should tell you whether a dog's condition is likely to respond to the alternative therapy and how long a trial period to give the therapy.

Betsy Brevitz, DVM

- Bonnie's K-9 Swim Therapy, 136 Ninth Avenue (19th Street), Manhattan, 212-414-2500. www.k9-swimtherapy.com
- Biscuit and Bath's Doggy Village, 227 East 44th Street (2nd and 3rd Aves), Manhattan, 212-692-2323.

For practictioners of Tellington-Touch massage, which is said to be effective for behavioral problems such as fearfulness and aggression as well as physical conditions such as wound healing and nerve damage, visit Linda Tellington-Jones' Web site at tteam-ttouch.com/index.html. For information about Reiki massage, in which practitioners use their hands and energy to unblock the flow of "ki," or "chi," much like in acupuncture, see this Web site: www.opcweb.com/reiki/.

Holistic Medicine: Holistic medicine combines elements of traditional and alternative medicine in a treatment plan. For example, a holistic treatment plan for a dog with lymphoma might include traditional chemotherapy plus a specially designed natural diet, herbs to bolster the immune system and counter stress, and massage and acupuncture to increase strength and relieve discomfort. To find a holistic vet, visit the American Holistic Veterinary Medical Associations Web-based directory at www.altvetmed.com/ahvmadir.html or call 410-569-0795.

9 lostandfoundhound

HOW TO KEEP YOUR DOG SAFE

In 2000, more than 3,000 New Yorkers called the city pound looking for a lost dog. And though the pound reunited 268 lost dogs with their families, the ratio of lost to found dogs isn't high. So practice prevention: read this chapter for tips on keeping your hound safe. Also, what do you do if you find a lost or stray dog on the streets? For the answer, turn to page 148 in this section.

Loss Prevention

Don't leave your dog unattended. It's a fact: dogs are stolen. Some are sold to research labs. In its July 2000 issue, the Atlantic Monthy reported that labs will pay upwards of $800 for some breeds. Others are held for ransom or used as bait for animal fighting rings. Bottom line: don't tie your dog up while you run into a store.

Don't let your dog off the leash—unless he's absolutely trustworthy. To give your dog more freedom to roam if she can't be off the leash, use a retractable leash or a long lead.

Use the right collar. Your dog should wear a collar with ID at all times. A leather or cloth collar that buckles is the safest choice. To reduce wear and tear, don't clip the leash to it: use a secondary collar just for the leash. Periodically inspect the collar to make sure it is not frayed or worn, that the hooks holding the tags are not bent, and that the tags are legible. If you use a metal choke collar, or a prong collar, always use a cloth slip collar as well: a prong collar can snap off without warning. Using a back-up collar is also a good idea if you use a head collar like a Gentle Leader or Halti, as dogs can wriggle out of them.

Have proper tags. Even if your dog has a microchip or a tattoo (see page 146), he should wear at least two tags at all times. First, an ID tag with your name and phone, cell phone and pager numbers on one side; and "Reward For Return" written on the other. Secondly, your numbered NYC dog-license tag (to license your dog, call 212-676-2100 or visit www.ci.nyc.ny.us/html/doh/html/vet/vet-dog.html). If you received a rabies tag from your vet, make sure your dog wears that one too: if your dog is lost and bites someone, she may be put down if it's not clear that her rabies shot is current.

If you find the noise of jingling tags annoying, wrap the tags with sturdy duct tape or a layer of clear Contac paper. You can also buy a dog tag silencer (clear plastic that you shrink around the tags with a hair dryer) from http://members.tripod.com/TagSilencers.

Get a tattoo. Tattoos are placed inside the ear fold or preferably on the inside of the rear leg. To be effective, the tattoo must be registered with one of the main registry services, and that registration must be kept up to date. Your groomer or vet may be able to tattoo your dog (a painless procedure); otherwise, get references from one of the big pet tattoo registries, listed in the chart opposite.

Get a microchip. Because tattoos can be hard to read, and can be removed or altered, microchips have become more popular. A pet ID microchip is about the size of a grain of rice. It is inserted using a needle in the area around your dog's shoulder blade, where it will remain for life. A growing number of places, including Singapore and the U.K., require that any dogs entering the country have a microchip.

Be aware that not all microchips and scanners are compatible, meaning that one company's scanner may not be able to read another company's chip. Many shelters carry more than one scanner, or a scanner that reads more than one chip, and the major microchip companies are working to eliminate this problem: for example, AVID's new EuroChip can be read by all the major scanners. Do your research before you decide which chip to use.

Your vet may be able to microchip your dog. If not, most larger veterinary clinics will, including the ASPCA's Bergh Memorial Hospital, the Bide-A-Wee Clinic, and The Humane Society of New York. The CACC holds free microchip clinics throughout the year (call 212-722-3620 for information). Manhattan's Have A Heart Clinic (355 W. 52nd St., between 8th and 9th Aves, 212-977-6877) will microchip your dog for $20, less than half what your vet is likely to charge. Microchips are provided to all pets adopted from the ASPCA and the CACC, among other shelters.

Once the chip is inserted, you must register it with at least one of the major chip companies listed in the chart opposite (if you don't register, the chip can still be traced back to the clinic that injected it). As with tattoos, a microchip is useless if you do not keep your contact information up-to-date.

Lost Dogs

If your dog is lost, act quickly: the longer your dog is gone, the slimmer the chance of recovery. Enlist friends and family to help take the actions listed below and cover as wide an area as you can (dogs are often found many miles from home).

Scan the neighborhood. As quickly as you can, walk the area where your dog was lost. If you can get help, have a friend take a cab to the other end of the neighborhood and work in the opposite direction.

Microchip or Tattoo? The Pros and Cons

Device	Cost	Plusses	Minuses	Major providers
TATTOO	About $35, plus a one-time $38 registration fee. Significantly more if your dog has to be anesthetized for the procedure.	■ Requires no special equipment to view ■ Because it's visible, it may deter theft	■ Hair in area must be kept shaved ■ Application may require sedation ■ Can be hard to read; may be altered	■ National Dog Registry: 800-637-3647 or www.natldogregistry.com ■ Tattoo-A-Pet: 800-TATTOOS or www.tattoo-a-pet.com ■ American Kennel Club Companion Animal Recovery: 800-252-7894 or www.akc.org/love/car
MICROCHIP	About $50, plus a $15 one-time registration fee.	■ Can't be altered or removed ■ Quick and painless to insert and read	■ Can't be seen without a scanner	■ American Veterinary Identification Devices: 800-336-AVID or www.avidid.com ■ Identichip: 800-926-1313 or www.identichip.com ■ HomeAgain (American Kennel Club Companion Animal Recovery): 800-252-7894 or www.akc.org/Car.htm

Call the shelters. Immediately contact all the shelters listed in Chapter One (page 22) and give them a description of your dog. Send them a fax that they can post with a photo of your dog and a description (see "Make and Distribute a Flyer," page 148). Also contact the city's Animal Rescue Unit, which picks up strays, at 718-649-8600. Search all the shelter's Web sites, and browse PetFinder.com as well. The CACC, the city pound, has a section of its Web site devoted to lost dogs at www.nycacc.org/lostfound.htm.

Call vets and animal hospitals. If your dog was injured, she may have ended up at a vet's office. Use the phone book to contact all of the vets in your area. Fax them a flyer with a photo and description of your dog. Contact the major emergency facilities: The Animal Medical Center at 212-

838-8100, the ASPCA Bergh Memorial Animal Hospital at 212-876-7700, and the Brooklyn Veterinary Emergency Service at 718-748-5180.

Make and distribute a flyer. Post and distribute the flyer as widely as possible, on the street and in heavily trafficked businesses, especially at all local vets, pet shops, and at police precincts. Distribute it to people walking their dogs, who may be more likely to spot yours. Fax copies to: the Animal Rescue Unit at 718-272-2659 and 212-722-4994; CACC headquarters at 212-442-2066; CACC shelters in Manhattan at 212-722-4994 and in Brooklyn at 718-927-1477 (you can also e-mail your flyer to the CACC at info@NYCACC.org). Your flyer should include:

- A current photo;
- Breed, sex, age, markings, and name;
- Collar type and tag types;
- Tattoo and microchip numbers, if any;
- Location and time when lost;
- Contact information, including phone, cell, and pager numbers, and an e-mail address;
- Offer a reward of at least $300.

Visit the shelters. Don't depend on shelter workers to spot your dog. Visit the shelters, especially the CACC, every day if possible.

Contact the police and Park Enforcement Patrol. Call police precincts near where your dog was lost. Fax or drop off a flyer. Call the Park Enforcement Patrol at 718-430-1815 and let them know if your dog was lost in or near a park. If you believe your dog has been stolen, file a report at your local precinct. A police report can be used as evidence in court if a suspect is brought to trial.

Found Dogs

In New York, the first reaction of people who find stray dogs is to call the city pound, or the Center for Animal Care and Control (CACC). Resist this response: the CACC is the only shelter in New York that euthanizes unadopted dogs in its care.

Instead, if you find a dog without ID tags, start by following many of the same steps listed in the previous section "Lost Dogs": call all the shelters (including the CACC), the police, the Park's Department, and veterinary clinics and give them a description of the dog. Post notices around your neighborhood, especially at vet's offices, pet shops, and other places where dog owners con-

Using the Internet to Find a Dog

There are many places on the Web to post an announcement of a lost or found dog. Most are free.

Local

- Brooklyn and Manhattan Dogchats: to subscribe to these e-mail forums, go to www.nycdog.org/forums.html
- Dog Owner Groups: listed at www.nycdog.org/comm.html, many have Web sites where they can post a lost/found dog message.
- Home Dogz: www.offleash.com/homedog.html
- Muffin's Pet Connection: lets you post photos at www.muffins.org
- Urbanhound.com: the message board has a section devoted to lost dogs at www.urbanhound.com.

National

- Acme Pet: http://acmepet.petsmart.com/club/bboard/lostdogs/index.html
- Dog-o-Mania: www.dogomania.com/dogs-in-need.shtml
- Find Fido: www.findfido.com
- Internet Lost and Found: http://internetlostandfound.com
- LostDog.com: www.lostdog.com
- Petfinder: www.petfinder.org/post/classifiedhop.html
- The USDA Missing Pet Network: www.missingpet.net/anlost.html

gregate, and on the Web (see box above). If you get a response, ask for some proof of ownership: ludicrous as it sounds, there are people who pose as a dog's owner so they can resell the dog.

Since the dog is likely going to spend at least some time in your home, he should be taken to the vet immediately to be vaccinated, dewormed and checked out for fleas or anything else he might pass on to your dog. Also, have the vet check for a microchip or tattoo. Many vets offer reduced rates for rescued dogs. For a list of clinics that provide low-cost care, see Chapter 7, page 127.

Ten Found Hounds

On January 4, 2000, the phone rang. It was Mark, the former dog walker of my dog Sara, who had died two years ago. He'd found a stray on Broadway and 100th Street. Was I ready for a new dog? I resisted. My daughter Lucy insisted.

We fell in love with Ella the moment she padded into our apartment, gazed up at us with her soul-melting eyes, chased one of our cats, followed us to the kitchen, and plopped down at our feet. She was around ten months old, a Rottweiler mix, loving, funny, calm, intelligent, loyal—and pregnant. On the morning of February 4th we went from one dog to ten dogs when Ella gave birth to nine puppies. We named them: Jacob, Malcolm, Lola, Samantha, Hope, Theo, Xerxes, Gia,and Harry.

If you think caring for one dog is hard work, consider having ten. They took over our apartment, made a heck of a mess, and required two nannies to care for them while I was at work. They also went through at least a thousand used copies of the New York Times, delivered to our back door by thoughtful neighbors.

Taking the puppies to the vet required complex logistics. At first, they were small enough so that three people could manage the job using two shopping carts, each packed with a box of pups. But by the second visit, we needed a car, plus two additional helpers from the vet's office.

Ella was a perfect Mom: she fed, cleaned, cared for and played with her pups all day. When she needed a break, she jumped over the gate and napped in the living room. Finally it was time to find the pups new homes. We interviewed about a hundred people, determined to find the perfect homes for all nine puppies. And we did! Jacob, Malcolm, Lola, Samantha, Hope, Theo, Xerxes, Gia, and Harry are now with loving families, one of which took two puppies. My daughter Lucy talked me into keeping Jacob.

Earlier this year, to celebrate their first birthday, we held a great reunion party for all the puppies. Ella was thrilled. I was amazed at how beautiful, and how different they'd all become. One puppy looks like a purebred Golden Retriever, another is the spitting image of Ella. Two of the bunch appear to be half-Rodesian Ridgeback, half-Vizla. There's a Gorden Setter among them, a Mastiff-Shepherd combo and one tricolored ball of fluff. With all these breeds, we figure they're not all descendents of the same father—but the only one who knows for sure is Ella, and she's not letting on.

Susan Yarnell

Unfortunately, most dogs found in New York are not lost—they're abandoned by their owners. If you make no headway in tracking down the dog's owners, and don't want to keep it yourself, here's how to go about finding the dog a new home.

Contact breed rescue. If the dog looks purebred, contact its local and national breed rescue group listed on the American Kennel Club Web site: http://www.akc.org/breeds/rescue.cfm. These groups work hard to prevent their breed from ending up in shelters: they'll help find a permanent home or a foster home.

Take the dog to a no-kill shelter or rescue group. This is a good option in theory, but not so easy in practice. Because no-kill shelters are drastically overcrowded, many will refuse to take in a stray. (An offer of a large donation may increase the chances that they will accept the dog.) But shelters and rescue groups can still can be a good resource. They may be willing to post a picture of the dog on their Web site, for example. Also, they can provide a copy of their adoption screening guidelines, which will help you to determine if someone who wants the dog can provide a good home. For the names and addresses of city shelters and rescue groups, see Chapter One, page 23.

Get word out. Make a flyer announcing that you have a dog who needs a new home and post it all over the neighborhood. Include a photo and detailed description. Emphasize that the dog is healthy, has all his shots, and mention his positive traits (is he housebroken? or obedience-trained?). People are far more willing to adopt a dog that's sweet-tempered and gets along with children and other dogs. To get the information out to a wider audience, post a photo and description of the dog on the Web sites listed in the box on page 149.

Have the dog spayed or neutered. By taking this step you will be making the dog more adoptable and helping to reduce the pet overpopulation problem. A dog can be fixed for as little as $30. See our list of low-cost clinics on page 127.

Find a foster home. Someone may be willing to house the dog while you work to find him a permanent home, especially if you offer to help cover expenses. Ask friends and family, your vet, and post an inquiry on the Brooklyn and Manhattan Dogchat lists (see box on page 149).

Board the dog. If you can afford to do so, board the dog with a sitter or kennel (see Chapter 6) while you seek a permanent home.

Teach Your Dog to Come

A dog who responds to a "come" command is less likely to run off and get lost. To teach your dog to come when called, begin in a quiet, safely enclosed area. Have a good supply of treats on hand.

1. Teach your dog to listen. Say your dog's name. If he looks at you, give him a treat and lots of praise. If he doesn't look, show him the treat he could have had, and try again.

2. Teach the meaning of "come." Call your dog's name, step away, and encourage him to follow you. Say "come" as he moves towards you. When he reaches you, greet him with a treat and lots of praise. Practice this over and over and over, gradually increasing the distance between you and your dog.

3. Have fun. Convince your dog that coming to you is a great game. Keep him begging for more! Offer different rewards. Play hide-and-seek and reward him lavishly for tracking you down.

4. Introduce distractions. Invite over a friend with a dog. As the dogs play, periodically grab your dog's collar, say his name, and give him a treat. Then begin to call him from a few feet away. Keep adding distance and distractions. (When you practice outside, use a long leash as backup, but don't reel him in: such prompting doesn't teach leash skills, it just becomes a crutch).

5. Develop consistency. Use the "come" command every day, especially when you are about to give your dog something he loves (dinner, a walk, or a belly rub). With treats in your pocket, practice at the dog run, in a back yard, in your hallway. Avoid asking your dog to "come" when you are about to do something unpleasant, like clipping his nails (instead, approach him calmly).

Andrea Arden, Manhattan Dog Training

10

houndafterlife

WHAT TO DO WHEN YOUR DOG DIES

Our Loved One, GRUMPY,

Aug. 4, 1913 to Sept. 20, 1926.

His sympathetic love and understanding enriched our lives.

He waits for us.

– **TOMBSTONE INSCRIPTION, HARTSDALE PET CEMETERY, NY**

As the inscription above demonstrates, New Yorkers were just as devoted to their dogs almost a century ago as they are now. And even then, the death of a pet was a serious matter. It's a heartbreaking subject, but here goes.

The Body in Question

When your dog dies, you are confronted with the gruesome task of disposing of the body. Although you are grieving, you must act quickly. What can you do? Some people freeze-dry their dead pets. It's true. Others spend thousands of dollars to mummify their pets. If you are interested in these procedures, visit this Web site: www.summum.org/mummification/pets. But most people opt for more traditional ways of handling the death of a beloved dog. Here they are:

DEPARTMENT OF SANITATION

For a no-frills disposal of a dead pet's body, call the city's Sanitation Department at 212-219-8090, weekdays between 7 A.M. and 4 P.M. They'll advise you to leave the body on the curb in a bag or box, and arrange for it to be picked up. There's no charge for this service.

CREMATORY AGENCY

There are two cremation options: group cremation, which means your dog will be cremated with others, and individual cremation, which costs more. (Note: To make absolutely sure that you are getting your dog's ashes, and hers alone, ask to witness the cremation.) Because dogs are most often euthanized at the vet's office, many people ask their vets to arrange a cremation. But you

Comparing Pet Cemeteries

Cemetery	History	Starting Rates	Getting There
Abbey Glenn Pet Memorial Park 187 Rte. 94 South Lafayette, NJ 800-972-3118 www.abbeyglen.com	**Founded:** 1982 **Size:** 14 acres Designed to look like a park. Grave markers are flush to ground, not upright. Your cremated remains can be buried with your pet.	**Plot:** $435 **Casket:** $165 **Marker:** $260 **Yearly maintenance:** $25 **Perpetual maintenance:** $530 **Transportation included**	55 miles from midtown Manhattan. Not accessible by public transit.
Hartsdale Pet Cemetery and Crematory 75 N. Central Park Ave. Hartsdale, NY 800-375-5234 www.petcem.com	**Founded:** 1896 **Size:** 7.5 acres Oldest pet cemetery in the US. Among the 80,000 buried are pets of Xavier Cugat, Diana Ross, and Mariah Carey. Landscaped grounds are planted with chrysanthemum and begonia.	**Plot:** $225 **Interment:** $125 **Casket:** $125 **Marker:** $395 **Yearly maintenance:** $32 **Perpetual maintenance:** $550 **Transportation:** $40	25 miles from midtown Manhattan. 45 minutes by Metro-North to Hartsdale, plus a 10-minute cab ride from the station.
Wantagh Pet Memorial Park 3300 Beltagh Ave. Wantagh, NY 516-785-6153 www.bideawee.org/memorial.htm	**Founded:** 1915 **Size:** 12 acres Run by nonprofit group Bide-a-Wee. Among the 50,000 pets here: President Nixon's dog, Checkers	$985 includes plot, burial, casket, transportation, and perpetual maintenance. **Optional marker:** $50	30 miles from midtown Manhattan. One hour by Long Island Rail Road to Wantagh, plus a 15-minute cab ride from the station.
Westhampton Pet Memorial Park 118 Old Country Rd. Westhampton, NY 631-325-0219 www.bideawee.org/memorial.htm	**Founded:** 1950 **Size:** 200 acres This is another cemetery operated by Bide-a-Wee.	$930 covers plot, burial, casket, transportation, and perpetual maintenance. **Optional headstone:** $50	75 miles from midtown Manhattan. 2 ½ hours by Long Island Rail Road to Speonk, plus a 5-minute cab ride from the station.

can arrange it yourself at any pet cemetery (see page 155) or through Brooklyn's Pet Crematory Agency (718-234-3653 or www.petcrematory.com).

The Pet Crematory Agency offers group cremation, including pick-up and delivery, for $114. Costs vary depending on a dog's weight and the urn you choose. This price, like others listed here, is for a 50-pound dog and a basic tin urn. An individual cremation is $227, but can go as high as $470 if you'd like a pewter urn. Cremations take place in West Babylon, Long Island. There's an additional $50 charge to attend.

No matter where you decide to cremate your dog, don't be pressured into buying an urn from them. Just about anything that seals tightly can be used as an urn. And there are dozens of places on the Internet that sell every imaginable pet urn, from bronze containers in the shape of your dog's breed to granite obelisks, and from lockets to pewter vases that display a photograph of your dog. Here are some Web sites worth browsing:

- www.petrelics.com
- www.foreverpets.com
- www.petsatpeace.com
- www.atpeace.com
- www.peturns.com

PET CEMETERIES

Burying your pet within city limits is apparently illegal in New York (we tried, but couldn't find the source of this law, or even learn why it exists). If you'd like, you can bury your dog at your country house (to preserve the body for around 24 hours, wrap it in plastic and keep it chilled with dry ice). Otherwise, there are some lovely pet cemeteries in the New York area.

The big pet cemeteries are full-service operations: pickup and transportation is provided; burials are offered but they also cremate animals and allow ashes to be scattered on their grounds. Caskets, urns, and grave markers or headstones are available, as are memorial services—both small (sitting quietly with your dog's body or inviting friends and family to read a poem or prayer) and large (a full funeral conducted by a member of the clergy).

For the rundown on the four best-known pet cemeteries used by New Yorkers, see the table on page 155. The rates included in the table are for the most basic service for a small dog. Listings of other pet cemeteries can be found at these Web sites:

- International Association of Pet Cemeteries: www.iaopc.com/memberlist.htm
- Pet Cemetery and Pet Crematory List: http://free.prohosting.com/~easyshop/petcem1.html#New%20York

Be warned: burial costs vary widely, and climb quickly. On top of paying for a plot, you'll also have to buy a casket and a marker, pay to transport your dog's body, and cover the cost of maintaining your dog's grave. You'll save money if you buy a casket and marker elsewhere. Doggone Purrrty (151 W. 25th Street, 212-22-0525) is the only store in the city we know of that sells grave markers for pets. Otherwise the Internet is your best bet. Here are some sites worth visiting:

- www.oldyeller.net
- www.carvedgraphics.com/petstones.htm
- www.c-dtags.com/f2order.html
- www.mycherishedpet.com/marker01.html

FUNERAL HOMES

To hold a formal memorial service for your dog in the city, there's only one place to go: All Pets Go to Heaven, 236 Carroll Street, Carroll Gardens, Brooklyn (718-875-7877 or www.allpetsgotoheaven.com). The closest subway stop is Carroll Street on the F train.

New York City's only full-service funeral home for pets, All Pets is owned by Kathleen and Raymond Leone, who also run Brooklyn's (humans only) Leone Funeral Home. The All Pets funeral home is in a brownstone with a Victorian-style non-denominational chapel and a statue of St. Francis of Assisi.

A two-hour service is $200 and includes grooming, casket rental, memorial cards, and supervision. Transportation of your pet's body to the funeral home is $50 from anywhere in Brooklyn, and $75 from other boroughs. All Pets will also arrange for individual cremations (rates start at $195) or burial of your dog at any pet cemetery.

Coping With Your Dog's Death

The pain of losing a dog can be compounded by the fact that friends and family members may not understand your loss. Here are other places to turn for help.

SUPPORT GROUPS AND COUNSELING

Liz Margolis, CSW is a psychotherapist who conducts a free pet-loss support group the first and third Wednesday of each month from 7:00 P.M. to 8:30 P.M. at Animal General, 140 West 67th Street between Amsterdam and Broadway in Manhattan. The group is small: two to six people attend each week. Call 212-712-9600 to reserve a spot.

How Do I Know When It's Time?

"I have a 13-year-old Samoyed who is very arthritic, deaf, and senile. He is on arthritis medication, but lately his hind legs have been giving out. Also, while he is lying down, he sometimes whines. How do I know when it's time to let him go? I don't want him to be in pain, but I don't want to lose him either." **Urbanhound.com's vet Betsy Brevitz, DVM, answers:**

One of the hardest things for dog owners to face is that our beloved companions don't live as long as we wish they did. Dog owners also have the weighty and sometimes unwanted responsibility to make choices about ending their dogs' lives. With such an emotional topic, it's helpful to set a rational framework for thinking through the issues. Remember, too, that you don't have to make a decision instantly. Give yourself time to think and discuss your situation with family members and friends. Here are some questions that can help you decide whether it's time to let go:

- How is your dog's overall quality of life? Is he still able to eat, rest, and enjoy your companionship? Does he have more good hours than bad hours, or more bad hours than good?
- What problems lessen his quality of life significantly? Do you have a definite diagnosis for each? Do you know and understand the different treatment options for each? For example, loss of strength in an older dog's hind legs can result from arthritis, or it could be due to overall weakness from heart disease or another condition that could potentially be treated. Senility, or canine cognitive dysfunction, can sometimes be helped with medication. Talk to

The Animal Medical Center Pet Loss Support Group, conducted by Paul Weinberg, CSW, meets every other Saturday from 2:00 P.M. to 4:30 P.M. at Manhattan's AMC, 510 East 62nd Street, between York Avenue and the FDR, in the 5th-floor seminar room. About six to 12 people attend each week. A $20 donation is suggested. For more information, call 212-838-8100, x 7342. The recorded message also includes a listing of private counselors (not affiliated with the AMC) who commonly deal with pet loss in their practices.

Bide-A-Wee offers one-on-one bereavement counseling with Jill Lauri at 410 East 38th Street,

your vet to be clear about the causes of each problem and whether different treatments might be worth trying.

- Can you adjust your dog's environment to help him be more comfortable? For example, if your dog loses his footing on bare floors, you can put down large carpet remnants to give him better traction. If he has trouble climbing stairs, you can use a bath towel as a sling under his lower abdomen, just in front of his hind legs, to help support him as he goes up and down.
- Do you have the physical, emotional, and financial resources to continue to care for your dog? It can be extremely difficult for people who have physical problems of their own to care for a large dog that cannot walk well. You need to be fair to yourself and consider your own health as well as your dog's.
- Have you discussed your dog's condition with family members and friends to get their help and emotional support?

Many dog owners feel better about making the decision to euthanize a seriously ill dog when they know they've carefully considered the treatment options available to them and tried the ones with the best chances of success. If you would feel better getting a second opinion from a veterinarian other than your regular vet—perhaps a specialist in neurology or orthopedics—by all means do so. Your regular vet will understand your desire to get all the information you can about your dog's prognosis.

Pet-loss hotlines and support groups can also be immensely helpful while you're caring for a sick dog and grappling with your choices. See page 157 for information about NYC pet-loss groups and hotlines.

All caring dog owners empathize with your pain and your desire to do the right thing. Don't rush into a decision, and trust yourself to be your dog's loving advocate.

between First Avenue and the FDR in Manhattan and at 19 W. 34th Street between Fifth and Sixth Avenues. There is no charge for up to three sessions. Call 212-289-3540 or visit www.bideawee.org for more information.

TELEPHONE SUPPORT

Stephanie LaFarge, PhD, Director of Counseling Services at the ASPCA, is an invaluable resource for anyone coping with the death of a pet. She provides free information by phone on such issues as deciding on euthanasia, making arrangements for your pet's remains, and helping kids cope with the loss of a pet. She can be reached weekdays from 9 A.M. to 4 P.M. at 212-876-7700, x 4355. At other times, she can be paged at 800-946-4646 (use your telephone keypad to enter PIN number 140-7211; then enter your phone number when you hear the beep). Dr. LaFarge can also be reached by e-mail at StephanieL@aspca.org.

NATIONAL HOTLINES

Many veterinary schools around the country have pet-loss support hotlines staffed with vet students. The hotlines are free (you only pay for the cost of the call). Here are three of the best known support lines:

Colorado State University Veterinary Teaching Hospital, 970-491-1242
Hours: Monday, Tuesday, Thursday and Friday, 9 A.M. to 5 P.M. Mountain Time

Cornell University School of Veterinary Medicine, 607-253-3932
Hours: Tuesday to Thursday, 6 P.M. to 9 P.M.

Tufts University School of Veterinary Medicine, 508-839-7966
Hours: Weekdays, 6:00 P.M. to 9:00 P.M.

BOOKS

Many books address pet-loss issues, and each one varies in its approach. Here we list just four that are frequently recommended. For others, visit a bookstore, or get a recommendation from the experts at the Dog Lover's Bookshop (212-369-7554 or www.dogbooks.com).

Coping with Sorrow on the Loss of Your Pet by Moira K. Anderson (Alpine Publications, 1998)
This practical guidebook discusses the grieving process and offers strategies to help adults, children, and other pets to deal with grief. It includes guidelines for making the decision to euthanize, and choosing what to do with your dog's remains.

When a Pet Dies by Fred Rogers (First Experiences, 1998)
Written by the star of "Mister Rogers' Neighborhood," this paperback book is for children between four and eight. It helps them share feelings about the loss of a pet and assures them that grieving is a natural part of the healing process.

When A Pet Dies by Wallace Sife (Howell Books, 1998)
A concise and compassionate guide by the founder of the Association for Pet Loss and Bereavement (www.aplb.org). It discusses handling friends and family who may not understand your grief, explains why the loss of a pet is so painful, and illustrates the stages of grief with case studies. Also, the book includes thoughts from religious leaders of various faiths on coping with pet loss.

Pet Loss: A Thoughtful Guide for Adults & Children by Herbert A. Nieburg, Arlene Fischer, and Martin Scot Kosins (Harper Perennial, 1996)
This book offers emotional support for passing through the stages of the grieving process. It includes practical advice on euthanasia, working with a vet to make funeral arrangements, helping children deal with the death of a pet, and how to decide when it's time to get a new dog.

WEB SITES

Pet-loss sites have proliferated on the Web. Some are good, some are dreadful; many are maintained by people who have recently lost their pet. Here, in alphabetical order, are a few of our favorites:

American Veterinary Medical Association: Pet Loss
www.avma.org/care4pets/avmaloss.htm

Association for Pet Loss and Bereavement
www.aplb.org

Cornell University School of Veterinary Medicine Pet Loss Support
http://web.vet.cornell.edu/public/petloss/

Dogheaven
www.dogheaven.com

In Memory of Pets
www.in-memory-of-pets.com

Petloss.com
www.petloss.com

Veterinary Information Network
www.vin.com/PetCare/Series/PetLoss.htm

Virtual Pet Cemetery
www.mycemetery.com/pet/index/html

Remembering a Dog Who Has Died

Giant tombstones aside, one of the best ways to memorialize dogs is with a donation to an animal welfare organization made in their name. One option is to give money to an animal shelter (see Chapter One, page 22, for a list of shelters in the New York area)—either a general donation or one earmarked for a particular dog. Another idea is to contribute to a not-for-profit veterinary group devoted to providing care for dogs in need. Here we list three such groups.

If you make the donation on behalf of a friend's dog, many nonprofit groups will send that person a card announcing your donation. Otherwise, if you're looking for sympathy cards designed for dog people, you can find them at this Web site: www.litterature.com/dogs/sympathy.htm.

Animal Medical Center, 510 East 62nd Street, Manhattan. 212-838-8100. www.amcny.org
The AMC is one of the world's best animal hospitals (see page 128 to find out why). But while it is a non-profit, AMC is still far too expensive for many New Yorkers to afford. Here there are three ways to make a donation:

- Good Samaritan Fund: Covers a 20 percent reduction in the cost of care for a sick or injured stray brought in by someone who has agreed to take financial responsibility for his care.
- Patient Assistance Fund: Offers financial assistance to low-income New Yorkers whose pets need emergency care.
- Senior's Animal Veterinary Effort (SAVE): Provides free or subsidized care to pets owned by low-income New Yorkers over 62.

Send donations to the AMC Development Office at the address above, specifing fund.

American Society for the Prevention of Cruelty to Animals, 424 East 92nd Street, Manhattan. 212-876-7700. www.aspca.org
The ASPCA's Trooper Fund pays for the treatment of stray or homeless pets at the organization's Berg Memorial Hospital. Send donations to ASPCA-Trooper Fund at the address above, and write Trooper Fund on the memo line of your check. For more information, call 212-876-7700, x 4516.

NY SAVE Save Animals in Veterinary Emergency, 331 West 57th Street, Manhattan. 212-246-3097. www.nysave.org
Started by a group of veterinarians in 1998, NY SAVE helps low-income New Yorkers pay for emergency veterinary care. The organization's Guardian Angel Fund accepts gifts in honor of people or pets. Contributions are acknowledged with a card sent to the honoree's family.

11

hound supplies

EVERYTHING YOU NEED TO SPOIL YOUR DOG

Who carries homeopathic flea powder? Where can I find a Burberry coat for my hound? Can I commission a portrait of my dog? Is there anyone out there who will "hand-strip" my wirehair terrier? If you're looking to indulge your dog, or just to buy the best supplies, read on.

Best Pet-Supply Stores

Looking for the city's best hound shops? Urbanhound's secret shoppers spend a great deal of time talking to dog owners and visiting stores. And they're demanding customers.

Chances are you've got a neighborhood favorite that's not included here, a place where they know your dog's name and remember that he gets the light version of California Natural. Don't worry: if your favorite isn't here, it's probably included in our list of the city's top neighborhood pet shops on page 170. The stores listed in this section aren't simply places we like, they're stores that are idiosyncratic. They're the ones worth visiting even if you don't live in the neighborhood.

BEST ALL-AROUND PET-SUPPLY STORE—MANHATTAN

Beasty Feast

630 Hudson Street (between Horatio and Jane Streets), Manhattan. 212-620-7099

Other locations:

680 Washington Street (Perry and Charles Streets), 212-620-4055

237 Bleecker Street (Leroy and Carmine Streets), 212-243-3261

The perfect neighborhood store. A giant selection—and great service too. Huge assortment of dog food, from super-premium (Solid Gold, Wellness, California Natural, Innova and the "home-made" Spot's Stew) to basic (Iams, Pedigree, Science Diet, Eukanuba, Alpo). Many vitamins and other supplements, plus brushes, shampoos, toys, crates, carriers and beds. The Hudson Street store offers grooming. As well, Beasty Feast will special order anything you need. Free delivery in the West Village or Chelsea ($30 minimum).

BEST ALL-AROUND PET-SUPPLY STORE—BROOKLYN

Pet Slope

814 Union Street (7th and 8th Aves.), Park Slope, 718-622-8554

This welcoming store is well-stocked with premium foods, toys, and treats, and it's a favorite with the large community of dog lovers in Park Slope. The informed staff is devoted to its canine customers. And they're conscientious too: when Proctor and Gamble bought pet-food maker Iams, Pet Slope posted signs informing shoppers that P&G conducts animal testing, and offered to recommend alternative foods.

BEST NEWCOMER

Four Paws Club

387 Bleecker Street (Perry and 11th Streets), Manhattan. 212-367-8265.

Soon after it opened in the spring of 2001, Four Paws was already a familiar hangout for neighborhood dogs and their people. The walls of this cheery West Village shop are decorated with wry portraits of dogs and cats by Portuguese muralist Bela Silva. The style and humor of the décor are matched in the selection of products, ranging from the practical (Nature's Miracle Pet Wipes) to the chic (Waggin' Wear raincoats that look like bright 1950s tablecloths, and collars patterned with grosgrain ribbons by Ella Dish) to the delicious (dog treats made with human-grade ingredients by Harry Barker and Taxi Dog Bakery).

BEST ALTERNATIVE PET SUPPLIES

Whiskers Holistic Petcare

235 East 9th Street (2nd and 3rd Aves.), Manhattan. 212-979-2532 or 800-944-7537.
http://choicemall.com/whiskers

Now that natural foods and homeopathic remedies are in fashion, more and more stores offer holistic pet supplies. But Whiskers is still the original and the best (as a matter of fact, it supplies its private-label line of food and supplements to many other pet stores). Whether you're looking for homeopathic flea solutions, herbal diarrhea relief, magnetic-healing pads, or grapefruit-seed-extract ear cleanser, you'll find it at Whiskers. Whiskers also stocks all-natural dog food (brands like Wysong, Solid Gold, Abady, Wellness and Innova), vegan treats, and raw meat. The staff is knowledgeable and friendly. If you can't get down to the East Village, Whiskers offers free next-day delivery anywhere in Brooklyn, Queens, and Manhattan (the minimum order is $25 or $50, depending on where you live). Out-of-towners can order from the Web site or by phone.

BEST OFFBEAT PET-SUPPLY STORE

Spoiled Brats

340 West 49th Street (8th and 9th Aves.), Manhattan. 212-459-1615.

www.spoiledbratsnyc.com

Perhaps it's the disco ball and the old LPs hanging from the ceiling. Or the dog toys strung overhead. Or maybe it's the collection of aromatherapy candles and incense. Whatever it is, this cramped store is not your typical pet supply shop. ("Spoiled Brats recognizes the spirituality of all animals," explains the store's Web site.)

Spoiled Brats promotes all-natural dog foods (California Natural, Abady and Spot's Stew among them), but also carries commercial brands (including Science Diet and Iams). A freezer is stocked with raw meat, and there are exotic dog treats (such as smoked bull penises and lamb hearts). Also, Spoiled Brats carries rain slickers by Doggiewear and handmade wool sweaters.

BEST SERVICE

Pet Stop

564 Columbus Avenue (87th and 88th Streets), Manhattan. 212-580-2400.

Your basic neighborhood pet-supply store, but with superb service. The staff will spend as much time as it takes helping you find the right food for your hound (they favor natural food, such as Wellness, Canidae and California Natural). You'll learn more about vitamin and herbal supplements than you ever wanted to know. They'll even send you home with a half dozen food samples.

BEST HIP ACCESSORIES—DOWNTOWN

Fetch

43 Greenwich Avenue (Perry and Charles Streets), Manhattan. 212-352-8591.

www.fetchpets.com

Stocked with some of the coolest dogwear in the City, Fetch carries smart dog beds by George and lined rubber raincoats by Wagwear. There are colorful plastic dog bowls from Italy, suede and shearling collars, Burt's Bees Pet Soap, Alpaca wool turtleneck sweaters, and soft travel cases in pink. It's hard to make it out of Fetch without buying something.

BEST HIP ACCESSORIES—UPTOWN

Barkley

215 East 76th Street (2nd and 3rd Aves.), Manhattan. 212-734-9373.

Shattering the myth that uptown hounds are stodgy, Barkley offers cutting-edge canine togs, including charming embroidered felt coats by Woofwear, contemporary collars by Wagwear, chic carriers by m. famous, and dog beds by K-9 sport in electric green and heather gray fleece.

BEST TRADITIONAL ACCESSORIES

Canine Styles

830 Lexington Avenue (63rd and 64th Streets), Manhattan. 212-751-4549 or 212-838-2064

As befits a store that's been in business on the Upper East Side since 1959, Canine Styles carries traditional supplies for the well-heeled hound. Burberry rain coats for dogs are a big seller (even at around $120 each, they're often out of stock). And there are Linda's Wool Sweaters (handknit for Canine Styles in Maine), handsome Foggy Mountain Dog Coats, bone china dog dishes, and English dog shampoo and cologne by Parness. Canine Styles also stocks dog food (Eukanuba, Science Diet, Triumph, Iams, and Nature Recipe, among the brands carried) and has a groomer on site.

BEST ACCESSORIES FOR DOGS THAT ARE ACCESSORIES

Karen's For People + Pets

1195 Lexington Avenue (81st and 82nd Streets), Manhattan. 212-472-9440.
www.karensforpets.com

Pony skin coats. Collars studded with Swarovski crystals. Special-order $3,900 Louis XIV dog beds, with carved-wood frames and embroidered throw cushions. Coats with faux fur collars and matching travel carriers. You get the idea. Karen has been in business since 1975. Fans say Karen's groomers, who work behind a glass window in the store, are among the best in the city.

BEST PET SUPPLIES PER SQUARE INCH

Dudley's Paw

327 Greenwich Street (Jay and Duane Streets), Manhattan. 212-966-5167.
www.dudleyspaw.com

It's hard to believe anyone could cram so much good stuff in such a tiny space. The back of the store is where food is stocked: many premium brands (among them, Wellness, California Natural and Innova), plus some bigger names like Iams and Science Diet. The fun stuff is kept in the front of the store: polar fleece coats for dogs, wonderful canvas Bowsers donut dog beds, tins of all-natural treats, and baskets of stuffed squeaky toys. Dudley's Paw is a classic neighborhood pet-supply store. Everyone in Tribeca knows the store's namesake, Dudley, a bear-like Akita mix.

BEST BREED PARAPHERNALIA

Zitomer Z-Spot

965 Madison Avenue (75th and 76th Streets), Manhattan. 212-472-4960.

www.zitomer.com

Tons of dog merchandise fills this spacious store, including a good selection of toys, some of which we haven't seen elsewhere; baked goods from Three Dog Bakery (see below) made of natural ingredients; and sweet houndwear, including a tiny red vinyl sailor collar and a blue suede yarmulke. But the real standout here is the vast selection of breed-related goods, ranging from a silk cravat imprinted with Golden Retrievers, to beer steins with the face of every breed you can imagine.

BEST (VIRTUAL) BOOKSTORE

Dog Lover's Bookshop

www.dogbooks.com

Originally a shop in midtown Manhattan, the Dog Lover's Bookshop is now going strong on the Web. Aside from stocking every new dog book out there, with an emphasis on small press publications, Dog Lover's carries an astonishing selection of hard-to-find used, out-of-print, and rare books, as well as videos and children's books. The site is updated weekly. Orders can also be placed by phone at 212-369-7554, by fax at 212-369-7554, or by snail mail at P.O. Box 117, Gracie Station, New York, NY 10028.

BEST HOME DELIVERY SERVICE

1-800-Pet-Food 800-738-3663.

www.800petfood.com

1-800-Pet-Food makes same-day deliveries of dozens of brands of dog food, including high-end lines like Spots Stew, Candidae, and Abady, plus toys and other necessities (Bitter Apple, Pet Dental toothpaste, Halti head collars, hair removal rollers). Prices are average, but the service is superb. The employees who take orders are cheerful and deliveries always arrive when promised. If you live outside of Manhattan, delivery charges are high, a charge waived if you have your food charged to your credit card and delivered automatically on a pre-arranged schedule. Steer clear of

1-800-Pet-Food's Web site. It's cumbersome, always under construction, and nowhere near as efficient as the phone service. You can request a catalog.

BEST RAW FOOD

Creature Features

21 East 3rd Street (Broadway and Lafayette), Manhattan. 212-473-5992

If you know what BARF stands for, and you're a believer, then this is the store for you (for those who still feed their dogs lams, BARF stands for Bones and Raw Food or Biologically Appropriate Raw Food, a diet that some believe is best for dogs). Creature Features is the place for anyone who wants unprocessed dog food, made of human-grade ingredients that are hormone- and antibiotic-free. Smaller than most Manhattan studio apartments, this store stocks flash-frozen raw meats for dogs; raw-food supplements from Pat McKay; plus prepared flash-frozen or freeze-dried raw meat-based brands of dog food like Steve's Real Food and Nature's Menu. The friendly, knowledgeable staffers can steer you toward the right fresh food for your dog.

BEST CANINE COLLECTIBLES

Doggie-Do & Pussycats Too

567 Third Avenue (37th and 38th Streets), Manhattan. 212-661-9111.

www.doggiedo.com

A tiny store packed with hand-crafted canine knick-knacks: clocks in the shape of a dog's head, tea pots decorated with brightly colored dogs, fanciful ceramic dog bowls, and giant $65 dog-themed snow globes. As well, there're plenty of accessories for glamorous pocket dogs: pink rhinestone collars, gold-trimmed leashes, chic carriers, an impressive collection of hand-knit woolens, and yes, $90 oiled, Burberry slickers.

BEST DOG BAKERY

Three Dog Bakery 1-800-4TREATS.

www.threedog.com

Sadly, Three Dog Bakery shut down its New York City store. But you can still order birthday and "bark-mitzvah" cakes for your hound through the Bakery's Web site. Deliveries are sent by second-day air.

Best Neighborhood Stores

Every dog owner needs a convenient source for a new Kong, a liver-treat fix, or the occasional Nylabone. This list includes the top neighborhood sources for pet supplies in the city (many also offer grooming).

MANHATTAN

Upper East Side

Animal Attractions
343 East 66th Street (1st and 2nd Aves.), 212-734-8400

Biscuits and Bath
255 East 74th Street (2nd and 3rd Aves), 212-585-1800

Calling All Pets
301 East 76th Street (1st and 2nd Aves), 212-734-7051
1590 York Avenue (83rd and 84th Streets), 212-249-7387

Dogs, Cats & Co.
208 East 82nd Street (2nd and 3rd Aves), 212-396-2585

Furry Paws
1705 Third Avenue (95th and 96th Streets), 212-828-5308

Le Chien
1044 Third Avenue (61st and 62nd Streets), 212-861-8100

Not Just Dogs
244 East 60th Street (2nd and 3rd Aves), 212-752-8669

Peter's Emporium for Pets
1449 Second Avenue (75th and 76th Streets), 212-772-3647

The Pet Market
1570 First Avenue (81st and 82nd Streets), 212-879-3888

Pet Necessities
236 E. 76th Street (2nd and 3rd Aves), 212-988-0769

Pets-on-Lex
1271 Lexington Avenue (85th and 86th Streets), 212-426-0766

Urban Pets
1661 First Avenue (86th and 87th Streets), 212-828-4254

Upper West Side

Furry Paws
141 Amsterdam Avenue (66th and 67th Streets), 212-724-9321

Little Creatures
770 Amsterdam Avenue (97th and 98th Streets), 212-932-8610

NY Aquatics and Pet Warehouse
209 West 96th Street (Broadway and Amsterdam Aves), 212-865-7500

Pet Bowl
440 Amsterdam Avenue (81st and 82nd Streets), 212-595-4200

The Pet Market
210 West 72nd Street (Broadway and West End Aves), 212-799-4200

Midtown

Animal Acts
233 W. 54th Street (Broadway and 8th Aves), 212-489-0568

Beekman Pet Emporium
900 First Avenue (50th and 51st Streets), 212-838-6480

Furry Paws
1039 Second Avenue (54th and 55th Streets), 212-813-1388

Chelsea

Barking Zoo
172 9th Avenue (20th and 21st Streets), 212-255-0658

Doggone Purrrty
151 W. 25th Street (6th and 7th Aves), 212-242-0525

New York Dog Spa and Hotel Boutique
145 West 18th Street (6th and 7th Aves), 212-243-1199

Pet Central
247 West 23rd Street (7th and 8th Aves), 646-486-1662

The Pet Parade
144 West 19th Street (6th and 7th Aves), 212-645-5345

Gramercy Park/Murray Hill

Animal World
219 East 26th Street (2nd and 3rd Aves), 212-685-0027

Natural Pet
238 Third Avenue (19th and 20th Streets), 212-228-4848

Furry Paws
120 East 34th Street (Lexington and Park Aves), 212-725-1970
310 East 23rd Street (1st and 2nd Aves), 212-979-0920

West Village

Beverly Hills Launder Mutt
45 Grove Street (Bedford and Bleecker Streets), 212-691-7700

The Four Paws Club
387 Bleecker Street (11th and Perry Streets), 212-367-8265

Groom-o-Rama
496 Sixth Avenue (12th and 13th Streets), 212-627-2899

Parrots & Pups
45 Christopher Street (7th Ave and Waverly Pl.), 212-352-8777

Pet Palace
109 W. 10th Street (6th and Greenwich Aves), 212-727-0525

Urban Pets
18 Christopher Street (Gay St and Waverly Pl), 212-727-0448

East Village

Animal Crackers
26 First Avenue (1st and 2nd Streets), 212-614-6786

Mikey's Pet Shop
130 East Seventh Street (1st and 2nd Aves), 212-477-3235

Pet's Garden
239 East Fifth Street (2nd Ave and the Bowery), 212-533-5304

SoHo

Alternative Pet
33 Howard Street (Broadway and Crosby Streets), 212-941-5083

The Pet Bar
132 Thompson Street (Houston and Prince Streets), 212-253-9250

Tribeca

Another Barking Zoo
368 1/2 Greenwich Street (Harrison and Franklin Streets), 212-233-0226

Dog Essentials
86 Franklin Street (Church St and Broadway), 212-343-9553

Battery Park

Le Pet Spa
300 Rector Place (South End Ave and the Esplanade), 212-786-9070

BRONX

Morrisania

Animal Feeds
3255 Park Avenue (at 163rd Street), 718-293-7750

Riverdale

Fieldston Pets
3476 Bailey Avenue, 718-796-4541

Pet-o-Rama
5705 Mosholu Avenue, 718-432-6000

BROOKLYN

Bay Ridge

A World of Pets

538 86th Street, 718-238-PETS

Brooklyn Heights

Pets Emporium

103 Montague Street, 718-624-2533

Carroll Gardens/Cobble Hill

Pet Treats

370 Court Street, 718-243-1919

Smith Street Pet Food

118 Smith Street, 718-625-9300

Flatbush

Pet Obsession

2196 Flatbush Avenue, 718-338-1208

Puppy Paradise

2082 Flatbush Avenue, 718-252-7877

Park Slope/Windsor Terrace

All For Paws

216 Prospect Park West, 718-788-7052

Four & A Tail

240 7th Avenue, 718-832-2717

Mothers Pet Food

370 7th Ave, 718-788-8688

VC Pet Supply

284A 9th Street, 718-499-9565

Williamsburg

B.Q.E. Pet Food

253 Wythe Avenue, 718-486-7489

One Stop Pet Shop

161 North Seventh Street, 718-218-7513

QUEENS

Astoria

Pet Stop Discounts

21-72 31st Street, 718-545-8972

Flushing

Mamas & Papas

45-10 Parsons Boulevard, 718-353-8698

Forest Hills

Wagging Tails

105-19 Metropolitan Avenue, 718-575-8245

Jackson Heights

Original Pet Deli

8216 31st Avenue, 718-565-6624

STATEN ISLAND

Manor Heights

Feed-Rite Pet Food & Supplies

945-947 Manor Rd, 718-698-7666

Best Catalogues

Doctors Foster and Smith
800-826-7206, www.drsfostersmtih.com

J-B Wholesale Pet Supplies
800-526-0388, www.jbpet.com

The Natural Pet Care Catalog
800-962-8266, www.allthebest.com

New England Serum Company
800-637-3786, www.neserum.com

R.C. Steele Pet Supplies
800-872-3773, www.rcsteele.com

Waggin' Tails
800-946-8245, www.waggintails.com

Best Groomers

New York does not require groomers to be licensed or insured, so beware. Get recommendations from friends, trainers, or vets. Some grooming shops let you roll up your sleeves and hose down your hound yourself. Others are elegant salons that paint a dog's nails (!) and use hairspray. And while a complete beauty treatment can cost between $60 and $300, many groomers will let you pop in with your dog for a quick $5 nail clip or ear cleaning.

Your dog's daycare center or your neighborhood pet store may offer grooming. Here we only list the city's best-known groomers.

MANHATTAN

Upper East Side

Biscuits & Bath's Grooming & Goodies
1535 First Ave. (between 2nd and 3rd Aves), 212-585-1800
This grooming shop, which is part of the growing Biscuits & Bath dog empire, charges between $65 and $125. Although this is the main grooming shop for Biscuits & Bath, grooming is available at the other locations: 255 East 74th Street (2nd and 3rd Aves) and 227 East 44th Street (2nd and 3rd Aves).

Canine Styles
830 Lexington Avenue (between 63rd and 64th Streets), 212-751-4549 or 212- 838-2064

The oldest grooming shop in NYC, Canine Styles has been operating in the same small retail front since 1959. The shop grooms only a few dogs a day; there's a big emphasis on personal service. Complete grooming costs $70 to $300.

Karen's For People + Pets

1195 Lexington Avenue (81st and 82nd Streets), 212-472-9440. www.karensforpets.com

Owner Karen Thompson has been in the business for more than 25 years and has a good reputation and the latest equipment (see Best Pet-Supply Stores, page 167). Her staff claims to groom 100,000 dogs a year. Complete grooming costs $80 to $100.

Petco

147 East 86th Street (Lexington and Third Aves.), 212-831-8001.

www.petco.com

The chain provides quality grooming at reasonable prices. The cost is $40 to $100, depending on the size and condition of your dog.

Upper West Side

A Cut Above

207 West 75th Street (Broadway and Amsterdam Aves), 212-799-8746

On the premises of the Canine Country daycare facility, and upstairs from Ansonia Veterinary Center, this salon is convenient for clients of both. Grooming runs $50 to $80.

Hydrosurge Holistic Bathing Center

207 West 80th Street (Broadway and Amsterdam Aves), 212-787-3073

This small, no-frills salon lets you wash your dog yourself, with a Hydrosurge—a handheld nozzle that shoots a water and soap mixture that is said to be helpful for dogs with skin allergies. Self-service baths costs $25 to $75, depending on size of dog. Full-service grooming services run $65 to $100.

Murray Hill

Doggie-Do and Pussycats Too

567 Third Avenue (37th and 38th Streets), 212-661-9111.

www.doggiedo.com

For an extra $25, Doggie-Do will pick up and deliver your dog for grooming, which takes place in a room at the back of the retail store (see Best Pet-Supply Stores, page 169). Hand clipping is offered here. Grooming starts at $60 and quickly climbs.

Best Online Shopping

Shopping online isn't what it once was. In the olden days of dot-com mania, e-commerce companies practically gave their stuff away, and shipping was free. Now they're mostly out of business. It's a shame. But the three big pet-supply e-tailers remain, and though they now charge plenty for shipping, they all offer better prices and more selection than just about every store in New York.

Site	The Good News	The Bad News
DRS. FOSTER AND SMITH www.drsfostersmith.com	The best customer service in cyberspace (including online access to a vet if needed), plus a well-designed site, a library of educational veterinary material and no tax.	Doesn't sell dog food. Shipping costs can be high.
PETCO.COM (formerly Petopia.com) www.petco.com	Large selection; convenient food subscription service.	Site is hard to read and navigate. You pay sales tax. Service is average.
PETSMART www.petsmart.com	Easy to navigate site, good selection and no sales tax. Includes Acme Pet Community, one of the largest collections of pet-related bulletin boards out there	Customer service reps are well-intentioned but not particularly knowledgeable.

New York School Of Dog Grooming

248 East 34th Street (2nd and 3rd Aves), 212-685-3776

If you're willing to let grooming students practice on your dog, this place is a bargain: a full grooming costs just $20 to $35. One drawback is that grooming here usually takes far longer than at other salons.

Chelsea

New York Dog Spa and Hotel

145 West 18th Street (6th and 7th Aves), 212-243-1199.

www.nydogspa.com

A full-service grooming salon that offers hand-scissoring and -stripping. Prices start at $45 and rise depending on the size, breed and condition of the dog.

Gramercy Park/Union Square

Petco

860 Broadway (17th and 18th Streets), 212-358-0692

See entry on Petco page 175.

West Village

Beverly Hill's LaunderMutt

45 Grove Street (Bleecker and Bedford Streets), 212-691-7700

LaunderMutt is a long-time favorite of many hounds in the Village. Grooming costs $50 to $100.

Dog Wash

177 MacDougal Street (MacDougal Alley and W. 8th Street), 212-673-3290.

www.dogwashnyc.com

Just around the corner from the Washington Square Dog Run, Dog Wash doesn't require appointments to use its convenient self-service shower stalls (price: $16). Simple grooming, which includes having your dog washed, brushed and dried, costs $32 or $37, depending on the length of your dog's hair.

Four Paws Club

387 Bleecker Street (Perry and 11th Streets), 212-367-8265

Even before it opened in spring, 2001, the little Four Paws had already attracted attention. Bark magazine, for one, gave owner Laura Bilyeu the title of "Potentially Next Big Groomer." Prices start at $55.

Groomers Who Make House calls

Groomers that make house calls arrive with their own table, supplies and tools (but not towels: you need to provide those). Depending on what needs to be done, and how big or dirty your dog is, an in-house grooming session will last between one and three hours. Costs also vary tremendously, so be sure to get an estimate in advance. Travel may be an extra charge.

Grooming Just For You: Carolyn Yaciuk 917-686-3647
Areas served: Manhattan and Queens
Cost: Basic cut and grooming starts at $75.
Carolyn has been grooming dogs since the early 1990s. A graduate of the New York School of Dog Grooming, she specializes in precise scissor cuts (as opposed to cuts using blades or attachments). In 2001 she won a "Rising Star Award" in Intergroom, a national grooming competition. No stickler for show standards, Carolyn believes in grooming for a dog's comfort.

Ilys Posner 212-481-6131
Areas served: Manhattan

Lower East Side
Personalized Pet Care by Alice
90 Ludlow Street (Broome and Delancey Streets), 212-228-7894.
http://doggiediva.com
Alice, who also runs a dog daycare center here (see page 115), uses organic cleaning products, steering clear of chemical detergents and insecticides. Prices start at $40.

Soho
Alternative Pet Care
33 Howard Street (Broadway and Lafayette), 212-941-5083

Cost: Basic cut and grooming starts at $60

Ilys owns and runs a grooming shop and daycare center, Doggyland at Little Red Pet Shop (see page 114), but she is also a graduate of the New York School of Grooming who makes house calls on the side. Sticking to the basics, she offers straightforward haircuts and grooming to small "well-kept" dogs.

In House Grooming: Jim Sommer 212-750-7170
Areas served: Manhattan (Upper East Side, Midtown, Downtown)
Cost: Basic cut and grooming starts at $60

Another graduate of the New York School of Dog Grooming, Jim has been grooming dogs since 1980 and making house calls since the early 1990s. Clients describe him as thorough, professional, and willing to work at odd hours.

Two Dogs & A Goat: Charlotte Reed 212-631-1157. www.twodogsandagoat.com
Areas served: Manhattan and the Hamptons
Cost: Basic grooming starts at $100

Charlotte, a graduate of the New York School of Dog Grooming and CUNY's Veterinary Technology Associates Program, promotes her grooming sessions as the equivalent of a human day spa ("Your dog is left refreshed, relaxed, and rejuvenated"). Aside from the standard grooming services, she also offers canine clients massages and a teeth cleaning. Since starting Two Dogs & A Goat in 1996, Charlotte has added around 30 employees and opened a second office in Sag Harbor, Long Island. She also offers dog walking and sitting (see page 109).

This spot offers self-service dog washes for $25. Full-service grooming is $45 to $60. It's especially convenient for people who use Alternative's daycare (see page 115).

BROOKLYN

<u>Prospect Park</u>

Perfect Paws

276 Atlantic Avenue (Boerum Place and Smith Street), 718-852-6200

The Prospect Park dog community raves about Perfect Paws. Grooming costs $20 to $200.

<u>Carroll Gardens</u>

Woofs 'n Whiskers

95 Summit Street (Columbia and Van Brunt Streets), 718-237-0298. www.woofsnwhiskers.com

This dog daycare lets you wash your dog using their large shower stalls. Included in the price is shampoo, brushes, dryers, and a long rubber apron and boots to keep you dry.

QUEENS

<u>Astoria</u>

Carol's Ark

23-19 Steinway Street, 718-278-4677

Basic grooming and a bath is about $35. At the top end, a major haircut and cleaning is $60.

Best Pet Portrait Artists

Perhaps they've been inspired by William Wegman's whimsically photographed Weimaraners. Maybe they're determined to immortalize their canine companions in the style of England's landed gentry. Whatever the reason, more and more American dog owners are commissioning portraits of their pets—and a growing number of professional artists are making a living photographing and painting dogs. Herewith, a listing of the best hound portraitists who work in New York (or from photographs of New York dogs). For samples of their work, visit Urbanhound.com's Web page devoted to portraitists: www.urbanhound.com/houndServices/portraits.html.

PHOTOGRAPHERS

Derek Berg, 212-777-8607. derekbergpix@hotmail.com

Having worked as a photojournalist for the past 20 years, Derek brings a photojournalistic perspective to his black-and-white portraits of dogs. He is especially interested in how dogs interact with the human world that surrounds them. His favorite format is "A Day in the Life of Your Dog," for which he follows his subjects everywhere, photographing them on their morning walk, playing in the dog run, and meeting canine friends on the street. He develops all of his own prints on resin-coated, double-weight archival paper.

Derek's work has appeared in magazines such as *Forbes, Connoisseur*, and *Interview*. His photos of New York dogs are featured in a series of postcards and greeting cards produced by Fotofolio N.Y. and Borealis Press.

Location: Derek will work anywhere in the New York City area.
Cost: $400 includes a four-hour photo session and two 8 x 10 inch silver gelatin archival prints.
Production Time: Around three weeks.

Jim Dratfield, Petography, 212-245-0914. petography@redconnect.net
www.petography.com
Jim works in a classical fine-art style with elegant portraits of dogs posed on chairs or sofas (he has a talent for keeping animals still). When he is not shooting on location, Jim uses natural settings as a complementary backdrop, particularly in his color photographs where blooming flowers and foliage accent the textures and expressions of the animals. Apart from traditional prints, Jim will turn your dog's portrait into note cards, bound-book covers and even jewelry.

Jim's portfolio includes portraits of such celebrities as Jennifer Aniston, Kathy Bates, and Jenna Elfman and their pets. His books include *Pug Shots* (Penguin USA, 1999) and *The Quotable Feline* (Knopf, 1996).
Location: Based in New York, he will travel outside the area for an additional fee.
Cost: $895 covers a two- to three-hour photo session in the city and three matted prints (one 8 x 10 inch and two 5 x 7 inch) of three different images. As well, you get a choice of either a dozen notecards or a 4 x 6 inch print in a burled wood frame.
Production Time: Around four to six weeks.

Amanda Jones, 877-251-2390. ajphoto@amandajones.com.
www.amandajones.com
Amanda's style is cool and minimal. Working in a studio, she uses a white background that disappears against the strong presence of the animal's silhouette. Her closely cropped, black-and-white compositions are striking for powerful imagery that often borders on the abstract. Amanda's work has been featured on greeting cards and in TV and print advertisements.
Location: Based in San Francisco, with studios in New York and Los Angeles, Amanda makes at least four trips a year to New York City.
Cost: Portrait sessions start at $450.
Production Time: Around six weeks.

Kim Levin, Bark & Smile Pet Portraits, 212-714-3984. KimLevin@aol.com
www.barkandsmile.com

Kim's playful portraits capture the lively and humorous side of a dog's personality: that quizzical look; the cocked head; the pricked ears. Shooting outside, in parks or on the street, Kim's compositions are full of details that contrast her subject's liveliness to the seemingly inanimate world around them.

Kim's first book of photography, *Why We Love Dogs* (Andrews McMeel, 1998), has spawned a cottage industry: she now has greeting cards, coffee mugs, journals, and a calendar that feature her dog photos. Her other books include *Why We Really Love Dogs* (Andrew McMeel, 2000) and *Working Dogs: Tales from Animal Planet's K-9 to 5 World* (Discovery Books, 2000).

Location*:* Kim will go anywhere in the tristate area for a photo session.
She lives in Red Bank, New Jersey.

Cost*:* $375 for three 8 x 10-inch black and white prints; $425 for three 8 x 10-inch color prints.

Production Time: Around three weeks.

Michael Nastasi, 212-595-3353. nastasi@canisphoto.com
www.canisphoto.com

Michael's informal photographs appear throughout this book. He works mainly in black and white, and captures dogs at their most playful moments: stretching, jumping, or relaxing in the sun. He also shoots beautiful closeup portraits that give a real sense of a dog's personality. His favorite shooting locations are Manhattan's Riverside and Central Parks. If you're seeking the most bang for your buck, Michael is the one.

Location: Manhattan-based Michael will travel anywhere in the New York City area.

Cost: $180 for three 8 x 10-inch black and white prints; $320 for three 8 x 10-inch color prints. Additional prints cost between $6 and $30 depending on size and the number ordered.

Production Time: The final prints will be ready 30 to 45 days from the photo session.

Valerie Shaff, 212-965-1080.

Because Valerie works with a medium-format camera that produces large, detailed negatives, her sepia-toned images have an extraordinary clarity that's hard to achieve with a traditional camera. Her prints are square. Using a soft-focus background that makes the dog stand out sharply, Valerie shoots everything from close-ups and outdoor action shots, to interior portraits with dogs seated on furniture. She prides herself on spending the time to learn her subjects' personalities and habits before taking their photographs.

Valerie's work has appeared in *The New Yorker, Harper's,* and *Cigar Aficionado*. Her books include *I Am Puppy Hear Me Yap: The Ages of Dogs* (HarperCollins 2000) and *If Only You Knew*

How Much I Smell You: True Portraits of Dogs (Bulfinch, 1998).
Location: Based in Manhattan, Valerie usually works in or around a client's home. She brings with her a "portable studio" that includes various hand-painted backdrops.
Cost: Fees start at $1,000.
Production Time: Contact sheets are available within a week.

PAINTERS

Angi Laframboise, portraits@mindspring.com
www.pastelportraits.com
Most of Angi's work is in pastel. She uses intense color, yet draws with a softness—a combination that gives her work texture and helps bring out her subjects' features. Angi also decorates Christmas-tree ornaments with pet portraits.
Location: From her home in Georgia, Angi works from photographs.
Cost: Prices start at $175 for charcoal, $275 for pastel, and $450 for oil and acrylics (plus $20 for shipping). Standard sizes are: 12 x 16 inches, 16 x 20 inches, and 18 x 24 inches. Christmas ornaments cost $40 each, plus shipping ($8 for up to six ornaments).
Production Time: Charcoal and pastel portraits: three to four weeks; oil and acrylic: six to 12 weeks; ornaments: two to three weeks.

Arlene Sibley, 801-277-0745. SibleyA@aol.com
www.animals-with-attitude.com
Working from several of your favorite snapshots, Arlene constructs a vibrant composition that uses lush flowers and patterns as background for your dog's portrait. She uses a traditional oil painting technique developed during the Renaissance which begins with the application of several layers of underpainting and ends with glazes that give the finished surface depth and luminosity. Unlike portrait artists who attempt to render a photographic likeness, Arlene makes paintings that are equal parts reality and imagination. To add to the character of the portrait, she requests lots of information about her subjects: from size and eye color, to personality and habits.
Location: Arlene works from her homes in Utah and Wyoming.
Cost: Portraits start at $450 (plus $30 for shipping). Standard canvas sizes are: 12 x 16 inches, 16 x 20 inches, 18 x 24 inches, and 20 x 24 inches.
Production Time: Around eight weeks.

Sarah Theophilus, Pets in Pastel. portraits@petsinpastel.com
www.petsinpastel.com
Sarah works either in oil or pastel using a photograph of your pet. Her meticulous technique captures every detail, often making it difficult to distinguish the painting from the original image. Most of Sarah's portraits are of a dog's face against a white background. She goes out of her way to seek your input; sending the work-in-progress via e-mail and asking for your feedback so that the final portrait is as close to your pet's likeness as possible. Also, for the quality of her work, Sarah offers bargain prices.
Location: Sarah works from her home in Qualicum Beach, British Columbia.
Cost*:* Between $135 and $245 depending on complexity and size (shipping is included). Standard sizes are: 9 x 12 inches or 11 x 14 inches.
Production Time: Three to six weeks.

Anne Watkins, 212-866-0057.
Anne's expressive watercolor sketches capture the essence of a particular dog without focusing on details. She prefers to work from life, in a spot where the dog feels comfortable, so she can observe his characteristic poses. She's known for stylish images of the life of the city dog. Her portraits of "shop dogs" of Manhattan's East Ninth Street have been published in *Bark* magazine. Samples of Anne's work can be found at the Web site for the Animal Haven shelter (www.animal haven.com), to which she donates her animal watercolors. A set of eight notecards costs $16 (plus $2 shipping).
Location: Anne will work anywhere in the NYC area.
Cost*:* $250 and up for an unframed 11 x 15-inch painting, $350 and up for a framed image.
Production Time: Two to three weeks.

Barrie Barnett and Christine Merrill, The William Secord Gallery
212-249-0075, 52 E. 76th Street, Manhattan
www.dogpainting.com
Barrie Barnett and Christine Merrill are two well-known dog portraitists represented by the William Secord Gallery, which specializes in hounds. Barrie, who began her formal art training at the age of nine, works exclusively in pastel. Christine, who spent five years at the traditional Schuler School of Fine Art in Baltimore, paints oils in the style of 18th-century English portraits; her work has been exhibited around the world.

You can see samples of both artists' work at the William Secord Gallery, and on its Web site. The gallery is worth a visit even if you're not looking to commission a painting. Its impressive collection includes collars, porcelains, terra cottas, rare books about dogs, and twentieth-century etchings and drawings of dogs. The gallery's owner, William Secord, was the founding director of The Dog Museum of America and is the author of *Dog Painting, 1840-1940, A Social History of the Dog in Art* and *Dog Painting, The European Breeds*.

Location: Christine lives in Maryland, but as long as travel expenses are covered, she comes to New York for sittings. Barrie includes one sitting in New York or Baltimore in her prices; each additional sitting, if needed, costs $150. Unlike Christine, Barrie will work off a photograph or videotape.

Cost: Barrie charges between $6,000 and $8,000 for a pastel on paper. Christine's oil portraits start at $9,000 for a 14 x 18-inch canvas.

Production Time: Both artists have waiting lists, sometimes of a year or more, but once work is begun, it takes about six months to complete.

SCULPTOR

Stanley Taub, 212-777-5548

www.taub-sculptor.com

Stan started his career as a plastic surgeon; he's now a full-time sculptor who's won many awards and commissions. Recently he has begun to sculpt dogs. In late 2000 he completed a beautiful bronze of a Labrador Retriever, commissioned by the New England Antivivisection Society. Other examples of Stan's work include the "SoHo Muse," a cherub on a 14-foot column that stands on the southeast corner of Manhattan's Houston Street and West Broadway; "Healing," a sculpture of a doctor caring for a patient located in the outdoor garden of the Grossman Burn Center at Sherman Oaks Hospital in Los Angeles; and a bust of Arthur Rubenstein on permanent exhibition at New York's Steinway Hall.

Location: Stan is based in New York City.

Cost: Fees vary tremendously depending on the size and material used. As an example, an 8-inch-high figure is around $4,500 in bronze and about $3,700 in bonded bronze (pulverized bronze mixed with polyester resin).

Production Time: It takes three to six weeks to complete a bust, then another two to four weeks for casting.

12 urbanhoundyellowpages

These pages represent the most complete list of New York City's canine-related businesses. Listings are divided by borough, then by category.

We've continually updated and added to the Urbanhound.com Yellow Pages since they were first posted on our Web site. Still, in this city, businesses come and go before you can say Urbanhound, so we apologize in advance for any listings that are out of date. Visit www.urbanhound.com for the most current listings.

MANHATTAN

Boarding & Daycare

Alternative Pet Care, 33 Howard St., 941-5083

Animal General, 140 W. 67th St., 712-9535

Bed & Biscuit, 475-6064

Biscuits & Bath Doggy Gym, 1535 1st Ave., 794-3600

Biscuits & Bath Doggy Village, 227 E. 44th St., 692-2323

Camp Canine, 46 W. 73rd St., 787-3647

Canine Country, 207 W. 75th St Fl # 2, 877-7777

Cat Practice, 137 5th Ave., Fl # 2, 677-1401

Dog Wash, 177 Macdougal St., 673-3290

Doggie Day Care: The Wagging Tail, 354 Greenwich St., 285-4900

Doggie-Do & Pussycats Too, 567 3rd Ave., 661-9111

Le Chien Pet Salon, 1044 3rd Ave., 861-8100

Little Red Pet Shop, 202 E. 25th St., 481-6131

New York Dog Spa & Hotel, 145 W. 18th St., 243-1199

No Standing Anytime, 515 W. 29th St., 268-7370

Pampered Pets Dog Walking & Boarding, 677-6965

Paws Inn, 189 9th Ave., 645-7297

Personalized Pet Care By Alice, 90 Ludlow St., 228-7894

Pet Superette, 187 E. 93rd St., 534-1732

Run Spot Run, 415 E. 91st St., 996-6666

Sit Stay Play, 140 West 67th St., 712-9535

Sutton Dog Parlour, 311 E. 60th St., 355-2850

University Animal Hospital, 354 E. 66th St., 288-8884

Wagging Tail Doggie Day Care, 354 ½ Greenwich St., 285-4900

Groomers

A Cut Above, 207 W. 75th St., 799-8746

Alternative Pet Care, 33 Howard St., 941-5083

American Kennels, 798 Lexington Ave., 838-8460

Amsterdog Groomers, 586 Amsterdam Ave., 496-6117

Anitra Cat Grooming Plus, 309 W. 99th St., 663-0122

Beekman Pet Emporium, 900 1st Ave., 838-6480

Before & After Dog Salon, 104 W. 83rd St., 799-9287

Beverly Hill's Launder Mutt, 45 Grove St., 691-7700

Biscuits & Bath Grooming & Goodies, 255 E. 74th St., 585-1800

Camp Canine, 46 W. 73rd St., 787-3647

Canine Country, 207 W. 75th St., 877-7777

Canine Styles, 830 Lexington Ave., 751-4549

Creature Comforts, 2778 Broadway, 864-9964

Creature Features, 3 Great Jones St., 473-5992

Dog Grooming School Of New York, 248 E. 34th St., 685-3776

Dog Wash, 177 Macdougal St., 673-3290

Doggie Dearest, 543 E. 5th St., 254-3204

Doggie-Do & Pussycats Too, 567 3rd Ave., 661-9111

Dogs Cats & Co, 208 E. 82nd St., 396-2585

East Bay Animal Clinic, 612 2nd Ave., 481-7999

East Side Animal Hospital, 321 E. 52nd St., 751-5176

Elite Grooming Salon, 242 E. 36th St., 686-5722

Find A Pet, 27 1/2 Essex St., 674-7488

Finishing Touches By Stephanie, 414 E. 58th St., 753-8234

Four Paws Club, 387 Bleecker St., 367-8265

Groom-O-Rama, 496 E. 6th St., 627-2899

Happy Pet All Breed Dog, 202 W. 80th St., 877-9658

Happy Trails & Tails, 1535 1st Ave., 737-2345

Hydrosurge Holistic Bathing, 207 W. 80th St.,787-3073

Karen's For People Plus Pets, 1195 Lexington Ave., 472-9440

L B Pet Supply, 326 E. 78th St., 737-3647

Le Chien Pet Salon, 1044 3rd Ave., 861-8100

Le Pet Spa, 300 Rector Place, 786-9070

Lexington Veterinary Group, 133 E. 39th St., 889-7778

Little Creatures, 126 Saint Marks Place, 473-2857

Little Red Pet Shop, 202 E. 25th St., 481-6131

Natural Animal Grooming, 1572 3rd Ave., 410-2150

Natural Pet, 238 3rd Ave., 228-4848

New York Dog Spa & Hotel, 145 W. 18th St., 243-1199

New York School of Dog Grooming, 248 E. 34th St., 685-3776

New York's Original Best Pets, 205 Dyckman St., 569-7401

Pampered Pets, 150 E. 69th St., 772-2181

Paws Inn, 370 W. 35th St., 736-7297

Personalized Pet Care By Alice, 90 Ludlow St., 228-7894

Pet Stop, 1572 3rd Ave., 410-4100

Pet Superette, 187 E. 93rd St., 534-1732

Petco, 860 Broadway, 358-0692

Petco, 542 2nd Ave., 779-8791

Petco, 147 E. 86th St., 831-8001

Poodle Cut, 14 Bedford St., 929-0137

Run Spot, 415 E. 91st St., 996-6666

Shaggy Dog, 400 E. 88th St., 289-0198

Sutton Dog Parlour, 311 E. 60th St., 355-2850

Towne House Grooming, 369 W. 19th St., 929-2910

Two Dogs & A Goat, 326 E. 34th St., 631-1157

University Animal Hospital, 354 E. 66th St., 288-8884

Urban Pets, 18 Christopher St., 727-0448

Ursula Lehnhardt Canine Styles, 830 Lexington Ave., 838-2064

Wagging Tail Doggie Day Care, 354 Greenwich St., 285-4900

Yuppie Puppy Pet Care, 274 W. 86th St.,877-2747

Obedience Trainers

A M Animal Training, 720 Lenox Ave., 491-4750

All About Dogs, 210 E. 23rd St # 3r, 481-2656

Allan Michael, 172 E. 4th St., 505-8714

American Dog Trainers Network, 161 W. 4th St., 727-7257

Andrea Arden Dog Training, 145 West 18th St., 213-4288

Animal Learning Center, 230 W. 105th St., 864-4973

ASPCA Center For Behavioral Therapy, 424 E. 92nd St., 876-7700

City Dog Obedience School, 158 W. 23rd St., 255-3618

Dogs In Motion, 30 W. 63rd St., 262-7000

Dogs-in-the-Hood Training, 25 West 87th St., 595-3353

Follow My Lead, 117 W. 74th St., 873-5511

Ivan Kovach Canine Academy, 535 5th Ave., 682-6770

Manhattan Dog Training, 145 West 18th St., 213-4288

Mutts & Jeff, 12 E. 72nd St., 516-383-6555

N Y Pet Co, 508 E. 12th St., 501-6972

Pet Get-Away, 1623 3rd Ave., 534-7924

Puddles Pet Service, 410-7338

Puppy Paths, 1636 3rd Ave., 736-7400

Red Dog Training, 16 E. 98th St., 534-1290

Samantha Schmidt, 55 E. End Ave., 737-0065

Two Dogs & A Goat, 326 E. 34th St., 213-6979

Vancouver Dog Training, 393 W. End Ave., # 6F, 877-7116

Walk This Way Canine Behavior Therapy, 195 Stanton St. 260-8423

Who's Walking Who, 319 Ave. of the Americas, 414-1551

Pet Supply Stores

All Pet, 410 W. 220th St., 567-2102

Alternative Pet Care, 33 Howard St., 941-5083

American Kennels, 798 Lexington Ave., 838-8460

Animal Acts, 233 W. 54th St., 489-0568

Animal Attractions, 343 E. 66th St., 734-8400

Animal Crackers, 26 1st Ave., 614-6786

Animal World, 219 E. 26th St., 685-0027

Another Barking Zoo, 368 1/2 Greenwich St., 233-0226

Barking Zoo, 172 9th Ave., 255-0658

Barkley, 215 E. 76th St., 734-9373

Beasty Feast, 237 Bleecker St., 243-3261

Beasty Feast, 630 Hudson St., 620-7099

Beasty Feast, 680 Washington St., 620-4055

Beekman Pet Emporium, 900 1st Ave., 838-6480

Beverly Hill's Launder Mutt, 45 Grove St., 691-7700

Biscuits & Bath, 255 E. 74th St., 585-1800

Blonde With Beagle Production, 545 W. 34th St., 695-1430

Blue Ribbon Dog Co, 20 W. 22nd St., 929-2252

Bonnie's K-9 Swim Center, 737 Washington St., 414-2500

Calling All Pets, 301 E. 76th St., 734-7051

Calling All Pets, 1590 York Ave., 249-7387

Canine Castle, 410 W. 56th St., 245-1291

Canine Styles, 830 Lexington Ave., 751-4549

Creature Features, 21 E. 3rd St., 473-5992

Dog Essentials, 86 Franklin St., 343-9553

Doggie-Do & Pussycats Too, 567 Third Ave., 661-9111

Doggie Wear, 85 E. End Ave., 288-3921

Doggone Purrrty, 151 W. 25th St., 242-0525

Dogs Cats & Co, 208 E. 82nd St., 396-2585

Dudley's Paw, 327 Greenwich St., 966-5167

Elbario Pet Shop, 122 E. 116th St., 426-5269

Fetch, 43 Greenwich Ave., 352-8591

Four Paws Club, 387 Bleecker St., 367-8265

Finishing Touches By Stephanie, 414 E. 58th St., 753-8234

Furry Paws 1, 120 E. 34th St., 725-1970

Furry Paws 2, 1705 3rd Ave., 828-5308

Furry Paws 3, 1039 2nd Ave., 813-1388

Furry Paws 4, 141 Amsterdam Ave., 724-9321

Furry Paws 5, 310 E. 23rd St., 979-0920

Groom-O-Rama, 496 Sixth Ave., 627-2899

Grooming All Pets, 1590 York Ave., 327-3600

Houndz In The Hood, 241 W. 108th St., 316-0468

I C Pet Place, 518 W. 181st St., 740-7900

Ideal Pet Warehouse, 356 E. 116th St., 876-5093

International Kennel Club, 1032 2nd Ave., 755-0100

J B Pets, 111 E. 125th St., 987-2786

JBJ Discount Pet Shop, 151 E. Houston St., 982-5310

Karen's For People + Pets, 1195 Lexington Ave., 472-9440

Le Chien Pet Salon, 1044 3rd Ave., 861-8100

Le Pet Spa, 300 Rector Place, 786-9070

Little Creatures, 770 Amsterdam Ave., 932-8610

Little Red Pet Shop, 202 E. 25th St., 481-6131

Lolly's Pet Salon, 228 E. 80th St., 517-3371

Metropets Corp, 594 9th Ave., 757-2924

Mikey's Pet Shop, 130 E. 7th St., 477-3235

Natural Pet, 238 3rd Ave., 228-4848

New York Dog Spa & Hotel Boutique, 145 W. 18th St., 243-1199

Not Just Dogs, 244 E. 60th St., 752-8669

NY Aquarium & Pet Supplies, 215 E. 23rd St., 481-7387

NY Aquatics & Pet Warehouse, 209 W. 96th St., 865-7500

NYC Pet Place, 431 W. 125th St., 864-2600

Outsect, 147 W. 22nd St., 807-9713

Parrots & Pups, 45 Christopher St., 352-8777

Pet Bar, 132 Thompson St., 253-9250

Pet Bowl, 440 Amsterdam Ave., 595-4200

Pet Canteen, 219 Mulberry St., 226-3683

Pet Central, 247 West 23rd St., 646-486-1662

Pet Club, 244 E. 13th St., 475-5244

Pet Garden, 239 E. Fifth St., 533-5304

Pet Market, 1570 2nd Ave., 879-3888

Pet Market, 210 W. 72nd St., 799-4200

Pet Necessities, 236 E. 75th St., 988-0769

Pet Palace, 109 W. 10th St., 727-0525

Pet Party, 1431 York Ave., 717-2524

Pet Stop, 564 Columbus Ave., 580-2400

Pet Superette, 187 E. 93rd St., 534-1732

Pet Supplies, 1931 Madison Ave., 876-4199

Petco, 860 Broadway, 358-0692

Petco, 560 Second Ave., 779-4550

Petco, 147-149 E. 86th St., 831-8001

Peters Emporium For Pets, 1449 2nd Ave., 772-3647

Petland Discounts, 1954 3rd Ave., 987-6714

Petland Discounts, 85 Delancey St., 477-6293

Petland Discounts, 7 E. 14th St., 675-4102

Petland Discounts, 304 E. 86th St., 472-1655

Petland Discounts, 132 Nassau St., 964-1821

Petland Discounts, 530 E. 14th St., 228-1363

Petland Discounts, 312 W. 23rd St., 366-0512

Petland Discounts, 389 Ave. of the Americas, 741-1913

Petland Discounts, 404 3rd Ave., 447-0739

Petland Discounts, 734 9th Ave., 459-9562

Petland Discounts, 976 2nd Ave., 755-7228

Petland Discounts, 137 W. 72nd St., 875-9785

Petland Discounts, 2708 Broadway, 222-8851

Petography, 25 Central Park West, 245-0914

Pets Kitchen, 116 Christopher St., 242-3924

Pets On Lex, 1271 Lexington Ave., 426-0766

Shaggy Dog, 400 E. 88th St # 400, 289-0198

Sherpa's Pet Trading Co, 135 E. 55th St. Fl # 6, 838-9837

Spoiled Brats, 340 W. 49th St., 459-1615

Sutton Dog Parlour, 311 E. 60th St., 355-2850

The Pet Parade, 144 W. 19th St., 645-5345

Uptown Pets, 4232 Broadway, 740-4457

Urban Pets, 18 Christopher St., 727-0448

Video Couch & Pet Supplies, 715 2nd Ave., 972-1076

Whiskers Holistic Pet Care, 235 E. 9th St., 979-2532

Zitomer Z-Spot, 965 Madison Ave., 472-4960

Pet Taxis

Paw Mobile, 594-7087

Pet Chauffeur, 152 E. 35th St., #3G, 696-9744

Pet Taxi, 227 E. 56th St., 755-1757

Petex, 480 Second Ave., 685-1173

Shelters & Rescue Groups

ASPCA, 424 E. 92nd St., 876-7700

Bide-A-Wee, 410 E. 38th St., 532-4455

Center for Animal Care and Control, 326 E. 110th St., 722-3620

Humane Society Of New York, 306 E. 59th St., 752-4840

I Love Animals—Animal Aid, 120 E. 73rd St., 628-7100

New Yorkers For Companion Animals, 427-8273

Sitters & Walkers

A Buddy For Hire, 697-0507
Aid Girl, 9 Post Ave., 544-0534
All Creatures Great And Small, 241 Central Park West, 580-6030
Animal Associates, 580-2065
BBZee Pet Care, 67 West 69th St., 496-6044
Biscuits & Bath Doggie Gym, 1535 First Ave., 794-3600
Biscuits & Bath Doggy Village, 227 E. 44th St., 692-2323
Cat Sitting & Dog Walking Service, 500 E. 77th St # 2019, 734-0052
Central Bark West, 917-856-7955
City Pet Care, 80 Central Park W, 874-8272
Dog Wash, 177 Macdougal St., 673-3290
Dog's Best Friend, 161 West 86th St., 724-4901
Doggie Kitty Nanny, 516 8th Ave., 249-0877
Dr. Larrys Animal Service, 544 W. 113th St., 222-9732
Family Affair Pet Care, 446 E. 86th St., 249-0839
Fur Fin & Feather Pet Service, 323 E. 9th St., 529-0658
Grossman Katia , 500 E. 77th St., 734-0052
Hoffmann Liz, 247 W. 76 St., 873-6199
K-9 Club, 225 E. 96th St., 410-3764
Mensch Petsitters, 831-6137
Michelle's Pied Piper Pet Services, 410 W. 46th St., 245-4704
New York Dog Spa & Hotel, 145 W. 18th St., 243-1199
Pampered Pets, 677-6965
Pampered Pets, 150 E. 69th St., 772-2181
Paws Inn, 370 W. 35th St., 736-7297
Pet Aways, 420-7638
Pet Care Network, 201 W. 85th St., 580-6004
Pet Get-Away, 1623 3rd Ave., 534-7924
Pet Mates, 414-5158
Pet Trekkers, 145 E. 35th St., 481-4111
Pets Please, 135 W. 79th St., 873-2724
Puddles Pet Service, 410-7338
Puppy Paths, 1636 3rd Ave., 736-7400
Purrfect Cat Care, 170 W. End Ave., 362-2175
Stichinsky, Barbara 503 E. 78th St., 861-3413
The Dog House, 665-4320
Three Dog Knight, 51 W. 88th St., 724-1379
Two Dogs & A Goat, 326 E. 34th St., 631-1157
Upper East Side Dog Walking Service, 311 E. 109 St., 860-3749
Urban Animal, 969-8506
Vancouver Dog Training, 393 W. End Ave., # 6F, 877-7116
Village Pet Care, 800-426-9439
Wagging Tail Doggie Day Care, 354 Greenwich St., 285-4900
Wagz!, 796 9th Ave.,. #2, 917-701-6373

Walkee Doggie, 69 Leonard St., # 5B, 925-8100

Whiskers Walkabout, 325 W. 16th St., 989-5073

Veterinarians, Vet Clinics & Animal Hospitals

145th St. Animal Hospital, 454 W. 145th St., 234-3489

A House Call Service, 349 E. 49th St., 838-2569

ABC Animal Hospital, 49 Ave. B, 358-0785

Abingdon Square Veterinary Clinic, 107 Greenwich Ave., 242-9169

All Pets Veterinarian, 1737 2nd Ave., 831-0410

Alternative Veterinary Care, 219 W. 79th St., 787-1993

Animal Clinic Of New York, 1623 1st Ave., 628-5580

Animal Emergency Clinic, 240 E. 80th St., 988-1000

Animal General, 140 W. 67th St., 712-9600

Animal General, 558 Columbus Ave., 501-9600

Animal Hospital Of Chelsea, 164 W. 21st St., 243-3020

Animal Medical Center, 510 E. 62nd St., 838-8100

Ansonia Veterinary Center, 207 W. 75th St., 496-2100

Ashley, Nancey DVM, 220 W. 83rd St., 580-1800

ASPCA Bergh Memorial Hospital, 424 E. 92nd St., 876-7700

Attas Amy DVM, 101 W. 57th St #14B, 581-PETS

Balch, David DVM, 801 W. 187th St., 923-1991

Barnett, Lisa DVM, 227 E. 84th St., 249-8802

Berger, Sherri DVM, 240 E. 80th St., 988-1000

Berman, Lewis DVM, 52 E. 64th St.

Bernstein, Marcella DVM, 227 E. 84th St., 249-8802

Bide-A-Wee Clinic, 410 E. 38th St., 532-5884

Bilsky, Jeremy DVM, 348 E. 9th St., 477-2688

Bodkin, Katherine DVM, 220 W. 83rd St., 580-1800

Brasher, April DVM, 220 W. 83rd St., 580-1800

Burya, Erin DVM, 348 E. 9th St., 477-2688

Cabrini Veterinary Hospital, 839 W. 181st St., 740-3819

Cantor, Karen DVM, 220 W. 83rd St., 580-1800

Carnegie Hill Veterinarians, 201 E. 89th St., 369-5665

Cat Practice, 137 5th Ave., Fl # 2, 677-1401

Cathedral Dog & Cat Hospital, 250 W. 108th St., 864-3631

Cavanagh, Paul G DVM, 220 W. 83rd St., 580-1800

Center For Veterinary Care, 236 E. 75th St., 734-7480

Chelsea Dog & Cat Hospital, 303 W. 20th St., 929-6963

Clinton Veterinary Center, 357 W. 52nd St., 333-5548

Cohen, Howard A DVM, 236 E. 75th St., 734-7480

Cole Animal Clinic, 230 W. 97th St # 1d, 222-6664

Columbia Animal Hospital, 229 W. 101st St., 864-1144

Cotter, Patrick M DVM, 310 E. 65th St # 1c, 396-3020

Country Vets, 430 E. 75th St., 535-3250

Culbert, Laura DVM, 240 E. 80th St., 988-1000

Cutler, Sarah J DVM, 52 E. 64th St Fl # 1, 832-8417

De Lorenzo, Dianne M DVM, 23 E. 9th St., 10003, 674-1670

Dillon, Christopher DVM, 220 W. 83rd St., 580-1800

Downtown Veterinary Clinic, 148 9th Ave., 463-8705

Downtown Veterinary House Call, 295 Greenwich St., 619-9119

East Bay Animal Clinic, 612 2nd Ave., 481-7999

East Harlem Veterinary Clinic, 2296 1st Ave., 348-8314

East Side Animal Hospital, 321 E. 52nd St., 751-5176

East Village Veterinarian, 241 Eldridge St. # 241, 674-8640

Fallek, Marcie DVM, 247 W. 11th St., 741-2459

Feibusch, Karen DVM, 37 E. 19th St., 477-4080

Feldman, Lori H DVM, 52 E. 64th St., Fl # 1, 832-8417

Ficarra, Janet, 295 Greenwich St., 855-5850

Fried, Richard DVM, 140 W. 67th St., 712-9600

Fund For Animals Have a Heat Clinic, 355 W. 52nd St., 977-6877

Gagliardi, John DVM, 240 E. 80th St., 988-1000

Gibson, Mark DVM, 240 W. 10th St., 718-832-3988

Gotham Animal Clinic, 329 2nd Ave., 777-7299

Gramercy Park Animal Hospital, 37 E. 19th St., 477-4080

Greene, Richard W. DVM, 236 E. 75th St., 734-7480

Gross, Stephen DVM, 1623 1st Ave., 509-4166

Haberkorn, R. DVM, 240 E. 80th St., 988-1000

Halligan, Bridget DVM, 203 10th Ave., 645-2767

Happy Tails Veterinary Service, 333 E. 66th St # 10n, 794-4993

Hayre, Michael DVM, 227 E. 84th St Fl # 1, 249-8802

Heart Of Chelsea Animal Hospital, 257 W. 18th St., 924-6116

Higashimura, Kayo DVM, 240 E. 80th St., 988-1000

Ho, Edwina DVM, 37 E. 19th St., 477-4080

Home Veterinary Service, 340 E. 80th St., 421-0553

Howell, Paul DVM, 140 W. 67th St., 712-9600

Humane Society of NY, 306 E. 59th St., 752-4840

Joseph, Richard DVM, 220 W. 83rd St., 580-1800

Kalvig, Barbara DVM, 321 E. 52nd St., 751-5176

Kantor, Amy DVM, 140 W. 67th St., 712-9600

Kantor, Amy DVM, 558 Columbus Ave., 501-9600

Kasanofsky, Steven DVM, 250 W. 100th St., 865-2224

Keating, Mary Lee, 1435 Lexington Ave., 876-8253

Keatings Animal Hospital, 1435 Lexington Ave., 876-8253

Kent, Susanne M DVM, 52 E. 64th St. Fl # 1, 832-8417

Korin, George M DVM, 349 E. 49th St., 838-2569

Kosovsky, Jane DVM, 140 W. 67th St., 712-9600

Kosovsky, Jane DVM, 558 Columbus Ave., 501-9600

Kosovsky, Jane DVM, 220 W. 83rd St., 580-1800

Lenox Hill Veterinarians, 204 E. 76th St., 879-1320

Lexington Veterinary Group, 133 E. 39th St., 889-7778

Lexington Veterinary Group, 145 W. 18th St., 243-1199

Lobasso, Thomas DVM, 37 E. 19th St., 477-4080

Lowenstein, Bruce DVM, 220 W. 83rd St., 580-1800

Mac Lean, Laura DVM, 348 E. 9th St., 477-2688

Manhattan Veterinary Group, 240 E. 80th St., 988-1000

Marquis Veterinary, 1676 1st Ave., # Fl1, 369-3962

Mc Caw, Michael C DVM, 705 Washington St., 633-7400

Mendelsohn, Gary A DVM, 236 E. 75th St., 734-7480

Mercy Veterinary Hospital, 134 E. 82nd St., 861-5601

Midtown Animal Hospital, 256 E. 33rd St., 683-0309

Morris, Julie B DVM, 52 E. 64th St., 832-8417

Moscovich, O. DVM, 241 Eldridge St., 674-8640

Mullings, Suzanne J DVM, 705 Washington St., 633-7400

Murray Hill Animal Hospital, 47 E. 30th St., 685-2857

Nenner, Jacqueline DVM, 321 E. 52nd St., 751-5176

New York Dog Spa & Hotel, 145 W. 18th St., 243-1199

New York Veterinary Hospital, 150 E. 74th St., 717-7222

Park East Animal Hospital, 52 E. 64th St Fl # 1, 832-8417

Pet Trekkers, 145 E. 35th St., 481-4111

Peterson, Dennis C. DVM, 2296 1st Ave., 348-8314

Petmenders Animal Hospital, 158 Duane St., 406-0970

Pigman, Carole DVM, 204 E. 76th St., 879-1320

Pirotin, Debra DVM, 1533 1st Ave., 879-0700

Post, Gerald S. DVM, 140 W. 67th St., 712-9600

Post, Gerald S. DVM, 558 Columbus Ave., 501-9600

Ramos, Rosado Javier S. DVM, 801 W. 187th St., 923-1991

Ravitz, Suzane DVM, 403 E. 37th St., 213-9885

Rhein, Alison G. DVM, 5 Lispenard St., 925-6100

Rivergate Veterinary Clinic, 403 E. 37th St., 213-9885

Rivergate Veterinary Clinic, 1535 1st Ave., 249-6080

Riverside Animal Clinic, 801 W. 187th St., 923-1991

Riverside Animal Hospital, 250 W. 100th St., 865-2224

Riverside Veterinary Group, 219 W. 79th St., 787-1993

Robbins, Laura J. DVM, 236 E. 75th St., 734-7480

Rocha, Timothy DVM, 240 E. 80th St., 988-1000

Rosenthal, Kim DVM, 207 W. 75th St., 501-9450

Rubin, Dale DVM, 37 E. 19th St., 477-4080

Schlereth, David DVM, 430 E. 75th St., 535-3250

Shimel, Kevin DVM, 137 5th Ave., Fl # 2, 677-1401

Soho-Tribeca Animal Hospital, 5 Lispenard St., 925-6100

Solomon, Gene A. DVM, 236 E. 75th St., 734-7480

St Marks Veterinary Hospital, 348 E. 9th St., 477-2688

Stein, Lauren DVM, 348 E. 9th St., 477-2688

Stern, Irving DVM, 8 W. 86th St., 362-2141

Symphony Veterinary Center: Rebecca Campbell, D.V.M, 698 Amsterdam Ave., 866-8000

Tehrani, Joy DVM, 164 W. 21st St., 243-3020

Tennenbaum, June DVM, 321 E. 52nd St., 751-5176

Tierney, Frederick DVM, 310 E. 65th St., 988-9390

University Animal Hospital, 354 E. 66th St., 288-8884

Veterinary House Call Service, 886 10th Ave., 581-5720

Veterinary Medical Association of New York City, 331 W. 57th St # 293, 246-0057

Vet-Med Impex, 47 E. 30th St., 684-3824

Village Veterinarian, 204 E. 10th St., 979-9870

VIP Veterinary, 16 Christopher St., 691-9270

Washington Heights Animal Hospital, 2414 Amsterdam Ave., 927-6070

Washington Square Animal Hospital, 23 E. 9th St., 674-1670

West Chelsea Veterinary Hospital, 203 10th Ave., 645-2767

West Parc Veterinary Clinic,
8 W. 86th St., 362-9100

West Village Veterinary Hospital,
705 Washington St., 633-7400

Westside Animal Hospital,
733 9th Ave., 247-8600

Westside Veterinary Center,
220 W. 83rd St., 580-1800

Wilbourn, Carole DVM,
220 W. 83rd St., 580-1800

Winters, Tracy DVM,
203 10th Ave., 645-2767

Yorkville Animal Hospital,
227 E. 84th St., 249-8802

Zausner, Gail DVM,
204 E. 76th St., 879-1320

BROOKLYN

Boarding & DayCare

Dog Abby Daycare,
60 Metropolitan Ave., 718-387-7767

Dog and Company,
North 11th St., 718-302-3955

Puppy Paradise,
2084 Flatbush Ave., 718-258-2342

Woofs 'n Whiskers,
59 Summit St., 718-237-0298

Groomers

A Tailored Pet,
89 Pineapple Walk, 718-875-7387

Animal Kind Veterinary Hospital, 365 7th Ave., 718-832-3899

Animal Massage Center,
44 Remsen St., 718-694-9030

Bed Stuy Animal Spa,
413 Tompkins Ave., 718-574-4870

Billy & Tommy's Doggie Salon, 109 Conklin Ave., 718-272-3611

Bonnie's Classy Canines,
9106 Flatlands Ave., 718-257-9283

BQE Pet Food Exchange,
253 Wythe Ave., 718-486-7489

Chere's Pet Salon,
410 7th Ave., 718-499-9197

Dapper Dawg, 2270 Bath Ave., 718-372-9083

Dyker Dog Salon, 7618 13th Ave., 718-680-3600

Gentle Touch Dog Grooming,
3415 Ave., S, 718-998-5474

Gloria's Dog Beauty Salon,
2192 Flatbush Ave., 718-253-7338

Gloria's Dog Beauty Salon Too, 2216 65th St., 718-837-8034

Groom Room, 5005 Ave., N, 718-258-4678

Happy Tails, 35 N Henry St., 718-383-2590

Heavenly Pets Grooming Salon, 182 Ave. S, 718-627-5816

House Of Pets, 8 Neptune Ave., 718-646-2622

J & K Dog Grooming, 1907 W. 9th St., 718-373-5646

Let's Pet, 402 Henry St., 718-797-9289

Love On A Leash,
2709 Coney Island Ave., 718-934-5550

Margaret's Dog Grooming,
6702 20th Ave., # B, 718-837-1887

Mobile Grooming, 2106 81st St., 718-837-6600

Olga & Irina Grooming Store,
118 Ditmas Ave., 718-435-8921

Park Slope Pet Salon, 453 7th Ave., 718-768-3617

Patty's Grooming Shop, 133 Ave. S, 718-996-8680

Paws N Claws, 57 Bay Ridge Ave., 718-836-8345

Paws R Us, 719 86th St., 718-745-9797

Penny's Poodle Parlor, 2178 64th St., 718-259-4177

Perfect Paws, 226 Atlantic Ave., # A, 718-852-6200

Personality Pup, 276 73rd St., 718-745-3640

Pet Hide-A-Way, 6205 11th Ave., 718-256-6521

Pet Obsession, 2196 Flatbush Ave., 718-338-1208

Pet Parade, 718 Ave. U, 718-336-6635

Pick O The Litter, 7120 Fort Hamilton Parkway, 718-836-0062

Polina's Grooming & Supplies, 9718 3rd Ave., 718-921-7366

Puppy Paradise, 2082 Flatbush Ave., 718-252-7877

Shiral's Show Dog, 953 Newkirk Ave., 718-435-3287

Viva La Pooch Pet Salon, 7225 New Utrecht Ave., 718-234-7695

White Poodle Image, 102 W. End Ave., 718-648-4348

Woofs 'n Whiskers, 59 Summit St., 718-237-0298

Obedience Trainers

American Canine Security, 100 Emerson Place, 718-783-7700

Animal Behavior Consultants, 102 Canton Court, 718-891-4200

Canine Counseling, 440 Lenox Rd., 718-693-3839

Carr's Canine Training Service, 1835 Harina St., 718-376-7297

Dingo Girl Dog Training, 359 Metropolitan Ave., 718-599-2625

Empire of the Dog, 12 A Catherine St., 917-723-5233

Happy Tails Family Dog Training, 150 Prospect Park West #1E, 718-788-3898

Intelligent K-9, 1110 Caton Ave., 718-941-0515

Jo-Tan Obedience Training, 2196 Flatbush Ave., 718-338-1208

K-9 Control, 4766 Bedford Ave., Brooklyn, 718-769-7278

K-9 Powerhouse Kennels, 313 Butler St # A, Brooklyn, 718-694-0600

Laughing Dog Training & Service, 251 Smith St., 718-625-8135

Majestic Securities & Guard, 1705 Ralph Ave., 718-968-2500

MetroDog, 155 Nelson St., 718-246-0855

Pet Hide-A-Way, 6205 11th Ave., 718-256-6521

Ronnie's School For Dogs, 346 39th St., 718-965-4109

The Educated Puppy & Dogs, Too, 571 Ninth St., 718-788-3602

Tyril Frith, 718-252-8501

Pet Cemeteries, Crematoriums & Funeral Homes

Pet Crematory Agency, 1724 Bath Ave., 718-234-3653

All Pets Go To Heaven, 236 Carroll St., 718-875-7877

Pet Supply Stores

A Grand Little Pet Shop, 479 Grand St., 718-218-7745

A Pet Shop, 7407 5th Ave., 718-238-3777

A World Of Pets, 538 86th St., 718-238-7387

Acme Pet Food, 628 Vanderbilt Ave., 718-789-8062

Al's Aquarium, 1504 Nostrand Ave., 718-462-2848

All For Paws, 216 Prospect Park West 718-788-7052

Animal Angels Pet Food Delivery, 488 President St., 718-625-8365

Animal Fare, 153 Prospect Park SW, 718-853-5664

Animal Krackers, 480 Myrtle Ave., 718-230-8561

Animal Pantry, 697 86th St., 718-680-2220

Atlantic Pets & Supplies, 2999 Atlantic Ave., 718-827-0154

Beastly Bite, 140 Court St., 718-522-5133

Bed Stuy Animal Spa, 413 Tompkins Ave., 718-574-4870

Bedford Pet Shop, 199 Bedford Ave., 718-387-6606

BQE Pet Food Exchange, 253 Wythe Ave., 718-486-7489

Carroll Hill Pet Supplies, 577 Henry St., 718-522-5972

Center For Animal Care & Control, 2336 Linden Blvd., 718-272-7200

Ciro's Pet Shop, 1729 Bath Ave., 718-837-2583

Dog Delight, 6215 18th Ave., 718-837-5118

Dog Delight, 300 Kings Highway, 718-339-7800

Dog Delight, 756 3rd Ave., 718-788-7970

Dog Delight, 8510 21st Ave., 718-714-0588

Doggie Bag, 321 Graham Ave., 718-218-7359

Duke's Pet Food & Supplies, 1501 Newkirk Ave., 718-941-4563

Dyker Dog Salon, 7618 13th Ave., 718-680-3600

Four & A Tail, 453 4th St., 718-832-2717

Gloria's Dog Beauty Salon, 2192 Flatbush Ave., 718-253-7338

Gloria's Dog Beauty Salon Too, 2216 65th St., 718-837-8034

Grand St. Pet Shop, 631 Grand St., 718-388-5337

Groom Room, 5005 Ave. N, 718-258-4678

Happy Tails, 35 N Henry St., 718-383-2590

Heavenly Pets Grooming Salon, 182 Ave. S, 718-627-5816

House Of Pets, 8 Neptune Ave., 718-646-2622

International Pet Center, 4766 Bedford Ave., 718-934-3382

J G's Quality Kennels, 2434 Stillwell Ave., 718-449-7944

Jormora Industries, 3052 Fulton St., 718-647-3609

Klassy Kats, 473 Hemlock St., 718-235-7387

Let's Pet, 402 Henry St., 718-797-9289

Margaret's Dog Grooming, 6702 20th Ave., # B, 718-837-1887

Marine Systems, 4116 10th Ave., 718-437-3232

Metro Pet Plus, 161 Myrtle Ave., 718-855-5855

Mothers Pet Food, 370 7th Ave., 718-788-8688

My Best Friend Also, 5908 5th Ave., 718-439-4848

Myrtle Pets, 642 Myrtle Ave., 718-783-6298

Brooklyn Pet Supplies, 983 63rd St., 718-680-0176

One Stop Pet Shop, 161 North Seventh St., 718-218-7513

P C Ocean Corp, 2539 Ocean Ave., 718-648-1655

Penny's Poodle Parlor, 2178 64th St., 718-259-4177

Perfect Paws, 226 Atlantic Ave., # A, 718-852-6200

Pet City, 122 Graham Ave., 718-963-4030

Pet Essentials, 1623 W. 9th St., 718-266-3578

Pet Express, 1611 Sheepshead Bay Rd., 718-615-1562

Pet Foods Plus, 495 Kings Highway, 718-375-1110

Pet Hide-A-Way, 6205 11th Ave., 718-256-6521

Pet Obsession, 2196 Flatbush Ave., 718-338-1208

Pet Parade, 718 Ave. U, 718-336-6635

Pet Paradise, 295 Flatbush Ave., 718-783-1856

Pet Slope, 814 Union St., 718-622-8554

Pet Treats, 370 Court St., 718-243-1919

Pet Warehouse 3, 1101 Liberty Ave., 718-348-8323

Pet's Emporium, 105 Montague St., 718-624-2533

Pete's Pet Supplies, 9603 Glenwood Rd., 718-257-1776

Petland Discount, 846 Manhattan Ave., 718-349-8370

Petland Discount, 968 Flatbush Ave., 718-284-8806

Petland Discounts, 72 Willoughby St., 718-834-0769

Petland Discounts, 6608 18th Ave., 718-837-8959

Petland Discounts, 8403 5th Ave., 718-745-7673

Petland Discounts, 2205 86th St., 718-837-7780

Petland Discounts, 717 Brighton Beach Ave., 718-891-3955

Petland Discounts, 2046 Rockaway Parkway, 718-241-2787

Petland Discounts, 510 5th Ave., 718-369-1786

Petland Discounts, 5015 5th Ave., 718-871-7699

Petland Discounts, 1618 Kings Highway, 718-376-0157

Petland Discounts, 5700 Ave. U, 718-951-8571

Pets For Less, 490 Court St., 718-222-9132

Pet Obsession, 2196 Flatbush Ave., 718-338-1208

Pets Playground, 2833 Atlantic Ave., 718-277-7387

Pick O The Litter, 7120 Fort Hamilton Parkway, 718-836-0062

Puppy City, 2539 Ocean Ave., 718-332-3400

Puppy Paradise, 2082 Flatbush Ave., 718-252-7877

Quality Canines, 2434 Stillwell Ave., 718-946-7014

Smith St. Pet Food, 118 Smith St., 718-625-9300

V C Pet, 284 9th St # A, 718-499-9565

Vinney's Pet Shop, 272 Bay Ridge Ave., 718-745-9074

Wet Pets, 15 Putnam Ave., 718-789-7800

White Poodle Image, 102 W. End Ave., 718-648-4348

Woodhulls Pet Supplies, 304 Ellery St., 718-302-1677

Shelters & Rescue Groups

Center For Animal Care and Control, 2336 Linden Blvd., 718-272-7200

Brooklyn Animal Resource Coalition, 253 Wythe Ave., 718-486-7489

Mighty Mutts, P.O. Box 140139, 718-946-1074

Sitters & Walkers

A Personal Touch Pet Sitters, 2766 E. 16th St., 718-368-1750

A Tailored Pet, 89 Pineapple Walk, 718-875-7387

Critter Sitters, 718-768-0372

Four Paws Dog Walking, 718-852-6359

K-9 Control, 4766 Bedford Ave., 718-769-7278

Tailwaggers, 718-834-5985

Urban Spot, 214 Sterling Place, 718-857-5424

Veterinarians, Vet Clinics & Animal Hospitals

9th St. Veterinary Clinic, 336 9th St., 718-965-3411

A House Call For Pets, 365 7th Ave., 718-832-3988

AAHA Animal Medicine Clinic, 9518 Ave. L, 718-444-5151

Abbey-Midwood Animal Hospital, 1909 Flatbush Ave., 718-338-9600

Abraham, Brian DVM, 3411 Ave. S, 718-382-9177

Animal Clinic, 8317 20th Ave., 718-372-6600

Animal Clinic of Bath Beach, 2125 Bath Ave., 718-373-5126

Animal Clinic of Bay Ridge, 689 86th St., 718-833-0700

Animal Clinic of Bensonhurst, 2249 65th St., 718-837-9711

Animal Clinic of Canarsie, 9605 Glenwood Rd., Brooklyn, 718-257-1010

Animal Clinic of Sunset Park, 5908 5th Ave., 718-492-9090

Animal Emergency Service, 2084 Flatbush Ave., 718-377-0330

Animal Hospital Of Brooklyn, 2270 Flatbush Ave., 718-258-0500

Animal Kind Veterinary Hospital, 365 7th Ave., 718-832-3899

Animal Medicine & Surgery Clinic, 2016 Bath Ave., 718-266-4000

Animal Medicine Clinic, 9518 Ave. L, 718-444-5151

Battiato, Frank V DVM, 7303 13th Ave., 718-621-1629

Bay Ridge Animal Hospital, 6803 5th Ave., 718-748-1047

Bay Veterinary Clinic, 2579 E. 17th St., 718-891-7811

Boccia, Carmine DVM, 3411 Ave. S, 718-382-9177

Bregman, Eric DVM, 1899 Coney Island Ave., 718-645-7666

Brooklyn Veterinary Emergency Service, 453 Bay Ridge Ave., 718-748-5180

Brooklyn Veterinary Group, 7624 New Utrecht Ave., 718-331-7775

Brooklyn Veterinary Group, 3411 Ave. S, 718-382-9177

Brooklyn Veterinary Hospital, 411 Vanderbilt Ave., 718-638-2276

Burns, Alan DVM, 411 Vanderbilt Ave., 718-638-2276

Canarsie Animal Hospital, 8423 Flatlands Ave., 718-444-8798

Castellano, Joann DVM, 2084 Flatbush Ave., 718-377-0330

Cobble Hill Animal Clinic, 173 Court St., 718-834-1800

Crown Heights Animal Clinic, 744 Nostrand Ave., 718-778-4265

Demmerle, Richard DVM, 6803 5th Ave., 718-748-1047

Doloroso, Lily DVM, 6803 5th Ave., 718-748-1047

Donchik, Peter J. DVM, 6803 5th Ave., 718-748-1047

Douglas, A.G. DVM, 1946 Bath Ave., 718-449-7800

Eisner, Barbara DVM, 233 Berry St., 718-387-0541

Felton, Elaine L. DVM, 897 Metropolitan Ave., 718-486-5634

Field, Philip DVM, 207 6th Ave., 718-789-7170

Fifth Ave. Veterinary Hospital, 9102 5th Ave., 718-748-1066

Foley, Robert DVM, 1899 Coney Island Ave., 718-645-7666

Fried, Derek DVM, 3411 Ave. S, 718-382-9177

Fuerst, David DVM, 3411 Ave. S, 718-382-9177

Gateway Animal Hospital, 1909 Flatbush Ave., 718-338-9600

Givan, Gerald DVM, 207 6th Ave., 718-789-7170

Grand Animal Clinic, 518 Grand St., 718-388-4746

Greenpoint Veterinary Clinic, 98 Norman Ave., 718-389-8866

Hallinger, C. DVM, 365 7th Ave., 718-832-3899

Heights Veterinary Hospital, 59 Hicks St., 718-625-7111

Horowitz, E. DVM, 689 86th St., 718-833-0700

Jacobson, Linda DVM, 291 Kings Highway, 718-376-8957

Jaffe, Kenneth DVM, 94 Ave. U, 718-373-0240

Kandl, J.F. DVM, 689 86th St., 718-833-0700

Kessler, Jeffrey DVM, 3411 Ave. S, 718-382-9177

Kings Bay Veterinary Hospital, 2560 Coney Island Ave., 718-339-0557

Kolbert, Steven DVM, 411 Vanderbilt Ave., 718-638-2276

Konstalid, S. DVM, 689 86th St., 718-833-0700

Krumenauer, J. DVM, 689 86th St., 718-833-0700

Lanarone, Pat DVM, 3411 Ave. S, 718-382-9177

Leiman, Daniel DVM, 233 Berry St., 718-387-0541

Maddon, Eric DVM, 105 Prospect Park West, 718-494-4497

Manhattan Beach Animal Clinic, 102 W. End Ave., 718-616-0964

Marine Park Animal Hospital, 3616 Quentin Rd., 718-382-8100

Marine Park Veterinary Group, 3411 Ave. S, 718-382-9177

Mateyak, Karen DVM, 365 7th Ave., 718-832-3899

Mid-Brook Animal Hospital, 1899 Coney Island Ave., 718-645-7666

Miyashiro, Linda DVM, 105 Prospect Park West, 718-768-6125

Mobile Veterinary Unit, 94 Ave. U, 718-373-0240

Narrows Animal Hospital, 9107 4th Ave., 718-238-5055

Norton, C. DVM, 59 Hicks St., 718-625-7111

Park Slope Animal Health Center, 250 Flatbush Ave., 718-230-5300

Parker, Tom DVM, 173 Court St., 718-832-8130

Pernice, Salvatore DVM, 3411 Ave. S, 718-382-9177

Pet Haven Animal Hospital, 290 McDonald Ave., 718-435-6900

Prospect Park Animal Clinic, 105 Prospect Park West, 718-768-6125

Ramos, Rosado Javier S. DVM, 5th Ave., 718-492-9090

Robert Composto DVM, 6803 5th Ave., 718-748-1047

Robinson, Donald DVM, 9518 Ave. L, 718-444-5151

Roffey, D. DVM, 689 86th St., 718-833-0700

Saint Francis Animal Hospital, 7303 13th Ave., 718-621-1629

Scandaglia, Frank DVM, 3411 Ave. S, 718-382-9177

Sheepshead Bay Veterinary Group, 2206 Ave. U, 718-368-1863

Sinha's Animal Clinic, 1946 Bath Ave., 718-449-7800

Sixth Ave. Animal Clinic, 207 6th Ave., 718-789-7170

Smith, Marsha DVM, 453 Bay Ridge Ave., 718-748-5180

Spiegel, H. DVM, 365 7th Ave., 718-832-3899

Star, Russ DVM, 3411 Ave. S, 718-382-9177

Tripodi, Lynn DVM, 365 7th Ave., 718-832-3899

Vent, George DVM, 9518 Ave. L, 718-444-5151

Veterinary Medical Center, 5010 Kings Highway, 718-338-1221

QUEENS

Boarding & DayCare

A Woodhaven Boarding Kennels, 7623 Jamaica Ave., 718-296-8244

Afternoon Groomer, 6167 Maspeth Ave., 718-416-0771

Animal Hospital Of Queens Boulevard, 13954 Queens Blvd., 718-291-0200

Animal Hospital—The Rockaways, 11410 Beach Channel Drive, 718-474-0500

Astoria Animal Center, 2564 Steinway St., 718-278-1084

Astoria Animal Hospital, 2127 21st Ave., 718-267-7140

Bayside Veterinary Center, 20418 46th Ave., 718-229-2460

Boarding Kennel Co, 5884 57th Rd., 718-416-2059

Carol's Ark, 2363 Steinway St., 718-278-4677

City Pet, 5612 Roosevelt Ave., 718-672-9722

Critter Care of Queens, 7131 Park Dr E, 718-263-3770

Dog & Cat Spay Clinic, 2022 College Point Blvd., 718-353-1522

Everglades Pet Shop, 8024 Northern Blvd., 718-639-0485

Feline Inn, 7025 83rd S, 718-894-4228

Lenny Ross Dog Training, 7039 57th Drive, 718-639-9002

Little Dog House, 2022 College Point Blvd., 718-939-2211

Mossland Kennels, 1429 128th St., 718-539-0520

Pet Doctor of Flushing, 2562 Francis Lewis Blvd., 718-886-6661

Queens Boarding Kennels, 18519 Hillside Ave., 718-526-7045

Vet Port, Bldg # 189, Cargo C, JFK Airport, 718-656-8295

Whitestone Animal Hospital, 14938 14th Ave., 718-767-3396

Whitestone Pet Grooming Center, 1249 150th St., 718-767-7445

Groomers

A Dog's Best Friend, 6278 Woodhaven Blvd., 718-335-0110

All Seasons Pet Grooming, 8768 Van Wyck Expressway, 718-526-5802

Alleycat Pet Supplies, 5916 Main St., 718-358-2761

Animal Hospital—The Rockaways, 11410 Beach Channel Drive, 718-474-0500

Anita's Dog Grooming, 4370 Kissena Blvd. # 5q, 718-631-1025

Astoria Animal Center, 2564 Steinway St., Queens, 718-278-1084

Astoria Animal Hospital, 2127 21st Ave., 718-267-7140

Bayside Zoo-Rama, 4017 Bell Blvd., 718-631-4669

Bob's Tropical Pet Center, 9110 Jamaica Ave., 718-441-3273

Canine Club, 4347 44th St., 718-729-0664

Carol's Ark, 2363 Steinway S, 718-278-4677

Chris & Roe's Dog House, 8409 Rockaway Blvd., 718-296-1690

Claws & Paws, 6909 Myrtle Ave., 718-366-7788

Dog & Cat Spay Clinic, 2022 College Point Blvd., 718-353-1522

Doggie Style, 7735 164th St., 718-591-3647

Grooming Gallery, 9408 Jamaica Ave., 718-849-5081

Happy Pawz, 102-30 Queens Blvd. 718-261-1175

Happy Pet Tails, 3645 Bell Blvd., 718-224-3150

Merrick Boulevard Animal Hospital, 11531 Merrick Blvd., 718-526-5328

Mobile Clipper Dog Grooming, 6128 65th St., 718-417-3051

Mon-Ami Dog Grooming, 15211 Northern Blvd., 718-358-0183

Moretti Deborah, 14008 Beech Ave., 718-961-1122

Mossland Kennels, 1429 128th St., 718-539-0520

My Best Friend Too, 9722 66th Ave., 718-897-7171

Pampered Poodle Palace, 4320 Broadway, 718-274-8255

Paul's Poodle Salon, 6512 Fresh Pond Rd., 718-366-2371

Personal Care Pet Grooming, 14616 Rockaway Blvd., 718-659-9216

Pet Gallery, 21519 39th Ave., 718-224-6580

Pet Menu, 19115 Northern Blvd., 718-939-4738

Pets-Erria, 7804 67th Drive, 718-894-5226

Poodle Emporium, 3080 51st St., 718-545-4644

Rainbow Pet Supplies, 6303 39th Ave., 718-426-0222

Shaggy Dog Inn, 145 Beach 116th St., 718-474-2880

Sophisticated Dog, 9234 Queens Blvd., 718-476-6866

Sterlings Discount Pet Supplies, 8266 Austin St., 718-849-2220

Teachers Pet School, 7333 Grand Ave., 718-446-1511

U S Pets, 3150 Steinway St., 718-545-7387

Whitestone Pet Grooming Center, 1249 150th St., 718-767-7445

Woodhaven Grooming, 7510 Jamaica Ave., 718-296-6646

Obedience Trainers

Academy Canine Education, 7563 185th St., 718-454-5800

Animal Behavior Center of New York, 8908 Eliot Ave., 718-205-8607

Lenny Ross Dog Training, 7039 57th Drive, 718-639-9002

Shear Delight Grooming, 3260 86th St., 718-458-3967

Pet Supply Stores

A OK Pet & Plant Supplies, 8602 117th St., 718-441-3004

Ace Pet Shop, 13517 Northern Blvd., 718-359-3336

Alleycat Pet Supplies, 15605 45th Ave., 718-661-9333

Aqua World Pet Shop, 11510 Liberty Ave., 718-323-2365

Astoria Animal Center, 2564 Steinway St., 718-278-1084

Bayside Zoo-Rama, 4017 Bell Blvd., 718-631-4669

Cameo Pet Shop, 11523 Jamaica Ave., 718-849-6678

Center For Animal Care and Control, 9229 Queens Blvd., 718-997-6330

Everglades Pet Shop, 8024 Northern Blvd., 718-639-0485

Flushing Aquarium & Pets, 4184 Main St., 718-539-7413

Grand Ave. Pet Center, 7315 Grand Ave., 718-476-2877

Happy Pet Tails, 3645 Bell Blvd., 718-224-3150

Home Of The Puppies, 14008 Beech Ave., 718-961-1122

Home Of The Puppies, 4355 Kissena Blvd., 718-359-8686

Horizon Pet Shop, 8820 37th Ave., 718-476-0394

House Of Fish & Pets, 16905 Jamaica Ave., 718-739-3090

International Pet Broker, 4355 Kissena Blvd., 718-359-3636

K-9 Caterers, 8202 Cooper Ave., 718-894-2416

L & A Aquarists, 1801 College Point Blvd., 718-463-4932

Lefferts Pet Caterers, 16026 84th St., 718-641-3346

Loving Pets, 21023 Jamaica Ave., 718-468-8826

Maspeth Pet Shop, 7111 Grand Ave., 718-429-9443

Mister B's Pet Depot, 2644 211th St., 718-423-0082

Mamas & Papas, 45-10 Parsons Blvd., 718-353-8698

Mon-Ami Dog Grooming, 15211 Northern Blvd., 718-358-0183

My Best Friend Too, 9722 66th Ave., 718-897-7171

Original Pet Deli, 8216 31st Ave., 718-565-6624

Pampered Poodle Palace, 4320 Broadway, 718-274-8255

Paul's Poodle Salon, 6512 Fresh Pond Rd., 718-366-2371

Pet Edibles, 25407 Northern Blvd., 718-229-8976

Pet Mart, 13720 Crossbay Blvd., 718-323-8933

Pet Menu, 19115 Northern Blvd., 718-939-4738

Pet Oasis, 24615 Jamaica Ave., 718-347-6463

Pet Stop Discounts, 2172 31st St., 718-545-8972

Petco, 15720 Cross Bay Blvd., 718-845-3331

Petland Discounts, 7417 Grand Ave., 718-779-4992

Petland Discounts, 9418 63rd Drive, 718-830-0957

Petland Discounts, 7044 Austin St., 718-268-1864

Petland Discounts, 6626 Metropolitan Ave., #19, 718-381-8021

Petland Discounts, 25915 Union Turnpike, 718-343-6755

Petland Discounts, 9108 Atlantic Ave., 718-843-3112

Petland Discounts, 11908 Liberty Ave., 718-845-5933

Petland Discounts, 17129 Hillside Ave., 718-657-7182

Petland Discounts, 3460 48th St., 718-937-9317

Petland Discounts, 7139 Kissena Blvd., 718-969-0588

Petland Discounts, 3028 Steinway St., 718-278-6921

Petland Discounts, 3720 Main St., 718-886-6061

Petland Discounts, 6144 Springfield Blvd., 718-224-5557

Petland Discounts, 3755 82nd St., 718-565-7171

Pets Asylum Grooming, 6302 Fresh Pond Rd., 718-456-7285

Pets N Stuff, 4505 162nd St., 718-359-3651

Pets Unlimited, 4510 46th St., 718-392-0395

Rainbow Pet Supplies, 6303 39th Ave., 718-426-0222

Shaggy Dog Inn, 145 Beach 116th St., 718-474-2880

Sterlings Discount Pet Supplies, 8266 Austin St., 718-849-2220

Tropical Island Pets, 4184 Main St., 718-539-7613

U S Pets, 3150 Steinway St., 718-545-7387

U S Pets, 3023 Stratton St., 718-888-0383

Wagging Tails, 105-19 Metropolitan Ave., 718-575-8245

Whitestone Pet Grooming Center, 1249 150th St., 718-767-7445

Pet Taxi

Animals Away, 2238 121st St. Rear, 718-461-5684

Shelters & Animal Rescue Groups

Animal Behavior Center of NY, 8908 Eliot Ave., 718-205-8607

Animal Haven, 35-22 Prince St., 718-886-3683

Center For Animal Care and Control, 9229 Queens Blvd., 718-997-6330

S.A.V.E., PO Box 570173, 718-358-0774

Sitters & Walkers

Canine Club, 4347 44th St., 718-729-0664

Critter Care Of Queens, 7131 Park Drive East, 718-263-3770

Reliable Pet Sitting & Grooming, 16242 96th St., 718-835-7487

Veterinarians, Vet Clinics & Animal Hospitals

A Animal Clinic of Queens, 6512 Fresh Pond Rd., 718-729-0664

Ackerman, Fred A. DVM, 7102 35th Ave., 718-639-5210

Alario, Anthony DVM, 11249 Queens Blvd., 718-261-1231

All Pets Veterinary Care, 3507 Ditmars Blvd., 718-956-7387

Alvarez, Louis DVM, 7102 35th Ave., 718-639-5210

Animal Clinic of Hillside Ave., 25918 Hillside Ave., 718-343-0810

Animal Clinic of Queens, 7846 Metropolitan Ave., 718-821-0100

Animal Clinic of Woodhaven, 7623 Jamaica Ave., 718-296-0500

Animal Clinic of Long Island City, 3304 36th Ave., 718-729-1495

Animal Hospital of Queens Boulevard, 13954 Queens Blvd., 718-291-0200

Animal Hospital—The Rockaways, 11410 Beach Channel Drive, 718-474-0500

Animal House Calls of Queens, 1 Bay Club Drive # 19j, 718-631-1396

Animal Medicine & Surgery, 4741 Little Neck Parkway, 11362, 718-423-5038

Antelyes Animal Hospital, 6209 Fresh Pond Rd., 11379, 718-386-0655

Astoria Animal Hospital, 2564 Steinway St., 718-274-2867

Astoria Veterinary Group, 2354 Steinway St., 718-777-0100

Bayside Animal Clinic, 3643 Bell Blvd., 718-224-4451

Bayside Veterinary Center, 20418 46th Ave., 718-229-2460

Belle Harbor Animal Clinic, 457 Beach 129th St., 718-474-1010

Bellerose Animal Hospital, 24201 Jamaica Ave., 718-347-1057

Boulevard Animal Clinic, 11249 Queens Blvd., 718-261-1231

Brew, Patricia DVM, 24201 Jamaica Ave., 718-347-1057

Corona Heights Animal Health, 10601 Corona Ave., 18-592-2022

Corwin Animal Hospital, 13621 Hillside Ave., 718-526-1422

Crum, Alberta DVM, 24201 Jamaica Ave., 718-347-1057

Defeis, Frank J. DVM, 11249 Queens Blvd., 718-261-1231

Dinetz, Bruna M. DVM, 9212 Liberty Ave., 718-738-6666

Dinetz, Scott I. DVM, 19209 Union Turnpike, 718-776-1165

Dog & Cat Spay Clinic, 2022 College Point Blvd., 718-353-1522

Estates Animal Hospital, 18519 Hillside Ave., 718-297-5400

Ferber, Michael DVM, 21214 Northern Blvd., 718-423-9600

Flushing Veterinary Hospital, 4024 Murray St., 718-445-0410

Flushing Veterinary Medical Center, 4424 College Point Blvd., 718-886-4416

Fresh Meadows Liberty Clinic, 19209 Union Turnpike, 718-776-1165

Gapas, Emma DVM, 3507 Ditmars Blvd., 718-956-7387

Glendale Animal Clinic, 7333 Grand Ave., 718-417-6767

Hatzidimitriou, Peggy V DVM, 3304 36th Ave., 718-729-1495

Heights Veterinary Hospital, 7102 35th Ave., 718-639-5210

Howard Beach Animal Clinic, 16311 Crossbay Blvd., 718-848-6803

International Animal Clinic, 8904 Northern Blvd., 718-507-5600

Klemenger, Cathy DVM, 24201 Jamaica Ave., 718-347-1057

Laurelton Animal Clinic, 11334 228th St., 718-341-2555

Lawrence Animal Hospital, 7723 Queens Blvd., 718-458-0500

Lefferts Animal Hospital, 8637 Lefferts Blvd., 718-849-3000

Liberty Animal Clinic, 9212 Liberty Ave., 718-738-6666

Little Dog House, 2022 College Point Blvd., 718-939-2211

Maspeth Animal Hospital, 7410 Grand Ave., 718-639-9339

Merrick Blvd. Animal Hospital, 11531 Merrick Blvd., 718-526-5328

Mobile Veterinary Animal Clinic, 10506 Metropolitan Ave., 718-575-5152

Nachamie, Howard DVM, 10506 Metropolitan Ave., 718-575-5152

Nebel, Matthew DVM, 4024 Murray St., 718-445-0410

New Hyde Park Animal Hospital, 2562 Francis Lewis Blvd., 718-961-4491

North Shore Animal Hospital, 21214 Northern Blvd., 718-423-9600

Orobello, Angela DVM, 2562 Francis Lewis Blvd., 718-886-6661

Ozone Park Animal Clinic, 10730 Rockaway Blvd., 718-843-7878

Pet Doctor Of Flushing, 2562 Francis Lewis Blvd., 718-886-6661

Petcare Animal Clinic, 4373 156th St., 718-762-4747

Queens Animal Hospital, 5612 Roosevelt Ave., 718-672-9722

Queens Midway Animal Hospital, 7746 164th St., 718-591-9223

Queens Village Animal Hospital, 22240 Jamaica Ave., 718-464-1471

Rego Park Animal Hospital, 9709 64th Rd., 718-263-4558

Riehle, Henry A. DVM, 7102 35th Ave., 718-639-5210

Rockaway Animal Hospital, 1833 Cornaga Ave., 718-327-7878

Rosenblum, Ronald DVM, 21214 Northern Blvd., 718-423-9600

Ryan, Deirdre DVM, 11912 9th Ave., 718-939-8804

Sakal, Anthony DVM, 2354 Steinway St., 718-777-0100

Simon, Allan B. DVM, 11410 Beach Channel Drive, 718-474-0500

Soliman, Sameh DVM, 2022 College Point Blvd., 718-353-1522

Steinway Court Veterinarian, 3241 Steinway St., 718-728-2822

Sunnyside Animal Clinic, 4527 47th St., 718-472-4600

Trylon Vet Care, 9883 Queens Blvd., 718-275-1800

Veterinary Care Unlimited, 8409 Rockaway Blvd., 718-296-7700

Veterinary Emergency Group, 18711 Hillside Ave., 718-454-4141

Veterinary Health Center, 2222 154th St., 718-661-2020

Veterinary House Calls, 3556 79th St., 718-457-8657

Veterinary Medical & Surgical, 6615 Woodhaven Blvd., 718-897-8200

Vet-On-Call, 2930 155th St., 718-886-6282

Whitestone Animal Hospital, 14938 14th Ave., 718-767-3396

Yousry, Gamal DVM, 7723 Queens Blvd., 718-458-0500

STATEN ISLAND

Boarding & Daycare Centers

Country Estate Kennels, 4838 Arthur Kill Rd., 718-356-3933

Groomers

All Pets Animal Hospital, 277 Van Duzer St., 718-442-1117

Andrew's Dog Grooming, 4131 Hylan Blvd., 718-948-8611

Aunt Phyllis's Dog Grooming, 583 Midland Ave., 718-980-1757

Clip & Fluff Boutique, 129 Port Richmond Ave., 718-447-2304

Clippendales, 539 Port Richmond Ave., 718-448-2200

Country Estate Kennels, 4838 Arthur Kill Rd., 718-356-3933

Diane's Pet Palace, 885 Annadale Rd., 718-356-5500

Dog House, 28 Hancock St., 718-979-5858

Feed Rite Pet Food & Supplies, 947 Manor Rd., 718-698-7666

Forest Animal Hospital, 1050 Forest Ave., 718-442-4377

Gateway Animal Hospital, 4236 Hylan Blvd., 718-984-1000

Gay Paree Canine Grooming, 640 Willowbrook Rd., 718-273-5445

Groomingdale's, 1230 Bay St., 718-273-9800

Groomingdale's, 125 New Dorp Lane, 718-980-2600

Groomingdale's, 640 Willowbrook Rd., 718-698-1400

Hylan Animal Hospital, 2115 Hylan Blvd., 718-987-8600

Kit-N-Shampoodle, 325 Nelson Ave., 718-966-8512

Mary's Tender Touch Pet Salon, 140 Main St., 718-317-7751

Noah's Ark Pet Center, 356 Sharrotts Rd., 718-227-3943

Pet Express-Dog & Cat Food, 519 Broadway, 718-447-3059

Pet Unisex Grooming, 141 Seaview Ave., 718-979-3774

Pooch Salon, 4282 Victory Blvd., 718-761-1235

Pretty Paws Dog Grooming, 4401 Arthur Kill Rd., 718-356-4023

South Animal Hospital, 45 Page Ave., 718-370-1102

St Francis Grooming Grotto, 499 Jewett Ave., 718-981-1780

Veterinary Emergency Center, 1293 Clove Rd., 718-720-4211

Obedience Trainers

Clip & Fluff Boutique, 129 Port Richmond Ave., 718-447-2304

Clippendales, 539 Port Richmond Ave., 718-448-2200

Holistic Animal Consulting Center, 29 Lyman Ave., 718-720-5548

Pooch Salon, 4282 Victory Blvd., 718-761-1235

Staten Island Companion Dog, 1309 Travis Ave., # B, 718-761-8048

Vontrapp Dog Training, 32 Allen Place, 718-967-2490

Pet Cemeteries, Crematoriums & Funeral Homes

Richmond Valley Pet Crematory, 4913 Arthur Kill Rd., 718-966-6381

Pet Supplies

Andrew's Dog Grooming, 4131 Hylan Blvd., 718-948-8611

Animal Kingdom Pet Center, 3894 Richmond Ave., 718-227-9453

Animal Pantry, 1801 Hylan Blvd., 718-979-1657

Animal Pantry, 3237 Richmond Ave., 718-966-0040

Annandale Animal House, 885 Annadale Rd., 718-605-9247

Arcadia Pets Welcome-to-the-Jungle, 4371 Amboy Rd, 718-967-7387

Aunt Phyllis's Dog Grooming, 583 Midland Ave., 718-980-1757

C G Country Feeds, 733 Sharrotts Rd., 718-356-0220

Center For Animal Care and Control, 3139 Veterans Rd. West, 718-984-6643

Clip & Fluff Boutique, 129 Port Richmond Ave., 718-447-2304

Excelsior K9 Academy, 59 Cypress Loop, 718-967-1843

Feed Rite Pet Food & Supplies, 947 Manor Rd., 718-698-7666

Noah's Ark Pet Center, 356 Sharrotts Rd., 718-227-3943

Pet A Believe It, 155 New Dorp Lane, 718-351-3332

Pet Locker, 95 Page Ave., 718-967-6100

Pet Savers Adoption Center, 35 Page Ave., 718-227-1892

Pet Unisex Grooming, 141 Seaview Ave., 718-979-3774

Petco, 1756 Forest Ave., 718-370-8820

Petland Discounts, 1495 Forest Ave., 718-981-0849

Petland Discounts, 2600 Hylan Blvd., 718-351-7811

Petland Discounts, 2795 Richmond Ave., 718-983-1158

Pooch Salon, 4282 Victory Blvd., 718-761-1235

Pretty Paws Dog Grooming, 4401 Arthur Kill Rd., 718-356-4023

Soft Paws Pet Sitting Service, 9 Iroquois St., 718-980-7297

Shelters & Rescue Groups

Center for Animal Care and Control, 3139 Veterans Rd. West, 718-984-6643

Staten Island Council for Animal Welfare, PO Box 120125, 718-761-6678

Pet Savers Adoption Center, 35 Page Ave., 718-227-1892

Sitters & Walkers

KCC Pet Sitting, 70 Escanaba Ave., 718-317-1464

Soft Paws Pet Sitting Service, 9 Iroquois St., 718-980-7297

Veterinarians, Vet Clinics & Animal Hospitals

Abraham, Brian DVM, 3875 Victory Blvd., 718-370-0390

Affiliated Animal Health, 1230 Bay St., 718-442-4100

All Pets Animal Hospital, 277 Van Duzer St., 718-442-1117

Andrew's Dog Grooming, 4131 Hylan Blvd., 718-948-8611

Animal Hospital-Staten Island, 640 Willowbrook Rd., 718-494-0050

Annadale Veterinary Clinic, 889 Annadale Rd., 718-984-4440

Apex Animal Hospital, 1409 Richmond Ave., 718-370-0700

AQL Dog & Cat Clinic, 3939 Amboy Rd., 718-227-0792

Boulevard Veterinary Group, 2300 Hylan Blvd., 718-980-6491

Brigande, Steven T. DVM, 39 Retford Ave., 718-966-4547

Cavallaro, Theresa A. DVM, 125 New Dorp Lane, 718-980-2600

Clemente, Joy DVM, 2115 Hylan Blvd., 718-987-8600

De Baecke, Phil DVM, 125 New Dorp Lane, 718-980-2600

Dongan Hills Veterinary, 289 Dongan Hills Ave., 718-987-7777

Eskanzi, Noreen DVM, 1230 Bay St., 718-273-9800

Esposito, Lisa A. DVM, 4915 Arthur Kill Rd., 718-948-3331

Flaig, Kenton D. DVM, 4236 Hylan Blvd., 718-984-1000

Forest Animal Hospital, 1050 Forest Ave., 718-442-4377

Gateway Animal Hospital, 4236 Hylan Blvd., 718-984-1000

Gordon, Keith D. DVM, 277 Van Duzer St., 718-442-1117

Green, Lynda DVM, 280 Marsh Ave., 718-761-8431

Hylan Animal Hospital, 2115 Hylan Blvd., 718-987-8600

Island Bird Cat & Dog Vet Group, 943 Manor Rd., 718-370-9472

Joyce, Pamla DVM, 125 New Dorp Lane, 718-980-2600

Landesman, Mark DVM, 2115 Hylan Blvd., 718-987-8600

Lipitz, Stacey DVM, 640 Willowbrook Rd., 718-698-1400

Maccia, John DVM, 4915 Arthur Kill Rd., 718-948-3331

Malihan Animal Clinic, 2221 Forest Ave., 718-981-1855

Marcovici, Oded I. DVM, 45 Page Ave., 718-227-2160

Mastrangelo, Lynn DVM, 125 New Dorp Lane, 718-980-2600

Mattera, Michele DVM, 125 New Dorp Lane, 718-980-2600

Northside Animal Hospital, 773 Post Ave., 718-981-4445

Richmond Valley Animal Hospital, 4915 Arthur Kill Rd., 718-948-3331

Roccaro, Gregory DVM, 4236 Hylan Blvd., 718-984-1000

Rosebank Veterinary Practice, 1230 Bay St., 718-273-9800

Salemi, Mark J. DVM, 773 Post Ave., 718-981-4445

San Giorgio, J. DVM, 1293 Clove Rd.., 718-720-4211

South Animal Hospital, 125 New Dorp Lane, 718-370-1102

South Richmond Veterinary, 277 Nelson Ave., 718-227-1313

South Shore Veterinary Medical, 125 New Dorp Lane, 718-980-2600

Stapleton Animal Hospital, 97 Broad St., 718-727-3331

Staten Island Animal Hospital, 640 Willowbrook Rd., 718-698-1400

Staten Island Veterinary Group, 3875 Victory Blvd., 718-370-0390

Teacher Christopher DVM, 45 Page Ave., 718-227-2160

Tottenville Animal Hospital, 45 Page Ave., 718-227-2160

Veterinary Emergency Center, 1293 Clove Rd., 718-720-4211

Veterinary Service, 39 Retford Ave., 718-966-4547

Veterinary Surgical Associates, 1230 Bay St., 718-442-7220

Veterinary Surgical Associates, 45 Page Ave., 718-605-0600

Viado, Daniel DVM, 640 Willowbrook Rd., 718-698-1400

Victory Veterinary Practice, 4316 Victory Blvd., 718-983-1811

Well Care Veterinary Clinic, 280 Marsh Ave., 718-761-8431

Werner, Michelle I. DVM, 277 Van Duzer St., 718-442-1117

Wicinski, Joseph M. DVM, 4915 Arthur Kill Rd., 718-948-3331

Wolfe, Carol DVM, 125 New Dorp Lane, 718-980-2600

THE BRONX

Animal Hospitals/ Boarding & Day Care Centers

Concourse Pet Center, 2324 Grand Concourse, 718-733-9333

Tri-Boro Animal Hospital, 604 Grand Concourse, Bronx, 718-292-1770

We Kare Kennels, 4363 Bronx Blvd., 718-547-7166

Groomers

All Paws Grooming, 3639 Bruckner Blvd., 718-824-3927

Bruckner Pet Land, 2922 Bruckner Blvd., 718-597-7120

Concourse Pet Center, 2324 Grand Concourse, 718-733-9333

Fieldston Dogs, 3476 Bailey Ave., 718-796-4541

In The Dog House, 1755 Jarvis Ave., 718-828-1117

Kennedy Canine Center, 6087 Broadway, 718-432-0471

Pet Center Bronx, 4412 White Plains Rd., 718-325-5647

Pet Center of Throggs Neck, 3800 E. Tremont Ave., 718-822-7387

Pet Stop, 3605 Riverdale Ave., 718-549-5900

Pets Plus Plants Ltd, 3197 Bainbridge Ave., 718-655-4054

Professional Grooming, 2561 Briggs Ave., 718-562-1545

Whiskers Pet Grooming & Supplies, 781 Van Nest Ave., 718-597-8844

Obedience Trainers

A Dog's World, 439 Morris Park Ave., 718-828-2700

Fieldston Dogs, 3476 Bailey Ave., 718-796-4541

Highlander Academy of Dog Training, 1956 Bronxdale Ave., 718-792-9421

Kennedy Canine Center, 6087 Broadway, 718-432-0471

New York Canine Service, 2040 Bruckner Blvd. #15M, 718-824-4279

Pet Supply Stores

A & V Nature's Pet Shop, 891 E. Tremont Ave., 718-328-7188

All Paws Grooming, 3639 Bruckner Blvd., 718-824-3927

Animal Feeds, 3255 Park Ave., 718-293-7750

Bronx Zoo Rama, 2566 E. Tremont Ave., 718-430-0909

Bruckner Pet Land, 2922 Bruckner Blvd., 718-597-7120

Canine Fencing Co, 3135 Godwin Terrace #1B, 718-548-2393

Center For Animal Care and Control, 464 E. Fordham Rd., 718-733-0743

Cevone's Dog House, 100 Alcott Place, 718-862-1127

China Pet Shop, 146 E. 170th St., 718-992-6888

China Pet Shop, 217 E. Tremont Ave., 718-716-7145

Christy's Pet Palace, 1011 Ogden Ave., 718-992-0155

Concourse Pet Center, 2324 Grand Concourse, 718-733-9333

Cross Bronx Pet Shop, 2064 Cross Bronx Expressway, 718-597-5652

Dave's Pet Shop Store, 3706 3rd Ave., 718-538-8076

Dave's World Pet Shop, 54 W. Kingsbridge Rd., 718-561-1155

Dave's World Pet Shop, 2914 3rd Ave., 718-585-5631

E & N Pet Paradise Shop, 289 E. Gun Hill Rd., 718-881-2870

Fieldston Pets, 3476 Bailey Ave., 718-796-4541

Fordham Pet City, 319 E. Fordham Rd., 718-295-3481

J & I Dog Grooming, 186 Mcclellan St., 718-588-7910

J & J Pet Shop, 715 E. Tremont Ave., 718-583-3350

Kennedy Canine Center, 6087 Broadway, 718-432-0471

Mad Dog Pet & Pet Supplies, 242 E. 167th St., 718-588-6055

Pet Center Bronx, 4412 White Plains Rd., 718-325-5647

Pet Center of Throggs Neck, 3800 E. Tremont Ave., 718-822-7387

Pet City, 108 E. Burnside Ave., 718-731-5787

Pet City, 1609 Westchester Ave., 718-378-8825

Pet City, 1764 Westchester Ave., 718-792-5876

Pet Island, 387 E. 138th St., 718-402-7457

Pet Master, 2212 Westchester Ave., 718-597-7387

Pet O Rama, 5705 Mosholu Ave., 718-432-6000

Pet Shop, 653 Elton Ave., 718-402-7279

Pet Warehouse II, 1535 Westchester Ave., 718-861-1252

Petland Discounts, 150 E. 188th St., 718-364-1948

Petland Discounts, 2188 Bartow Ave., 718-379-8385

Petland Discounts, 25 Westchester Square, 718-239-0250

Petland Discounts, 2175 White Plains Rd., 718-792-9408

Petland Discounts, 5550 Broadway, 718-543-5932

Petland Discounts, 3466 Jerome Ave., 718-231-9466

Pets Plus Plants Ltd, 3197 Bainbridge Ave., 718-655-4054

Professional Grooming, 2561 Briggs Ave., 718-562-1545

Stephanie Pet Center, 1099 Southern Blvd., 718-842-7651

Super Pet & Aquatics, 729 Allerton Ave., 718-652-5326

Third Avenue Petmaster, 3023 3rd Ave., 718-585-5463

Waggin' Tails, 1131 Rhinelander Ave., 718-597-5222

Whiskers Pet Grooming & Supplies, 781 Van Nest Ave., 718-597-8844

Shelters & Rescue Groups

Center For Animal Care and Control, 464 E. Fordham Rd., 718-733-0743

Sitters & Walkers

J.A.M. Pet Sitting Service, 5545 Netherland Ave., 917-689-0127

Veterinarians, Vet Clinics & Animal Hospitals

Abbey Veterinary Hospital, 322 W. 231st St., 718-543-6565

ABC Animal Euthanasia Center, 3325 Boston Rd., 718-547-6520

Animal Clinic, 451 Morris Park Ave., 718-828-6404

Animal Clinic & Surgery, 3800 E. Tremont Ave., 718-430-7000

Animal Hospital Of Morris Park, 1135 Morris Park Ave., 718-822-3309

Armory Dog & Cat Hospital, 18 E. Kingsbridge Rd., 718-367-4350

Avalon Animal Hospital, 1812 Westchester Ave., 718-829-2355

Bender Animal Hospital, 6118 Riverdale Ave., 718-549-8131

Broadway Animal Hospital, 5664 Broadway, 718-543-5600

Chondris, George DVM, 3800 E. Tremont Ave., 718-430-7000

Concourse Animal Hospital, 2356 Grand Concourse, 718-933-1002

Fletcher, Charles DVM, 322 W. 231st St., 718-543-6565

Lurting Animal Clinic, 3004 Lurting Ave., 718-881-1000

Middletown Animal Clinic, 2968 Middletown Rd., 718-824-8300

Pelham Bay Animal Clinic, 3077 Westchester Ave., 718-931-3139

Pereyra, Carlos DVM, 18 E. Kingsbridge Rd., 718-367-4350

Riverdale Animal Hospital, 3619 Kingsbridge Ave., 718-884-4133

Rosenberg, Mark DVM, 322 W. 231st St., 718-543-6565

Surgeon, Thoulton DVM, 18 E. Kingsbridge Rd., 718-367-4350

Tri-Boro Animal Hospital, 604 Grand Concourse, 718-292-1770

Wakefield Animal Clinic, 675 Nereid Ave., 718-994-7708

BEYOND NEW YORK CITY

Boarding

Almost Home Kennels, 176 Pudding St., Putnam Valley, NY, 845-528-3000

Barkingham Palace, 26 Davis Ave., Port Washington, NY, 516-944-5757

Best Friends Pet Resort, 825 Route 22 West, North Plainfield, NJ, 908-822-9200

Best Friends Pet Resort, 269 Red Schoolhouse Rd., Chestnut Ridge, NY, 914-371-4000

Grace Lane Kennels, 46 Grace Lane, Ossining, NY, 888-PET-CAMP

Rondout Valley Kennels, 4628 Route 209, Accord, NY, 914-687-4406

Rye Country Boarding Kennels, 21 Nursery Lane, Rye, NY, 914-967-4577

Woods End Kennels, 66 Woods End Rd., Putnam Valley, NY, 914-528-3211

Pet Cemeteries, Crematoriums & Funeral Homes

Abbey Glen Pet Memorial Park, 187 Route 94, Lafayette, NJ, 800-972-3118

Bide-A-Wee Westhampton Pet Memorial Park, 118 Old Country Rd., Westhampton, NY, 631-325-0219

Bide-A-Wee Wantagh Pet Memorial Park, 3300 Beltagh Ave., Wantagh, NY, 516-785-6153

Hartsdale Pet Cemetery & Crematory, 75 N. Central Ave., Hartsdale, NY, 800-375-5234

Regency Forest Pet Memorial Cemetery, 716 Middle Country Rd, Middle Island, NY, 800-372-7387

Shelters & Animal Rescue Groups

Central Westchester Humane Society: Elmsford Animal Shelter, 100 Warehouse Lane S., Elmsford, NY, 914-592-7362

North Shore Animal League, 25 Davis Ave., Port Washington, NY, 516-883-7575

Index

ABOUT THE AUTHORS

Nina Munk is the founder of the Web site Urbanhound.com. She is also an award-winning writer whose articles have appeared in *The New York Times Magazine*, *Vanity Fair*, *Fortune* and *The New Yorker*. From 1997 to 1999, she was a Senior Writer at *Fortune* and, for five years before that a Senior Editor at *Forbes*. She and her husband live in New York City with their urban hound, Mack, a Brittany who's fond of city pigeons. Her Web site can be found at www.ninamunk.com.

Nadia Zonis, Urbanhound.com's editor, has worked as an editor at SesameStreet.com, Good Housekeeping Online, Sesame Workshop, and *Ladies' Home Journal*. A PhD candidate in European History at Columbia University, Nadia and her Shepherd mutt Masha can frequently be found playing fetch in Central Park's East Meadow or trekking through The Ramble. Full disclosure: Nadia and Masha have a cat named Cyrus.

ABOUT URBANHOUND

Since it began as a Web site in June 2000, Urbanhound.com has received rave reviews, attracted millions of visitors and established itself as the voice for New York City's 1.1 million hounds. From the *Houston Chronicle* to the *Chicago Tribune* ("dog-ear this site"), praise for the site has been unanimous. *Forbes* calls Urbanhound.com "sophisticated and sassy." The *Wall Street Journal* says it's "wry" and "cool." Urbanhound's reporting on canine issues has been cited by *The New York Times, Ladies' Home Journal, Newsday,* NBC's Today Show, NewYork1, Fox News, the *New York Post*, and the Associated Press.

Urbanhound has been honored with the 2000 Applied Arts Award for Excellence in Web-Site Design; the Annual National Post Design Exchange for Interactive/New Media; the 2000 International Web Page Award's Creative Excellence Award; and, our favorite, the Dog Gone Good Award for Creativity, Excellence, and Commitment to the Animal Community. After you finish this book, visit Urbanhound.com and see for yourself what the hullabaloo is all about.

ABOUT THE PHOTOGRAPHER

Michael Nastasi is a New York City-based pet portaitist (see page 182) whose endearing photographs of city dogs appear regularly on the Urbanhound.com Web site. His Web site can be found at www.canisphoto.com.

Guides to the Best of New York

City Baby: The Ultimate Guide for New York City Parents from Pregnancy to Preschool	$18.95
City Wedding: A Guide to the Best Bridal Resources in New York, Long Island, Westchester, New Jersey and Connecticut	$17.95
The Cool Parents Guide to All of New York Excursions & Activities In & Around our City that Your Children Will Love and You Won't Think are Too Bad Either	$14.95
The Food Lover's Guide to the Best Ethnic Eating in New York	$14.95
Glory in Gotham: Manhattan's Houses of Worship— A Guide to their History, Architecture and Legacy	$14.00
Hampton's Survival Guide	$17.95
Heavenly Weekends: Travel Without a Car	$14.95
How to Live the Good Life in New York	$20.00
New York's 50 Best Bookstores for Booklovers	$12.00
New York's 50 Best Places to Discover and Enjoy In Central Park	$12.00
New York's 50 Best Places to Take Children	$12.95
New York's 100 Best Wonderful Little Hotels	$15.00
New York's 75 Best Weird and Wonderful Nights Out	$12.95
New York's 50 Best Places to Find Peace and Quiet	$12.95
New York's 50 Best Places to Keep your Spirit Alive	$12.95
New York's 100 Best Little Places to Shop	$15.00

"THESE BOOKS ARE FILLED WITH SHINY OBJECTS OF INFORMATION AND ADVICE, LIKE THE COUNTERS OF OLD-FASHIONED VARIETY STORES."

—*THE NEW YORK TIMES*